INTIMACY AND AGEING
New relationships in later life

Torbjörn Bildtgård and Peter Öberg

T0385533

First published in Great Britain in 2019 by

Policy Press
University of Bristol
1-9 Old Park Hill
Bristol
BS2 8BB
UK
t: +44 (0)117 954 5940
pp-info@bristol.ac.uk
www.policypress.co.uk

North America office:
Policy Press
c/o The University of Chicago Press
1427 East 60th Street
Chicago, IL 60637, USA
t: +1 773 702 7700
f: +1 773-702-9756
sales@press.uchicago.edu
www.press.uchicago.edu

© Policy Press 2019

British Library Cataloguing in Publication Data
A catalogue record for this book is available from the British Library

Library of Congress Cataloging-in-Publication Data
A catalog record for this book has been requested

ISBN 978-1-4473-2650-2 paperback
ISBN 978-1-4473-2649-6 hardcover
ISBN 978-1-4473-2653-3 ePub
ISBN 978-1-4473-2654-0 Mobi
ISBN 978-1-4473-2651-9 ePdf

The right of Torbjörn Bildtgård and Peter Öberg to be identified as authors of this work has been asserted by them in accordance with the Copyright, Designs and Patents Act 1988.

All rights reserved: no part of this publication may be reproduced, stored in a retrieval system, or transmitted in any form or by any means, electronic, mechanical, photocopying, recording, or otherwise without the prior permission of Policy Press.

The statements and opinions contained within this publication are solely those of the authors and not of the University of Bristol or Policy Press. The University of Bristol and Policy Press disclaim responsibility for any injury to persons or property resulting from any material published in this publication.

Policy Press works to counter discrimination on grounds of gender, race, disability, age and sexuality.

Cover design by Policy Press
Front cover image: istock
Printed and bound in Great Britain by by CPI Group (UK) Ltd, Croydon, CR0 4YY
Policy Press uses environmentally responsible print partners

Contents

Contents

List of figures and tables

Figures

Tables

Acknowledgements

Writing a book is hard work and demands much time and sacrifice. This book would never have been written without the support of institutions, colleagues and friends.

We would like to thank the research foundations that provided financial support for the two research projects that this book to a large extent is based on, the Swedish Research Council for Health, Working Life and Welfare (Dnr 2009–0720), and the Swedish Foundation for Humanities and the Social Sciences (P11: 0909–1). We would also like to thank Harald and Louise Ekman's Research Foundation for providing a one-week scholarship for writing at the Sigtuna Foundation's hotel and conference centre, and the Jonsered Foundation for providing a one-month scholarship for writing at Villa Martinson in Partille.

For valuable comments on the book manuscript we would like to thank the anonymous reviewer and the book series editors Chris Phillipson, Toni Calasanti and Tom Scharf. We thank Professor Emeritus Lars Andersson, and the social gerontology group at Uppsala University (Sandra Torres, Gunhild Hammarström, Ulla Hellström Muhli, Magdalena Kania Lundholm and Marianne Winqvist) for important feedback. We also thank Professor Susan Brown for providing us with statistics from the US.

Last, but not least, we thank our families and wives for invaluable practical and emotional support during the writing process.

We, the authors of this book, have in all parts contributed equally to the drafting of this book, including conception, research design, collection of data, analysis and writing.

Series editors' preface

Chris Phillipson (University of Manchester, UK),
Toni Calasanti (Virginia Tech, USA) and
Thomas Scharf (Newcastle University, UK)

As the global older population continues to expand, new issues and concerns arise for consideration by academics, policy makers and health and social care professionals worldwide. Ageing in a Global Context is a series of books, published by Policy Press in association with the British Society of Gerontology, which aims to influence and transform debates in what has become a fast-moving field in research and policy. The series seeks to achieve this in three main ways. First, the series is publishing books which rethink key questions shaping debates in the study of ageing. This has become especially important given the restructuring of welfare states, alongside the complex nature of population change, both of these elements opening up the need to explore themes which go beyond traditional perspectives in social gerontology. Second, the series represents a response to the impact of globalisation and related processes, these contributing to the erosion of the national boundaries which originally framed the study of ageing. From this has come the emergence of issues explored in various contributions to the series, for example: the impact of transnational migration, cultural diversity, new types of inequality, and contrasting themes relating to ageing in rural and urban areas. Third, a key concern of the series is to explore inter-disciplinary connections in gerontology. Contributions provide a critical assessment of the disciplinary boundaries and territories influencing the study of ageing, creating in the process new perspectives and approaches relevant to the 21st century.

Among the many changes influencing later life, new types of relationships and social ties must rank as one of the most important. In this respect, Torbjörn Biltgård and Peter Öberg's contribution to the series is especially welcome, providing a major assessment of changing patterns of intimacy in later life. The authors draw on their own original research in Sweden, together with a large number of international studies, to provide a comprehensive account of intimacy in later life. The book provides an exciting and challenging account, demonstrating the numerous ways in which older people are reshaping social and family life in the 21st century.

ONE

Introduction

This book is about late-life intimate relationships in cross-gender couples. Intimate relationships are among the most important relationships in our lives. They correspond to our longing to feel loved and appreciated, support our sense of self, give us a sense of belonging, and satisfy our physical desires. In other words they correspond to our deepest emotional, psychological and physical needs as human beings. Although these needs are arguably ageless, a widely held idea is that intimacy is associated with the earlier part of the life course, while later life is associated with the loss of intimate relationships and the decline of interest, expectations and physical abilities. This book will challenge this and other normative conceptions and stereotypes of late-life intimacy.

Stereotypes regarding older people's intimate relationships contribute to maintaining knowledge gaps with regard to late-life intimacy with consequences for ageing policy and practice, but also knowledge gaps in the wider fields of gerontology, family studies and sexology. Using international research, comparative international data and our own Swedish studies, this book will address these knowledge gaps by presenting a comprehensive overview of older people's attitudes, expectations and experiences of late-life repartnering.

Setting the scene

Consider the following two cohabiting persons who met late in life: Cohabiting Carl[1] is a 70-year-old man with a complex relationship career and several biological and step-children from different marriages. Raised by liberal parents, he had his sexual debut at the age of 15 and had a number of intimate relationships before he met his first wife-to-be at the age of 23. Soon after meeting they moved in together and only after she got pregnant did they marry. The marriage, established in the 1960s ('for love and friendship'), was not sexually exclusive, and other partners were accepted. After ten years Carl divorced. He then moved to Great Britain where he met his second wife, two years later. He describes the marriage as an emotional roller-coaster that ended in divorce 15 years later. Immediately thereafter he moved to an Asian country, where he met his third wife, whom he again divorced ten years later. After returning to Sweden he actively searched for a new intimate partner in online dating forums and dated a few women.

Two years prior to the interview Carl met his current cohabiting partner, Caroline. Now 72 years old, Caroline met her first intimate partner and had her sexual debut at the age of 17. Two years later, as soon as they found an apartment, they got married and moved in together and within a couple of years they had three children. The abusive marriage ended in a divorce 15 years later. After a couple of years she met her second partner, whom she married after some years of cohabitation. In her early 50s her husband, who was 20 years older than her, died. At that time, she recalls, she was convinced that she would never want a new partner again. However, after having lived alone for 20 years she met Carl at a local event and immediately fell in love.

Caroline initiated their relationship by revealing to Carl how she had fallen in love with him at first sight. He invited her over to his house for dinner and, as she recalls, they have shared a bed ever since. They soon bought a new house and moved in together. Carl explains that in later life there is little time left for hesitation. Carl and Caroline have discussed marriage, but Carl is unwilling, partly because he has experienced three divorces, but also for financial and inheritance reasons. However, the issue is still under negotiation.

Both Caroline and Carl describe the reactions of their friends and family to their relationship as overwhelmingly positive. Caroline recalls how her daughter telephoned her during their first date and wished her 'Good luck, mummy' and how the daughter shared the good news with her colleagues.

They both describe how they care for and support each other in several ways in everyday life. Caroline is frail and Carl helps her in physically challenging situations, such as walking outdoors, for example to doctor's appointments. Caroline takes care of Carl in a traditional housewife role. They both describe their sex life as intensive. Caroline recalls how she had worried before their first sexual encounter about how Carl would perceive her body and about not being able to perform sexually after 20 years of singlehood. However, now they both claim that sex and physical intimacy is a very important part of their relationship. Caroline says that she has never been happier. Carl ends his story by saying that he cannot imagine a better life than they have together, and he cannot imagine that it would end before one of them dies.

Carl and Caroline's relationship shows all the characteristics commonly included in definitions of intimacy in romantic relationships (see for example Moss and Schwebel's 1993 review of definitions of intimacy): it is a *committed* relationship. As Carl says, he can only imagine that the relationship will end through the death of one partner. It is characterised by *cognitive closeness*. Both Caroline and Carl describe how they are constantly aware of and think about each other. It is an *emotionally close* relationship, where they care for each other in many different ways in everyday life. Their relationship is *physically close*. Carl and Caroline sleep together, caress frequently and have an intense sex life. All of these aspects are clearly *mutual,* and both Carl and Caroline emphasise that all of these aspects of intimacy are important parts of their relationship.

Carl and Caroline's story could be understood from several perspectives. It could be understood in terms of historical change: from a *culture of marriage*, where marriage was an externally given norm for intimate relationships, supposedly for life, and divorce was a final resort, to a *culture of divorce* where relationships are shaped in negotiations between equal partners, where marriage is one relationship form among others, and divorce/separation is always a getaway (Hackstaff, 1999, see also Chapter two). It could also be understood in terms of the specific existential conditions surrounding relationships in later life: how are relationships affected by an awareness of the restricted remaining lifetime? Or it could be understood as an expression of the specific cultural context of state-supported individualism in late modern Sweden: how do different cultural contexts promote different attitudes towards late-life relationships and different relationship practices? It could also be understood in relation to how new partnerships in later life are shaped by earlier relationship history, where individual experiences of prior relationships, for example their quality and how they were dissolved (through divorce/separation or widowhood), might impact on attitudes towards new relationships.

The case of Carl and Caroline raises a number of questions that are generally relevant for the understanding of new intimate relationships in later life. While Carl actively searched for a new intimate partner after his last divorce, Caroline had no interest in finding a new relationship after being widowed: what attitudes do single[2] older people have towards forming new romantic relationships? And how do attitudes and experiences of new intimate relationships differ between men and women? Carl and Caroline became cohabitants but disagree about getting married: which union forms are chosen in new relationships initiated in later life? Both Carl and Caroline agree on the importance of the relationship for their quality of life: how do new romantic relationships affect loneliness and the well-being of older people?

And what are the social support benefits of having a new partner? Carl and Caroline's family and friends were enthusiastic about their relationship: how do family and friends react to older people forming new intimate relationships? Carl and Caroline enjoyed an intensive sex life: how important is sex and what are the experiences of sexuality in new romantic relationships? Both Carl and Caroline had earlier relationship experiences: how do new romantic relationships in later life differ from romantic relationships earlier in the life course and from lifelong marriages?

New intimate relationships in later life have become an increasingly popular subject of investigation in popular culture in the last couple of decades. In popular culture it has become increasingly common to portray older single people as interested in starting over in new romantic and sexual relationships. For example, older people are increasingly being portrayed as sexually active in mainstream feature films (Bildtgård, 2000; Vares, 2009); articles in retirement magazines increasingly encourage older people to 'start over' in new romantic relationships (Jönsson, 1998). At the same time it has become more common for older people to place personal ads, and Internet dating sites increasingly address older people (Butler & Lewis, 2002; Malta & Farquharson, 2014; Öberg, 2000). Furthermore, medical innovations have made it possible to treat male impotence and the female menopause. Thus, sexuality has been released to become part of the expectations of what successful ageing or a good old age should consist of, and sexual activity has become part of active ageing (see for example Katz & Marshall, 2003).

As part of the wider changes of the life course as a social institution (see for example Dannefer & Settersten Jr, 2010; Mortimer & Shanahan, 2003), it is reasonable to assume changes of intimacy patterns among older people. For example young-old people today were pioneers in the establishment of late modern society with its focus on the ego as a reflexive project created through lifestyle choices (cmpr. Giddens, 1991), and they are accustomed to choose their own lifestyles, also concerning intimate relationships. They also live longer, have a generally better financial situation and better subjective health than earlier generations and thus have the time and resources to pursue the lifestyles of the third age (Gilleard & Higgs, 2000) and to envision new intimate futures.

Still, for a long time the subject of new intimate relationships in later life suffered from a form of 'double blindness'. A common statement in the sociology of the family is that intimacy in late modern societies has been freed from its earlier reproductive functions, leaving space for new forms of intimacy. However, ironically, most family studies about the transformation of intimacy have focused on people of reproductive age. For a long time older people, for example, tended to be 'forgotten' in studies on sexual intimacy (Gott 2005; for Swedish examples, see for example Lewin, 2000; Zetterberg, 1969). Similarly, in social gerontology it has been common to argue that late modernity has given birth to a new life phase, the third age (Laslett, 1989), characterised by active identity formation and realisation of life plans. Still, although intimate relationships may be thought to play an important role in those plans, social gerontology was until recently blind to the intimate life of older people. Maybe this invisibility reflected a form of ageism, where the latter part of the life course was made visible primarily in terms of functional incapacity and dependency. In this book we hope that by focusing on transitions in the later part of the life course from a perspective of gains and potentials (new intimate relationships), rather than primarily loss and decline (for example widowhood), we will contribute to rethinking ageing.

Key takeaways

The last two decades or so have seen a growing research interest in older people's intimate relationships, and this growing interest has been accompanied by a small but steady trickle of research articles being published in the field. Now the field can probably be said to have reached a stage of early maturity. A pioneering collection of articles on this topic appeared in a special issue of the journal *Ageing International* that appeared in 2002 and was published two years later as an edited volume with the title *Intimacy in Later Life* (Davidson & Fennell, 2004). This book differentiates itself from the earlier collection by its comprehensive ambition. It brings together a wide range of international research published in English and adds the authors' own research from Sweden, in order to give an overview of intimacy and ageing. It investigates older people's attitudes, ideals and personal experiences of new intimate relationships and uncovers their structural preconditions. The book will be relevant to several audiences: researchers in gerontology, family studies and sexology, as well as to policy makers and practitioners.

The book will be useful for gerontologists by transcending the established view of old age as a period of loss and decline. It contributes to rethinking ageing in the context of the emergence of the third age and the new opportunities offered by consumer society and shows that later life can be a period of gains and development, also with regard to intimate relationships. It also contributes to rethinking ageing by stressing the importance of life phase for understanding later life in general and intimate relationships in particular. By uncovering the particular conditions of late-life intimacy we show that love is not ageless. But the book is also relevant with regard to mainstream gerontological concerns and gerontological practice. It illustrates the increased complexity of older people's family relationships in late modernity.and the implications for access to informal care and support.

The book will also be relevant to family researchers by challenging the image of older people as representatives of a conservative view on intimate relationships and the family – in particular the view of older people as defenders of the marital norm, both as ideal and practice. It contributes to the last two decades of research that has uncovered the increasing heterogeneity of older people's family lives (Allen, Blieszner & Roberto, 2000; Silverstein & Giarrusso, 2010). Many older people belong to generations that were agents behind the sexual and family revolution in the late 20th century and continue to revolutionise intimate relationships in later life. But this life phase is also characterised by its freedom from many of the normative restraints that shape relationships in early adulthood and mid-life and which are connected to reproduction and parenthood. As a consequence, older people are relatively free to shape their relationships according to their own preferences and can potentially be an avant-garde, inventing new ways of living together. Late-life intimate relationships are therefore a strategic place to study the future development of ideal-typically 'pure' relationships in Giddens' (1992) sense.

In the book we challenge the myth of older people as asexual. We show that sexual attraction and sexual activity are regularly a precondition for repartnering in later life. We also show the change of sexual norms during the life course of contemporary generations of older people, from 'sex, but marriage first' in their youth, to 'sex, but no marriage' in later life.

The book illustrates the problems of basing policy regarding older people on research and census data that use civil status as a measure of older people's relationship situations. As increasing numbers of older people live in non-marital relationships and have complex relationship biographies, civil status becomes increasingly irrelevant for capturing the complexity of older people's relationship situations and family lives – especially of those who have repartnered late in life – and risks being a blunt instrument for planning public efforts and services for older people.

The book is intended for an international readership. It is based on research from different Western countries and contexts. Despite obvious differences with regard to culture and social organisation, global trends such as increasing gender equality, increased longevity, increasing divorce rates and technological and digital innovations that facilitate repartnering create similar conditions for older people's relationships. By comparing cases, such as the US and northern and southern Europe, the book attempts to differentiate global trends from local realities and thereby help the international reader to imagine what late-life intimacy might look like in their countries in the future.

Finally, this book will hopefully help the generally interested reader to envision new intimate futures for later life.

Outline of the book

In Chapters two to four we investigate the changing structural preconditions of late-life repartnering from both a theoretical and empirical standpoint, focusing on the emergence of the third age and the transformation of intimacy. *Chapter two: Intimacy and ageing in late modernity*, lays the theoretical groundwork for the book. In the chapter we argue that the phenomenon of new intimate relationships in later life has to be understood in relation to the life course as a historically and culturally dependent social institution. Every cohort ages in its own particular way in a changing landscape of later life. We begin by discussing two recent historical changes to the institution of the life course with importance for late-life intimacy. One such historical change is the emergence of a *third age* that allows for new projects of self-development – including new intimate relationships. A second central historical change is *the transformation of intimacy*. Contemporary family theory often describes a historical move from a modern context where relationships were externally determined by a given form – marriage – to a late modern context where relationships are flexible arrangements that are the product of negotiation between relatively equal partners and constantly open to change. We discuss the relevance of this historical development for understanding the phenomenon of new intimate relationships in later life. But we also acknowledge social and cultural difference within the framework of these large-scale historical transformations. In the chapter we discuss the importance of cultural context and Sweden as a particular case of late modernity, with its typical Nordic form of state-supported individualism, which facilitates individual autonomy and equality in intimate relationships. Despite historical change and cultural difference in the landscape of ageing, the inevitability of death remains universal. At the end of the chapter we use developmental theory to discuss later life as a life phase with its own particular characteristics, which also shapes and differentiates intimate relationships late in life from relationships earlier in the life course.

In *Chapter three: The changing landscape of intimacy in later life*, we illustrate the changing structural preconditions for late-life intimacy outlined in Chapter two, using demographic data from different Western countries. The chapter emphasises the importance of increased life expectancy and the prolongation of the healthy lifespan for longer relationships, but also for making it possible to envision new intimate futures late in life, and thereby laying the ground both for a grey divorce revolution and a grey repartnering revolution. In the chapter we illustrate the shift from a culture of marriage to a culture of divorce and argue that this shift has had an important impact on the relationship careers of contemporary older generations. In later life it continues to have an impact by restructuring the population of older individuals towards an increase in the relative number of divorced older individuals – creating what we call a 'society of divorcees'. A consequence is that a larger number of older singles of both sexes become available, evening out the traditional gendered imbalance on the partner market over time. A third structural aspect with an impact on the landscape of ageing is technological change. At the end of the chapter we discuss the importance of new digital and transport technologies for bringing older single people together and present data on historically changing venues for meeting a partner.

In *Chapter four: From marriage to alternative union forms*, we look more closely at the development of new union forms as part of the historical deinstitutionalisation of marriage, and the relevance of these forms for late-life relationships. In the chapter we consider the historical development of cohabitation and Living Apart Together (LAT)[3] as union forms. We illustrate the shift with data that shows the increasing prevalence of cohabitation and LAT as alternative union forms among older people, and also how common these are in intimate relationships established late in life. We discuss whether cohabitation and LAT unions established late in life should be considered as alternatives, or preludes, to marriage. In the chapter we challenge the hypothesis that older people are carriers of a cultural lag with regard to relationship norms and necessarily prefer marriage as their union form. Instead we argue that older people, at least in some respects, could be viewed as pioneering explorers of new union forms. We criticise official census data and gerontological research mainly based on civil status for giving a partially false picture of older people's intimacy and family life. As a consequence of the biased focus on civil status, unmarried older people's romantic relationships as well as dissolutions by death or separation from these relationships remain invisible.

In Chapters five to seven we investigate how the structural changes described in Chapters two to four played out in individual lives and intimate relationships. First, in *Chapter five: A life of relationships*, we use survey data and individual biographies to illustrate the very heterogeneous relationship careers of contemporary older Swedes. In the chapter we question the idea that in their relationship careers older people in general have lived according to marriage cultural ideals, in particular the ideal of the single lifelong marriage. Instead, a substantial minority of the older population has experienced more than one intimate relationship and because relationship transitions accumulate over the life course, older people often have very complex relationship careers. Furthermore we investigate the importance that prior relationship experiences (such as widowhood, divorce, separation) have for choices regarding repartnering. Older divorcees tend to be more prepared to repartner than older widowed people. In the chapter we uncover the logic behind this preference, which is of central importance in a society where the number of older divorcees is growing.

In *Chapter six: Attitudes towards new romantic relationships* we focus on older people's attitudes to repartnering and their preferences for different union forms. How have the historical shift to divorce culture and the corresponding complex relationship careers of contemporary older people influenced relationship preferences? Prior research presents rather diverging results depending on *who* the studied respondents are and *what* they are asked about more specifically. Are the respondents divorcees, widowed or never married people? Are they men or women? Are they asked about dating, repartnering or remarriage? In the chapter we disentangle the inconsistencies in the results of prior research and also add our own survey data to produce a more comprehensive overview of older people's attitudes to repartnering. We criticise research that has focused on (re)marriage for underestimating older single people's interest in new intimate relationships. The chapter also illustrates the importance of gender for understanding attitudes to new intimate relationships.

A central assumption in much contemporary family theory is that relationships are increasingly shaped by negotiations between partners and less by external norms. In *Chapter seven: Initiation and development of new romantic relationships*, we ask how the development of relationships established late in life is negotiated. We present histories of newly formed relationships to illustrate the internal dynamics of late-life repartnering. We use four case studies representing different relationship stages, from dating to marriage, to illustrate the negotiations taking place during the successive establishment of a relationship and the questions that typically need to be resolved in order for the relationship to develop. We criticise prior research about older people's interest in remarrying for posing the wrong questions. We show that for older as well as younger people, the first question is normally whether you want a relationship or not, then if you should move in together or not. Questions of marriage are not normally actualised until a later stage of an established relationship – if ever.

In Chapters eight to nine we continue our investigation into the changing landscape of late-life intimacy by looking at the consequences of repartnering for the older individual's social integration and access to social support. The purpose of *Chapter eight: A new partner as a resource for social support* is to investigate the potential gains of repartnering in later life. In the chapter we discuss the importance of an intimate relationship for well-being. Previous research tends to support the common-sense assumption that a long-term intimate relationship prolongs life – but is this true also for relationships established late in life? In the chapter we argue that a new romantic partner can be an important resource for social support. As de Jong Gierveld (2002) has noted, without a partner all forms of support have to come from outside the household. We discuss the forms of companionate, practical and emotional support that a partner provides: a partner as a central source of companionship for travelling or visiting social occasions, restaurants, theatre and so on; a partner as a central source for care and for coping with practical challenges in everyday life; a partner as a primary confidant.

While Chapter eight investigated what a new partner could contribute in terms of social support, *Chapter nine: Consequences for social network and support structures* investigates how the introduction of a new partner in later life affects the wider network of social support providers. In the chapter we show how existing relationships are renegotiated as a consequence of repartnering. We show how a new partner tends to replace children and friends as the preferred provider of social support. We engage with social theories about the structure of care networks and argue that an intimate partner has the special characteristic of being able to fulfil a wide range of support functions, which makes him or her a particularly useful resource for achieving autonomy for the older individual and for unburdening alternative support providers, especially children. We argue that the model of

Nordic state-supported individualism tends to promote an ideal of autonomy in which the individual is encouraged to cultivate their own support networks, for example through repartnering, rather than relying on traditional relationships of duty. This ideal conforms to the idea of a 'chosen' family.

Chapter ten: Sex in an ideology of love investigates the role and meaning of sex in late-life relationships. Sex has for a long time been a neglected topic in gerontological research and often reduced to questions of sexual health and function. Studies on older people's sexual lives have tended to focus on quantitative measures of activity while the voices of the older people themselves have been forgotten. In the chapter we contribute to filling this blind spot by focusing on older people's personal testimonies of their sexual experiences over the life course and in their current late-in-life relationships, and we highlight different gender experiences. We show that sexual attraction is seen as a central part of a new late-in-life intimate relationship – companionship is not enough. But at the same time older people's ideas about sex tend to be framed in an ideology of love, where a loving relationship – not marriage – is seen as a requirement for sex, while sex outside of a monogamous relationship tends to be frowned on.

Is love 'ageless' or is there something that sets intimacy in later life apart from intimacy in earlier phases of life? If the previous chapters focused on the changing structural conditions for late-life intimacy, *Chapter eleven: Time as a structuring condition for new intimate relationships in later life* adds the persistent dimension of life's finality. We draw on Heidegger's (2008 [1927]) existential theory of time and argue that two aspects of time differentiate late-life relationships from relationships earlier in life: on the one hand increased free time, on the other hand limited remaining lifetime. These two aspects form the existential paradox of having a lot of free time after retirement and child rearing to allow for cultivating a relationship, but also having an increased awareness of the limited remaining lifetime that can be spent together – that the relationship can end any day. We argue that this existential paradox of time can be generalised to most older people, at least in the Western world.

In the final chapter we briefly summarise the major insights from the previous chapters and develop two themes of special importance for intimacy and repartnering in later life: first, the importance of the historical and socio-cultural context, particularly how late modern relationship norms are expressed in the Swedish case; and second the importance of life phase, particularly the social and existential structure of later life.

TWO

Intimacy and ageing in late modernity

In this chapter we will present different theoretical perspectives that we will use to discuss the structural preconditions for late-life intimacy in contemporary Western societies. In the chapter we discuss the rise of consumer society as a context for extending the lifestyles of mid-life into later life and the concurrent emergence of the third age as a historically new life phase of self-realisation. We also discuss the transformation of intimacy in the second half of the 20th century and how this transformation is shaped by different social and cultural contexts. Finally, we use developmental theory to consider the existential structure of the later phase of life and its implications for intimacy.

The changing landscape of later life

The life course is a social institution which varies by historical time and cultural context (Kohli, 2007). It determines the expected contents of the normal life and the timing of these events, for example education, work, marriage, parenthood and so on. As society changes, the institution of the life course will change as well and members of different cohorts will grow old in different ways (Riley, 1998). In the following we argue that the institution of the life course is a central structural condition that affects intimate relationships in later life. Opportunities for repartnering in later life will be different depending on the historical period in which individuals grow old and in which cultural context this takes place.

A central change in the institution of the life course in the last century, with important effects on the opportunity structure for new intimate relationships in later life, is the addition of years to the healthy lifespan. Together with improved material conditions and social reforms in many parts of the Western world it has given rise to a new phase of life, the third age (Laslett, 1989), a life phase between the second age of working life and the fourth age of frailty and dependence. The third age, which Laslett calls the 'crown of life', is characterised by active self-development and realisation of life plans. As part of the third age, the prolongation of life provides a central structural change of the life course that allows people to envision new intimate futures later in life. If, in earlier historical periods, there was little or nothing of the healthy lifespan left after working life to consider 'starting over', in many parts of the Western world people today can count on 10–20 good years after retirement – time that can be used for new intimate adventures.

To fulfil the promise of the third age the individual is encouraged to make deliberate lifestyle decisions, often based on advice and information offered by consumer culture. According to Gilleard and Higgs (2000) the rise of consumer society in the later part of the 20th century has meant that identities and lifestyles that used to be determined by the individual's social position have instead increasingly become determined by the individual's own choices on a market of lifestyles. New digital technologies have made information about alternative lifestyles increasingly available across cultures, age groups and other social divisions (cmpr. Appadurai, 1996). This has meant that the lifestyles of the young and middle aged have become increasingly available as part of the promises of what the third age could contain, such as travel, romance, entertainment and good health (Rees Jones et al, 2008). For many people an intimate partner might be an important part of the promises of the third age, or a resource for achieving these promises.

According to Bauman (2003) consumer society has also affected the way that people relate to partners and relationships, approaching them more like consumer goods. With the help of information offered in consumer society, for example about role models, older individuals can imagine different intimate futures for themselves: partnered individuals can imagine a life as separated, singles can imagine what life in a relationship would mean and what the perfect relationship should look like. New digital technologies have also lowered the threshold for repartnering, by creating new arenas for finding a new suitable partner, and enabled long-distance relationships to be formed and maintained, for example as LAT relationships.

Overly positive renderings of the possibilities offered by the consumer lifestyles of the third age should arguably be taken with a pinch of salt. From a critical gerontological perspective, these renderings tend to downplay difference within the community of older people and how social inequalities shape the opportunities for individual choice (cmpr. Katz & Calasanti, 2015). This is evident with regard to class and health – having or not having the resources needed to participate in consumer culture. In their later writings, Gilleard and Higgs (2010) describe the fourth age as a period with constrained agency that marks the collapse of the third-age project. Still, this criticism should not detract from the general insight that the emergence of the third age and consumer culture has transformed the later part of the life course into a period of growth for substantial parts of the older population in many late modern societies.

The transformation of intimacy

Besides the historical emergence of the third age described above the normative context for intimate relationships has also undergone an important transformation in the last half century. This transformation is an important topic in contemporary family and social theory.

Earlier family theory tended to portray marriage as an important social institution with a number of functions, such as the reproduction and socialisation of new generations, the stabilisation of the adult population's personalities and the fulfilment of their needs. Marriage played a central role in shaping the institutionalised life course, structuring and scheduling life course events – how and when to live together, have sex and have children. The institution of marriage defined roles and obligations between family members according to external social norms, in particular the division of tasks between husband (breadwinner) and wife (housekeeper), and made negotiations around family roles redundant. This division was seen as a rational solution to the external demands that the family had to meet and was sometimes viewed as natural (Parsons & Bales, 1955). In this model the family was often presented as a harmonic unit of social solidarity and a haven safe from the competition that characterised the society outside of the family.

However, with historical change social theory has also come to view the family in a different way. A central assumption in much contemporary family theory is that late modern relationships have been individualised and democratised and tend to be based on negotiations between relatively equal partners rather than on external norms and conventions. In response to a weakening of external conventions partners ideally strive to get to know each other intimately – personal ideals, goals, life story, lifestyle – and build their relationship on this close knowledge of the other.

For example, in family theory Cherlin (2004) has argued that marriage became deinstitutionalised in the last quarter of the 20th century, and that the relationship between married partners has become determined less by external norms and more by internal negotiations. Marriage has become more of a choice and less of a necessity, and is no longer a requirement for having sex or children. For example, the norm used to be that sexual intimacy should be practised exclusively in marriage, and the development of an intimate relationship was clearly ordered. First the couple was supposed to be wed, then move in together, become sexually active and have a first child one year later (Levin, 2004). As part of the deinstitutionalisation of marriage, this sequence has been broken up and individualised. People often have sex first, move in together, start a family and only then might they marry, but the sequence can be different from couple to couple and can also vary in different phases of life.

The transformation of intimacy has affected not only the *content* and *organisation* of the relationship between the involved partners – but also the union *form*. The hegemony of marriage as an exclusive union form has been challenged by other, less institutionalised ways of living together, as evidenced by the emergence of cohabitation and LAT as alternative union forms in the 1970s and 1980s. And these union forms are not necessarily only preludes to marriage, but also alternatives in their own right – people can choose to live together in these forms without getting married (Kiernan, 2002; Levin, 2004; Trost, 1978; Trost & Levin, 2000). Similarly, more and more people stay single, not because they have failed to find a partner, but by choice (Jamieson & Simpson, 2013; Klinenberg, 2012). In short the individual has increasingly become the basic unit of social life and relationships are increasingly being negotiated around individual wishes and life projects.

The transformation of intimacy has become a focal point for wider theoretical debates about social change. Perhaps most famously, Giddens (1991, 1992) uses late modern intimacy to illustrate his wider argument about the increasing pervasiveness of reflexivity in late modernity. According to Giddens even the individual's most intimate relationships are constantly evaluated in relation to what they offer the individual and their life projects. Giddens suggests that the late modern relationship tends to be 'pure', primarily based on the pleasure it gives the involved partners and less on social convention (such as male and female role expectations). These relationships are constantly open to change and mutual adaptation in order to avoid the 'threat' of separation. This frailty of relationships leads to a generalised separation anxiety and a need to constantly work on relationships – and get to know the intimate wishes of one's partner – as evidenced by the rise of couple's and family counselling and therapy.

Giddens (1992) contrasts the contemporary relationship ideal to a 19th-century ideal of romantic love. In the romantic ideal women and men were portrayed as equal but different (complementary) and the search for the perfect matching partner with whom to marry and raise a family was idealised. The ideal helped legitimise the modern one-earner family model with a clear division of roles between spouses. The ideal of romantic love reached its peak in the middle of the 20th century, when it started to be challenged by the entry of women into the labour force and a corresponding demand for more flexible family arrangements as well as increased gender equality. Instead, in the latter part of the 20th century, according to Giddens, the ideal of romantic love has been replaced by a new ideal of 'confluent love', a belief that romantic partners are equals who enter into relationships with their individual hopes and wishes and who strive to get to know each other intimately in order to be able to fulfil each other's relationship dreams. Relationships that fail to fulfil the individual's dreams can easily be terminated.

In this contemporary relationship ideal, disclosing intimacy is given special importance, as the force that keeps relationships together in a culture that provides few external forms or conventions for romantic relationships. In modernity, according to Luhmann (1986), a central social function of intimate relationships was as a support for identity in societies where identity was no longer determined and given stability by inherited social position. The intimate partner was often the most persistent point of confirmation for the self and in order to be mirrored in a continuous manner, mutual disclosure became central to the relationship. In Giddens' description of late modern relationships, intimate disclosure, or the sharing of confidences and other intimate knowledge of oneself with another person, takes on an even more central role as relationships are increasingly seen as electable venues to personal happiness and fulfilment. The relationship becomes a central part of the individual's life project and partner change can be part of the reinvention of the self throughout the life journey – finding a new partner quite literally becomes a way of finding a new 'me'.

Because of remaining gender differences, heterosexual couples seldom conform in full to the ideal type of a 'pure' relationship. Instead, Giddens uses gay couples as examples of what these relationships might look like. Because gay relationships are not tied by traditional relationship norms surrounding gender and reproduction, they are free to be negotiated by equal partners. In this sense the gay community might be viewed as an avant-garde that points to new possibilities also for heterosexual couple life as traditional norms weaken. Also heterosexual family relationships are increasingly chosen and not simply biologically given. The development towards pure relationships has fittingly been described as a 'queering' of heterosexual couple life (Weeks, 2007).

Giddens' argument has been widely recognised, but it has also encountered important criticism. For example, Jamieson (1988, 1999) has criticised the core idea that pure relationships are formed through negotiations between equal and reflexive individuals. According to Jamieson, Giddens does not distinguish enough between the ideology – as expressed in relationship literature – and the reality of late modern relationships. Despite all the talk of democratisation, empirical studies of couple relationships tend to show that intimate relationships are far from equal, and that men tend to have more influence over central relationship concerns such as family finances, and over their involvement in home work and child care. Rather than being 'pure' agreements between free and reflexive individuals, Jamieson argues that relationships are often influenced by external factors such as the labour market and pervasive gendered expectations. Loyalty means that partners will often work hard on relationships even when they are not satisfying, rather than break up, and although equality is important for most couples, more energy is normally directed towards creating the *appearance* of equality than in actually undermining gender differences.

It has also been argued that Giddens forgets the influence of linked lives. As Smart and Neale (1999) note, a common child can make a clean break very difficult to achieve. Even if a couple end their intimate relationship, they remain linked as parents and will need to continue to cooperate around parental decisions. Even in the best of situations this means having to sacrifice some of the freedom promised by single identity, and an ill-spirited former partner can exert power over the individual by refusing to cooperate (for example about schedules, decisions, new partners acting as step-parents, and so on).

Much of the critique levelled against the pure relationship seems reasonable when it comes to younger couples. However, Giddens' model might be better suited for describing repartnering in later life. Older people, who are no longer working and who are not expected to have children, might in many respects be as fitting an example of an ideal-typical pure relationship undetermined by external norms, as the gay couples in Giddens' example. In many ways older couples would seem to be freer from external demands than younger couples. Although they may have children, most often these children no longer need everyday support. And after retirement they are less dependent on an external labour market that might influence division of work in the home. This is not to say that older people's relationships are free from gendered habits and expectations, but they might be less determined by external demands.

A legitimate critique of Giddens' argument is that he underplays the importance of external structural factors in generating the conditions for intimacy. In a different, but in many ways similar, analysis of the transformation of intimacy, Beck and Beck-Gernsheim (2002) explain the transformation in terms of an increased individualisation of society which has affected not only the relationship between romantic partners, but the whole late modern family. There are two major reasons for this individualisation according to the authors. First, women have increasingly taken up employment outside the family and have consequently gained more financial independence. Second, the development of active welfare states that grant rights on an individual basis has made people less dependent on traditional units such as family, religious groups or the local community. As a consequence of this increased autonomy, individuals are liberated to leave relationships that are not perceived as rewarding. We find this line of argument sociologically relevant and in the book we will investigate the driving forces and structural conditions behind the changing landscape of late-life intimacy.

Another family theorist, Hackstaff (1999), uses a poignant conceptualisation for the transformation of intimacy that we will be using throughout the book. She describes it as a move from a *culture of marriage* to a *culture of divorce*. According to Hackstaff the culture of marriage was characterised by three beliefs: (a) that marriage was a given, (b) that it was supposed to last for life, and (c) that divorce was a final resort. The culture of divorce is characterised by three alternative beliefs: (a) that marrying is one option among others, (b) that marriage is a flexible arrangement between equal partners, and (c) that divorce/ separation is always a getaway. Where marriage culture was predicated on the complementary, but different, roles and responsibilities of males and females in the relationship, with a breadwinning, dominant husband and a caretaking and child-raising wife, divorce culture is based on two supposedly equal partners with few predefined roles and responsibilities, making negotiations central to the relationship. Taking the US as an example, Hackstaff argues that a tipping point was reached in the 1970s when divorce replaced widowhood as the primary cause for relationship dissolution.

The transformation of intimacy is highly relevant also for understanding the intimate lives of older people today. It is part of the changing landscape of later life. From a cohort-based perspective, it is often assumed that older people are carriers of a cultural lag, and that their relationship beliefs are still anchored in marriage culture. However, this is not necessarily the case. Contemporary cohorts of older people were young or middle aged during the transition from marriage to divorce culture in the 1960s and 1970s (depending on country). Some of today's older people were actively taking part in challenging the beliefs of marriage culture and shaping new and emergent forms of intimacy already in their young adulthood. Others experienced the transition later in their adult life but might well have assimilated the values of divorce culture and have been through one or more divorces or separations, sometimes followed by repartnering. Older individuals who have experienced the transition may have quite complex relationship careers. If they have had children (or reared children as step-parents) their family arrangements might be very heterogeneous – far from the expectations of the institutionalised nuclear family (see for example Ganong & Coleman, 2017). As older people, it is possible that they continue to live in accordance with the ideals of divorce culture. Also, it is possible that pure relationships are particularly suitable for later life, when relationships are no longer shaped by external responsibilities, for example child rearing and working careers, but can be formed freely as part of self-realisation in the third age.

The general relevance of the transformation of intimacy can be challenged. The acceptance of the new norms as well as the ability to act on them may vary with such factors as religious beliefs and financial resources. Most importantly, the normative change is related to the cultural and social policy context and unevenly spread across countries. In the following section we look at some important theoretical contributions that illuminate such differences.

Intimacy and cultural context

Despite its universal appearance, the historical transformation of intimacy described above is shaped by cultural context and social organisation (as can be derived from the argument above by Beck & Beck-Gernsheim, 2002). This context has clear consequences for attitudes towards living alone, divorce, gender equality and so on. Below we use theoretical models of differences in values and social organisation to try to disentangle some of these attitude differences across countries.

An excellent source for systematic cultural differences is the World Value Survey, which has studied social, cultural, religious and moral values in different countries around the world since the 1980s (see www.worldvaluessurvey.org). In one of the most famous representations of the survey's central findings Inglehart uses two value-dimensions to map cultural differences between the countries of the world (see Figure 2.1) (Inglehart, 2008; Inglehart & Baker, 2000; Pettersson & Esmer, 2008). The first dimension is traditional vs. secular/rational values. *Traditional values* emphasise the importance of religion, parent–child ties, respect for authority and traditional family values. Cultures in which these values are held in high regard tend to reject divorce. Cultures that, on the other hand, score high on *secular/rational values* tend to place less emphasis on traditional values and see divorce as relatively socially acceptable. The second dimension is survival vs. self-expression. Societies that emphasise *survival values* – often countries where the fulfilment of basic needs remains a challenge – prioritise family cohesion and emphasise financial and physical security, advocate traditional gender roles, and have low tolerance for minority groups (for example homosexuals). The other polarity, *self-expression*, characterises countries that emphasise tolerance, quality-of-life concerns, and the individual's right to make their own life choices.

Figure 2.1: Locations of different societies on two dimensions of cross-cultural variation

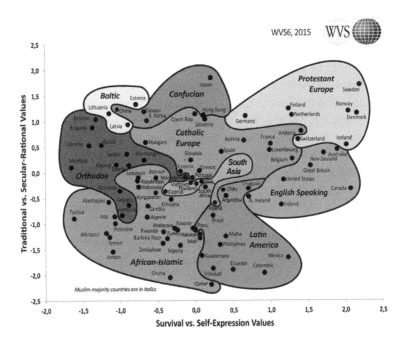

Source: World Values Survey 2015 (http://www.worldvaluessurvey.org/) [6th wave].

Most of the Western world can be found in the upper right corner of the map in Figure 2.1, signifying that they score high on secular-rational and self-expression values. In other words, in this corner we can find countries that place less emphasis on traditional family values and are more tolerant of the individual's right to make their own life and relationship choices. The transformation of intimacy (in terms of for example rates of divorce, non-marital cohabitation, children born out of wedlock) seems to be particularly evident in countries that score high on self-expression values, possibly underlining that in these countries intimate relationships are viewed as vehicles for individual happiness. However, there is much variation within the Western world. The north European Protestant countries tend to score higher on these dimensions than both the Catholic and the English-speaking part of the world. An extreme country in terms of both these dimensions is Sweden, where secular values and the individual's right to self-expression are held in high regard. The World Value Survey builds on time series data, and shows that for decades most of the countries – at least the Western ones – have moved in the general direction of the upper right corner of the map (on the World Value Survey's home page – www.worldvaluesurvey.org – it is possible to follow an interactive map with the transitions of different countries in Figure 2.1 from 1970 to 2014). From this point of view Sweden is an interesting case – it might be a forerunner and a strategic case study for understanding the future of intimate relationships in later life in many parts of the Western world.

According to Berggren and Trägårdh (2006; 2012) the underlying moral logic of the Nordic welfare model (of which Sweden is a case) is an ambition to liberate the individual from traditional relationships of dependence, such as the family and civil society – for example wives from husbands, children from parents – and to replace those dependencies with a relationship between the individual and the state. According to this moral logic, relationships of love and friendship are only possible between independent and equal individuals. Berggren and Trägårdh refer to this as a 'Swedish theory of love'. However, while Swedes tend to frown on unequal power relations between individuals and hierarchical institutions such as the traditional family, they tend to see the state as an ally in evening out social differences.

Basing themselves on Esping-Andersen's (1990) typology of three welfare regimes, Berggren and Trägårdh (2012) make a distinction between the Nordic countries and their Anglo-American and continental counterparts. As shown in Figure 2.2, the Nordic social contract as expressed by the case of Sweden is built on an alliance between the state and the individual (where rights and obligations are

Figure 2.2: Dynamics of power in modern welfare states, contrasting the position of state, family and individual in the US, Germany and Sweden

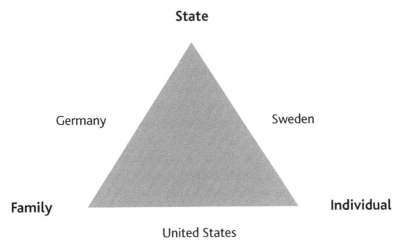

Power relations in modern welfare states

State

Germany   Sweden

Family   **Individual**

United States

Source: Berggren and Trägårdh (2012, p 20).

primarily conferred on the individual) – what Berggren and Trägårdh refer to as 'statist individualism'. It bypasses the dependency of the individual on the family. This can be contrasted with the Anglo-American social contract, as expressed by the case of the US, where the primary alliance is between the individual and the family, and where the state is looked on with suspicion. A third possibility is the continental alliance between the family and the state (where rights and obligations are primarily conferred on the family), as represented by the case of Germany.

Berggren and Trägårdh and the World Value Survey point to institutional and cultural differences that have practical and concrete implications for the transformation of intimacy in different countries. Obviously Berggren and Trägårdh's typology of welfare regimes, like that of Esping-Andersen, is an ideal type and all countries might not fit perfectly into the categories, although they help to illuminate contrasts. Below we try to tease out how these ideal-typical cultural and institutional models promote different normative models of intimacy in three concrete cases – Germany, the US and Sweden.

Germany scores relatively low on acceptance of self-expression values. Institutionally the German case is one of the clearest representatives of a traditional breadwinner/housewife centred policy model typical for many countries in continental Europe, which protects both marriage and the family (O'Hara, 1998; Orloff, 2006). German family policy supports a traditional family model by offering income support to parents who stay at home with their children, and as a consequence reinforce gender roles and obligations and undermines female independence and self-expression. Compared to, for example, the US and Sweden, Germany has seen relatively little change in family lifestyles in recent years and still has comparatively low divorce rates.

In contrast to Germany, the liberal US family policy model has minimised state involvement in family life and offers no direct public transfers to families. State support is instead primarily limited to tax credits for child care and parental incomes with the aim of supporting a universal breadwinner model for both men and women, whether living in couples or alone. Partly as a consequence of this policy the US has one of the world's highest rates of women's work force participation, also promoting gender equality and female financial independence (O'Hara, 1998; Orloff, 2006), central preconditions for intimate relationships based on negotiations between equal partners. The US scores relatively high on self-expression values, something that is also reflected in a high acceptance for individual relationship choices (Thornton & Young-DeMarco, 2001). At the same time, the lack of public support and services to individuals and families makes the individual more dependent on the family than in the Nordic countries. As a consequence the burden for individual welfare, also across generations, is primarily borne by the family and might cause strain on couple relationships. Increasing female independence and high strain on families is arguably a fertile context for divorce – the US has the highest divorce rates in the world (Brown & Lin, 2012).

Finally, a representative of the Nordic 'statist individualist' system is Sweden. In Sweden the ambition to support individual (and in particular female) independence became part of public policy in the 1960s, when legislation started to be revised to provide rights on an individual rather than on a family basis (Evertsson & Nyman, 2013; Hantrais, 1997). This is evident, for example, in the creation of systems for tax collection, sickness insurance, parental insurance and pensions, based on the individual's income and built on the assumption that both men and women participate in the workforce. At the same time a large part of the responsibility for child and elderly care was assumed by public institutions. For example, in the 1970s the formal obligation of adult children to care for their older parents was removed in the legislation. As a consequence the family has been relieved of some of its traditional social functions, and both its form and content have become more a question of negotiation and individual choices.

According to Evertsson and Nyman (2013) 'the deinstitutionalized family model of Swedish social policy, where benefits and rights follow the individual into whichever family form they choose, has led to a normalization of alternative family forms and lifestyles' (pp 63–64). This has had a tremendous impact on the Swedish family. As early as the 1980s, Popenoe (1987) argued that Sweden had moved farther from the ideal-typical nuclear family than any other industrial society, and this process has continued into the present.

As we have shown in this section, the cultural and institutional context of intimacy varies across the world. Attitudes and experiences of intimate relationships in later life will depend on the context in which people grow older. Thus, an older person in Sweden or the US will have lived their life during a historical period characterised by the deinstitutionalisation of marriage and the establishment of alternative union forms, and a wide acceptance of the individual's rights to choose both partner and form for a union. Based on these life course experiences, it is reasonable to believe that the conditions for repartnering in later life should be fertile in the US and Sweden. At the same time, the family arguably has a more central role in American life, which might point to a higher interest in repartnering in the US. However, this may not be the case where the family is still a more traditional institution and a more important unit for the organisation of social life, for example in continental Europe. This is also reflected in the research presented in this book. Germany and continental Europe figure rarely in this research, while North America and northern Europe, where repartnering is more acceptable, dominate prior research on the topic.

The importance of life phase: a developmental perspective

The emergence of the third age and the transformation of intimacy are two important historical changes of relevance to the landscape of late-life intimacy. In this section we will argue that developmental theory provides a third important perspective. A shared assumption in developmental theory is that life phase is central for understanding the individual's behaviour and life goals. For example, Cumming and Henry (1961), in their well-established – and criticised – Disengagement theory, assumed that people, as they grow old, withdraw from society (and that society likewise 'pushes' the individual away) in a functional preparation for death. A central driving force behind this disengagement, according to the authors, was an increasing awareness of life's finitude – a consciousness that life approached its end.

A very general consequence of this awareness was a decrease in social interaction and a discontinuation of certain relationships. Likewise, in Tornstam's (2005) Gerotranscendence theory – which suggests maturation into a new understanding of life, the self and others as a part of the process of ageing – it is assumed that people, as they age, tend to withdraw from superficial social relationships and instead focus on deeper personal relationships and positive solitude.

Carstensen's Socioemotional-Selectivity theory (Carstensen, 1992, 1995; Carstensen, Isaacowitz & Charles, 1999) is particularly relevant for describing the development of late-life relationships and has often been used in research on the topic. The theory combines two of the insights above – the importance of the awareness of finitude (cmpr. disengagement) and the reprioritisation of social contacts (cmpr. gerotranscendence). According to the theory, remaining lifetime constitutes an existential structure from which people plan and make central life decisions. Carstensen argues that social relationships are managed in order to fulfil two sets of life goals: the acquisition of knowledge and the regulation of emotions. The first goal corresponds to getting to know oneself and the surrounding world. The second goal corresponds to the need to control positive and negative emotions. According to Carstensen, early in life, when the time horizon is open, the goal of social contacts is primarily to gather information that is relevant for life planning. Individuals enter many social relationships in order to get to know themselves and the variety of opportunities that future life will offer. However, as the time horizon becomes more limited in old age, people tend to focus more on what is important in the immediate present, in particular emotional needs. As a consequence, older people tend to prioritise close and familiar social relationships where emotional reactions are predictable and normally positive. From the perspective of socioemotional-selectivity theory it is assumed that older people will primarily turn to social partners who are already familiar to them, such as family, close friends and in particular a spouse, for emotional support. As a consequence these relationships could be assumed to increase in emotional closeness in later life.

In our study of late-life relationships we have been much inspired by socio-emotional selectivity theory. However, a challenge to Carstensen's theory, in relation to the topic of this book, is that it takes as its point of departure the decline of social interaction in later life and focuses the selection and optimisation of *already existing* social networks as part of the ageing process. Although Carstensen's theory is inspired by Baltes and Baltes' Selection, Optimization and Compensation model of coping (Carstensen, 1992, p 338), in our reading the theory leaves little room for *compensation* through the initiation of new relationships. At least on an empirical level, it tends to assume that the existing social network can provide for all emotional needs. The problem with this assumption is perhaps best expressed when it comes to sexual intimacy. It can be very difficult to fill the need for sexual intimacy within the existing social network for those older people who have no sexual partner. But the social network might also be lacking in terms of other aspects of intimacy, which puts focus on the need to compensate through, for example, new intimate relationships. As a male informant in a new intimate relationship in one of our studies put it: 'The children are great, but you need somebody who you have something in common with', in reference to the fact that he and his new partner shared a common generational experience that he and his children did not.

On a more general level, we would argue that an awareness of life's finality can be used to understand not only decline, but also expansion, in social interaction. An awareness of the finality of life can be a motivation for fulfilling remaining life and relationship goals ('It's now or never'). For example, for the large part of the older population made up of singles, 'development' may have other meanings than just cultivating already existing close relationships. For these individuals, managing emotional needs may be more about envisioning a new intimate future for their remaining time.

A theoretical perspective that offers space for such an interpretation of the importance of finality is Heidegger's (2008 [1927]) existential theory of being and time. In his theory Heidegger argues that being, in a human sense, is a situated and concrete experience. Being is being-in-the world, or being consciously involved and engaged with the world. In other words, it is not an abstract subjectivity. This being is at its core temporal. It involves a present, a past and a future and also, importantly, an end. Individual being is engaging with the world in a present, in relation to future goals, from the horizon of past experiences. In this context, life's finality is a universal ruler against which life can be evaluated and measured, and an exhortation to live life deliberately. For us, Heidegger's argument is relevant because it does not necessarily equate coping with restrictive remaining time with decreased social contacts but just as well through an increased engagement with the world, which might include new intimate relationships. With the emergence of the third age, we would argue, this becomes even more important, as current generations of older people are 'thrown' into a historical context where the privilege of having the time and resources to live life deliberately has been afforded to larger sections of the older populations in many parts of the Western world, and where such an active outlook on later life is encouraged.

Conclusion

In this chapter we have presented some important tools that we will use to draw a map of the changing landscape of intimacy in later life. We have considered some important historical, cultural and existential conditions that shape late-in-life intimate relationships. These theoretical perspectives are particularly useful for making the upcoming empirical observations more analytically understandable and applicable in a wider cultural and historical context.

In the following empirical sections of the book, we will continue to investigate the changing landscape of late-life intimacy using these theoretical insights. Chapters three and four discuss the impact of the emergence of the third age and the transformation of intimacy for late-life repartnering in contemporary societies and put these historical developments in a comparative social and cultural context. In Chapters five to ten we investigate how these historical changes have shaped the relationship careers and late-life relationships of contemporary older Swedes and the role and meaning of sex in these relationships. And we discuss the social and personal consequences of late-life repartnering. Finally, in Chapter eleven, we turn our attention to the existential framework of later life and investigate the impact of this structure for new late-life intimate relationships.

The theoretical framework will help us discuss the extent to which the empirical insights generated by this book, are generalisable. Most relevant statistics, as well as empirical research, on repartnering in later life has been produced in North America and northern Europe. The above theoretical tools help us to make this uneven distribution of research understandable but also to predict how insights from this research might be applicable also to other countries and contexts. Our theoretical tools help us see and distinguish the general historical development from different social and cultural contexts, but also to see what constitute universal existential conditions.

THREE

The changing landscape of intimacy in later life

The title of this chapter alludes to Laslett's (1989) metaphor of the changing landscape of later life and refers to the changing conditions of late-life intimacy. While the previous chapter aimed to investigate the changing structural conditions for late-life intimacy from a *theoretical* perspective, the purpose of this chapter is to uncover the changing realities for repartnering using *empirical* data. In the chapter we show the prolongation of the lifespan in different countries and discuss its importance for older people's relationships and for envisioning new intimate futures. We illustrate the rise of divorce culture among older people using comparative data on divorce rates in different countries and show how this affects the partner market for older singles, by creating a 'society of divorcees' and potential for a 'grey repartnering revolution' – but also how the gendered structure of the partner market is affected by this change. Finally, we use survey data to show how new digital technologies have affected the dating arena by introducing new venues for meeting a new partner.

In this chapter and in the rest of the book we will be using three main sets of empirical data (described in detail in the methodological appendix at the end of the book): first, demographical data collected from Eurostat and a number of national census bureaus, including Statistics Sweden; second, a national representative survey with 1,225 responses from 60–90-year-old Swedes; and third, a qualitative interview study with 28 Swedes, 60–90 years old, who are currently dating singles or who have repartnered after their 60th birthday and are currently in a marital, cohabiting or LAT union.

The impact of the prolonged lifespan for envisioning new intimate futures

How people imagine their intimate futures is arguably affected by how much time they expect to have left in life in relatively good health (see also Chapter eleven). This perceived remaining healthy lifespan is likely influenced by the average length of life, which has increased in all countries of the Western world over the last half century (cmpr.

Vaupel, 2010). If we take the age of 65, which is the chronological age most often used as a reference point for the transition into later life, statistics from the EU countries show that in the last half century (1960–2013), life expectancy *at 65* has increased by on average five years. This development of increased survival in later life, for the years 1973–2013, is shown for a selection of countries in Figure 3.1. In 2012, the average life expectancy in the EU at the age of 65 was 82.1 years for men and 85.5 years for women. For the average person the main part of this remaining lifetime will be lived in at least fair perceived health – for example, in Sweden 16–18 years, in Greece 12–14 years (European Commission, 2009). Thanks to the development of pension systems, for many people it will also be spent in relatively good financial circumstances. This is the demographic background for talking about a third age of self-realisation (Laslett, 1989). Thus, at the age of 65, there is still considerable lifetime left to fulfil the promises of the third age, and for many an intimate partner might be an important companion for realising these late-life projects – or an intimate relationship might even be a late-life goal in itself.

Figure 3.1: Remaining life expectancy at the age of 65 in a selection of European countries, 1973–2013

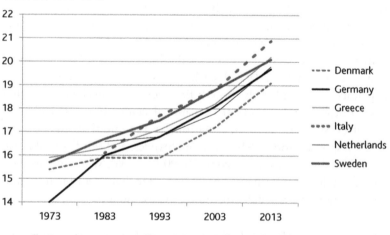

Source: Eurostat.

The prolongation of life means that couples who do not separate live longer lives together (co-survivorship) than in any previous historical period. As a consequence, the number of married people who get to celebrate their golden wedding anniversaries has increased in the last decades. For example, in Sweden the number of marriages having lasted 50 or more years increased from 32,000 in 1960 (Sundström & Johansson, 2004), to 153,000 in 2015 (Statistics Sweden) – almost a five-fold increase. Statistics from the US show the same pattern, with the number of marriages having lasted 50 or more years increasing from 558,000 in 1950 according to the US Census, to almost 4,464,000 in 2015, according to the American Community Survey (estimation by National Center for Family & Marriage Research, Bowling Green State University).

Statistics on golden weddings shows the impact that the prolonged life course has on intimate relationships. However, increased life expectancy also means more time to grow apart or to fall out of love, more time for potential conflicts to build up – and more time to divorce or separate (cmpr. Brown & Lin, 2012; Wu & Penning, 1997; Wu & Schimmele, 2007). This might be particularly relevant in a historical period promoting self-realisation, and is arguably one reason behind the historical increase in divorce rates. Also, and of special relevance to this book, increased life expectancy means more time to envision new intimate futures and to start over in a new intimate relationship. Thus, at the same time as the number of golden wedding anniversaries has increased it has become less common to spend one's whole life with the same partner.

A culture of divorce

Another condition shaping the opportunities for intimate relationships in later life is the culture of divorce, discussed above in Chapter two. The development of a culture of divorce is common to many parts of the Western world but depending on cultural context, contemporary cohorts of older people have experienced the introduction of this normative change at different points in their lives and it might be more or less relevant to them in later life.

The most important indicator of an emerging divorce culture is increasing divorce rates. From statistics of divorce incidence in European countries from 1960 onwards (Eurostat and OECD; Organisation for Economic Co-operation and Development), it is possible to make a crude distinction between 'two worlds of divorce'. In the Protestant northern European countries (for example Denmark, Sweden, the UK, the Netherlands) as well as Canada the increase in divorce started early in the 1960s, with a quick rise between 1970 and 1980, after which rates started to stabilise at new and higher levels than before the transition. In the US, the country that has the world's highest divorce rate, this transition seems to have started even earlier (Cherlin, 1992).

In southern Europe and Catholic Europe (for example Italy, Ireland and Greece) the process started later, from lower rates, and has increased at a much slower pace and divorce rates seem not yet to have stabilised. In this category the institutional support for marriage is still strong – in some countries divorce was not even possible by law until recently (in Italy not until 1970, Spain 1981, Ireland 1995, Malta 2011). Today, increasing divorce rates are a reality in most OECD states, although some countries in Catholic Europe are 'lagging' (and might never catch up). This change can be interpreted as an increased acceptance of the idea, fundamental to divorce culture, that relationships should contribute to individual happiness and that unsatisfying unions can, or even should, be dissolved.

From 'society of widows' to 'society of divorcees'

A consequence of the normalisation of divorce is that increasing numbers of individuals enter old age as divorcees or become divorced in later life. This has important consequences for the structure of the grey partner market. Figure 3.2 shows the change in civil status patterns in the Swedish 60–90-year-old population over a period of almost 50 years (1968–2015). The figure shows that the proportion of both marrieds and unmarrieds is largely constant over time. The marrieds constitute about half of the population and about one in ten has never married (except for 1968 when the proportion was somewhat larger).

However, of special interest for this book is the decrease in the proportion of widows/widowers and the concurrent increase of divorcees who, as will be shown later, tend to be more prone to repartner. The figure shows that the proportion (prevalence) of divorced Swedes in the age group 60–90 years has more than quadrupled during the last 48 years, from 4% to 18%. And since the general number of older people has increased during the period, the number of divorcees has increased even more – from 55,000 to 450,000. Since the year 2011 *the proportion of divorcees is for the first time larger than the proportion of widowed people* in this age group. This is a historically new phenomenon and comparisons with other European countries, using data from Eurostat in 2012 and other sources (Figure 3.3), shows that Sweden is extreme, but not unique, in this respect.

Figure 3.3 shows that it is considerably more common to be widowed than to be divorced in the 60–90-year-old age group in south European countries. The difference between the groups is generally smaller in the US and the northern European countries, especially in the Nordic countries, but with the exception of Sweden widows and

Figure 3.2: Swedes, 60–90 years old, by marital status (%)

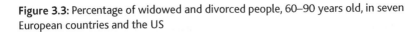

Source: Statistics Sweden (own calculations).

Figure 3.3: Percentage of widowed and divorced people, 60–90 years old, in seven European countries and the US

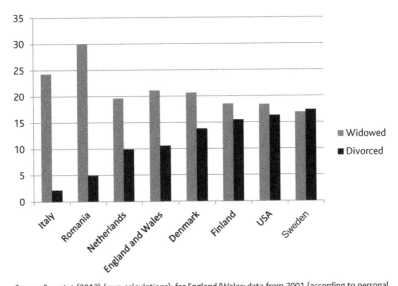

Source: Eurostat (2012) (own calculations); for England/Wales: data from 2001 (according to personal communication with Office for National Statistics the latest available census data); for US: data for 2014 from US Census Bureau, American Community Survey, personal communication with Susan Brown.

widowers remain the larger group. Because divorce creates two divorced individuals while death creates only one widowed individual, the proportion of divorcees is likely to soon surpass widowed people also in several other countries besides Sweden. To shed light on the changing structure of the community of older singles (the grey partner market), we have coined the concept 'society of divorcees', as a contrast to the concept 'society of widows' once suggested by Lopata (1973, 1996) for a community of women sharing a similar situation and social status.

The US is the country which resembles Sweden the most with regard to the proportion of divorcees. Considering that the US has a longer history of divorce and consistently higher divorce rates than Sweden, it might seem odd that Sweden has a higher prevalence of divorce in the older cohorts. Indeed in the general population divorce surpassed death as the main cause of relationship dissolution a full decade earlier in the US (the 1970s) than in Sweden (the 1980s). The larger proportion of older divorcees in Sweden relative to the US is primarily due to the fact that Swedes who have divorced earlier in life have remarried to a lesser extent than Americans, and have instead chosen alternative forms for their consecutive unions, thus the likelihood of being divorced increases by age. Of all divorcees in Sweden in 2015, almost half (46%) were 60 years or older (Statistics Sweden). This reflects both that older Swedes tend to have the means to live alone and that there is little social pressure to remarry for people in non-marital relationships.

The grey divorce revolution

Divorce culture is not only visible in increasing numbers of divorced older people, but also in increased numbers of people *getting divorced* in later life ('grey divorce'). The incidence of divorce (the proportion of married people who divorce during a given year) among older people has increased in large parts of the Western world. In the US the divorce rates among people 50+ doubled between 1990 and 2010 – from 4.9 to 10.1 divorced per 1,000 married individuals. This has motivated Brown and Lin (2012) to talk about a 'gray divorce revolution'. For Sweden the corresponding divorce rate for 50+ people in 2010 was 6.2. For an older group of Swedes *aged 60 and over* the divorce rate has almost doubled during the last decade: from 1.8 to 3.2 divorcees per 1,000 married individuals between 2001 and 2013 (Statistics Sweden). Cohabitation and LAT unions are common in Sweden, and if we were also to add those who separate from these unions, the rates would be even higher.

According to Wu and Schimmele (2007) longer life expectancies and higher expectations on marriages to be personally satisfying is putting lifelong marriages under severe pressure and increasing the risk of divorce. The expectation that a relationship should be personally satisfying is reflected in the increased acceptance of 'no-fault divorces', where the fault for separation is not attributed to any of the partners, but rather to the relationship as such and where people separate because they grow apart and fall out of love (see for example de Graaf & Kalmijn, 2006). In many Western countries the legislation was amended in the 1970s to reflect this shift in values. The expectation that a relationship needs to be personally satisfying seems to be accepted also by older people: in her investigation of late-life divorce in the US, Montenegro (2004) found that two out of the four most common reasons for divorce were 'no-fault' reasons, such as lifestyle differences and falling out of love, implying that the ideals of divorce culture have reached later life.

The grey divorce revolution implies that older people are increasingly prepared to leave unsatisfying relationships also in later life. The changing pattern for relationship dissolutions is important. A divorce releases twice as many individuals to a potential partner market as widowhood – and one of each sex. At the same time it is more common for divorcees to initiate new relationships than for widowed people (Calasanti & Kiecolt, 2007; Davidson, 2002; de Jong Gierveld, 2004a), partly because divorcees feel less loyalty towards their earlier partner (Brown, Lee & Bulanda, 2006; Brown & Lin, 2012). A growing number of divorces are consequently closely related to more positive attitudes to repartnering, and to a wider market of potential partners, *thus laying the foundation for a grey repartnering revolution.*

The gendered structure of the partner market

The cross-gender market of 'available' older singles is skewed in favour of men. The reason is that the widowed community is primarily made up of women and the gendered structure of the widowed population remains largely intact over time. This can be seen from Table 3.1: in both England/Wales and Sweden, the proportion of widows 65+ remains roughly three times larger than the proportion of same-aged widowers in this 30-year period. The main reason for the gender difference is that more men than women die married (in Sweden 7 in 10 men die married compared to 3 in 10 women). A central reason for this difference is the longer average lifespan of women, which means that more men die before their partner than vice versa. This difference is further accentuated by the cultural expectation that men should be older than women in marriages. As a consequence, the supply of opposite-sex partners is considerably smaller for older single women than for older single men, and this difference increases with age.

Table 3.1: Changes in marital status for the 65+ population over time in England and Wales compared to Sweden, 1981 to 2014 (%)

	1981		2014	
	E & W*	SE	E & W**	SE
	%	%	%	%
MEN				
Married	73	67	74	62
Widowed	18	16	12	10
Divorced	2	5	8	16
Never married	7	12	5	11
Total number (millions)	(3.0)	(0.6)	(4.6)	(0.9)
WOMEN				
Married	37	38	51	44
Widowed	49	43	36	30
Divorced	2	6	9	18
Never married	12	13	4	8
Total number (millions)	(4.6)	(0.8)	(5.6)	(1.0)

Sources: Statistics Sweden; *Arber, Davidson & Ginn (2003);**British National Statistics.

Of all Swedish men and women who were *not currently married* in 2013 a small majority of the young-old (60–74 years), but a substantial majority of the old-old (75–90 years), were women – 54% vs. 71% (Statistics Sweden). However, people who are not currently married can still be cohabiting or in an LAT union. If we exclude everyone who is living in a union (marrieds, cohabitants and LATs) and include only singles, the same gendered structure is evident. Our Swedish survey data showed that among all young-old singles, 59% were women. This number increased to 75% among old-old singles. In sum, there are more older female than male singles.

As a consequence the cross-gender partner market for older men is significantly larger than it is for older women, and the gap increases by age – a fact that had not escaped our older interviewees. Cohabiting Clint, an 82-year-old man, describes how he, after having been widowed, discovered the late-life dancing scene where he met his current partner:

> 'I'll be blunt and say that when you were young and went out dancing there was a lot of competition among the boys to invite the girls to dance. When you reach my age it has changed radically. On these dancing nights, there might be

150 people, of which the men count 50. So there is a fierce competition going on [between the women].'

The perspective from the point of view of older women is rather the opposite. Clint's cohabiting partner Cecilia, aged 78, talks about her fears of being widowed: "I'm terrified of being left by myself again. When you go out dancing, one third are men and two thirds women. The men can choose freely." Thus, the opportunity for finding a cross-gender partner in later life is structured by gender, in favour of older men. The same gendered structure has been reported from many Western countries (see for example Brown et al, 2006 for the US). However, and importantly, since the society of divorcees is more evenly gender structured than the society of widowed people, and since it grows over time, compared to the community of widowed people, the partner market for older singles is *becoming less skewed by gender*, as can be seen in the distribution of married men and women in Table 3.1, which is slowly evening out over time. And since divorced people are generally more open to repartnering, the rise of the society of divorcees means that *the gendered opportunity gap for dating in later life is slowly decreasing* over time, even if it will not close in the near future.

Changing venues for dating in later life

Another aspect of the opportunity structure for late-life repartnering is the availability of arenas for meeting a partner. Cohabiting Clint and Cecilia met on the dance floor. Where do people meet a new partner late in life? Has there been a change over time? There are quite a few studies that investigate dating in later life, looking, for example, at the desire for a new partner, the characteristics of daters and the different functions that dating fulfils (we will return to these topics in Chapter six). However, there are few studies of *where* older couples meet. Those that exist often look exclusively at one specific venue, such as Internet dating (Alterovitz & Mendelsohn, 2009, 2013; McWilliams & Barrett, 2014) or pensioners' dances (Ronström, 1998). Still, the structure of available dating venues is important, since it shapes the opportunities for finding a new romantic partner and changes in venues also affect these opportunities.

In our survey we have asked respondents in unions where they met their current intimate partner. As can be seen from Table 3.2, two continuously important arenas for meeting a partner in different life phases are networks of friends and dance halls. In the quotes above, Cohabiting Clint and Cecilia talked about the dance floor as a possible venue for finding a new partner, and as Table 3.2 shows, dancing is the most common arena in Sweden for meeting a partner throughout the life course – also in later life. Work is also an important arena, but less in later life than in mid-life – instead, travel and associations gain more importance.

Table 3.2: Venues for meeting a partne: how 60–90-year-old Swedes met their current partner, depending on their age when initiating the relationship (%)

	Age when meeting one's current partner		
	up to 24	**25–59**	**60–90**
Friends	28	20	16
Internet/personal ad	0	8	20
Dance	44	36	22
Travel	2	2	10
Association	6	6	10
Work	8	19	9
Other	12	9	13
Total	100	100	100

A noticeable life course difference visible in Table 3.2 is that the Internet and personal ads seem to become more important as an arena for finding a partner later in life, partly at the expense of dancing. This reflects the emergence of new digital technologies in the 1990s and their impact on the dating patterns for the studied cohorts. New digital technologies have lowered the threshold for searching for new partners and have contributed to making personal ads more socially acceptable. However, this is mainly a historical effect. Our Swedish survey data showed that almost no one (2%) had met their partner through 'Internet or personal ads' before 1990, but among those who had repartnered in 1990 or later, 15% had met their partner through this venue (not shown in the table). This reflects not only a technological change, but also a concurrent normalisation of personal ads, where it is seen as more acceptable both to place and respond to personal ads.

The rising importance of Internet dating can be explained in terms of filling a void. McWilliams and Barrett's (2014) interviewees described how dating venues that used to be important earlier in life, such as pubs, come to be seen as catering mainly to younger people, excluding older people. At the same time social networks diminish when same-aged friends and siblings die. In this situation the Internet provides a new and appreciated venue.

Some of our interviewees had met their current and prior partners at pensioners' dances as well as Internet dating sites, and comment on the differences between them. Single Sarah, 67 years old, who had been dancing a lot earlier in life and met some of her partners through dancing, describes how she did not feel at home at pensioners' dances, which she found de-eroticising: "Pensioners' dance? No, help me God, I've tried. I couldn't stand it when they paused and took out their packed coffee and sandwiches. So I left!" She had almost given up on finding a new partner prior to discovering Internet dating with the aid of her daughter:

> 'Where else could I have found them? It's not as if you can go out into the street calling for them. Eva [daughter] created an account for me on Cooldate (…). There were a couple of dead years after my second marriage but then along came the Internet, and God, I have met many men in the last few years. They have been short, almost exclusively sexual, relationships.'

In Sarah's case her daughter had been a support in introducing her to Internet dating and showing her how to get started. This was not uncommon among older interviewees who were not habitual IT users themselves. Thus the Internet can introduce adult children to a new social support function, as 'dating coaches' for their parents.

Digital technologies also have the advantage of transcending geographical distances, even national borders. Some of our interviewees had met their partners in other parts of Sweden or even abroad and used the Internet to stay in touch regularly when they did not meet in person. Others described how they had used the Internet to find and reconnect with intimate partners from their early adulthood. In short, although friends and dancing remain important dating venues, new digital technologies have provided new possibilities for finding a partner late in life.

Conclusion

In this chapter we have illustrated the changing landscape of intimacy in later life using empirical data from different countries. The purpose has been to map out some of the more important socio-historical conditions that shape late-life intimacy. The chapter has investigated the extension of the healthy life course and it has shown how increased longevity affects relationships by prolonging lifelong marriages, but also by increasing the risk of divorce and the opportunity for repartnering. We have also investigated the changing structure of the late-life partner market in the wake of the establishment of a culture of divorce, and the changing venues for meeting a partner.

The extension of the healthy life course is a precondition for what Laslett has referred to as the emergence of a third age between the productive phase of the second age and the frailty and dependency of the fourth age. This space is characterised by a relative freedom from the duties that characterised mid-life, but also by the increased intensity that is created by the realisation that life is limited. As a consequence the third age becomes a life phase that both allows and encourages the individual to pursue outstanding or new life goals. Within this new-found freedom, an old relationship can be a support for achieving these life goals, but a non-rewarding relationship can constitute an obstacle. This might partly explain the increase in late-life divorces. A couple of decades ago, when the healthy lifespan was shorter, personal finances more limited and the normative context less allowing, older people might have chosen to remain in a non-satisfying relationship for their last years. In contemporary consumer society older people are more prone to leave a non-rewarding relationship and either continue on their own as singles or try to find a new life partner who can accompany them in their pursuit of their life goals.

The increase in both the prevalence and the incidence of divorce in later life can be understood in relation to the emergence of the third age and the pursuit of happiness and self-fulfilment in later life, but also in relation to what Giddens refers to as the transformation of intimacy and a new view on relationships as tools for self-reflection and development. In an earlier historical period when marriage was for life, late-life divorce was difficult to achieve. But in late modern society, it becomes legitimate – or even an obligation to the self – to leave a relationship which is no longer seen as rewarding. The fact that it has become more common to be divorced, but also to get divorced, in later life, shows the power of this new normative frame.

As a consequence of these socio-historical changes the structure of the late-life partner market has changed. We have conceptualised this change in terms of the emergence of a society of divorcees which – as we will see later – consists of individuals who might be more inclined to repartner than widowed singles. And we have shown how this emergence will contribute to a decrease in the gendered opportunity gap for older dating singles over time.

Finally, we have investigated how technological change has contributed to a restructuring of the partner market for older single people. We have shown how the emergence of new digital technologies affects dating opportunities for older people by introducing new ways to meet, for example through Internet dating sites, but also to maintain relationships over geographical distance, even between countries, through new communications technologies.

FOUR

From marriage to alternative union forms

In this chapter we continue the empirical investigation into the changing landscape of late-life intimacy. A central aspect of the transformation of intimacy is the deinstitutionalisation of marriage and the concurrent emergence of alternative forms for intimacy. The purpose of this chapter is to investigate union form in older people's intimate relationships. Older people are often expected to be conservative in their choice of union form – because they grew up in a time when marriage was the norm for people in intimate relationships, they are assumed to still prefer marriage for their unions. In this chapter we question this assumption and show that at least with regard to union form, older people tend to follow the times they live in, being part of the transformation of intimacy described in Chapter two. But we also argue that the later phase of life seems to have its own conditions that shape the choice of union form, such as having a wealth of earlier relationship experiences, being in a phase beyond work and reproduction, and having a restricted remaining lifetime. By showing the importance of the historical transformation of intimacy and the particular conditions of later life for the choice of union form, this chapter provides a foundation for the arguments in the following chapters.

A smorgasbord of union forms

Contemporary older people can choose from a number of different union forms, ranging from different types of LAT relationships, to living together in non-marital and marital cohabitation. If marriage for a long time was the normative and established union form for an intimate relationship, this hegemony has for half a century been challenged, first by non-marital cohabitation and later by LAT relationships, both of which can be a prelude, or an alternative, to a formalised marriage.

Cohabitation can be defined as two people living in an intimate relationship and sharing the same household (cmpr. Chevan, 1996). In some countries non-marital cohabitation has become an accepted alternative to marriage, while in others it is still a marginal phenomenon.

Kiernan (2002) identifies four stages in the historical development of unmarried cohabitation: (1) a deviant avant-garde phenomenon, (2) a prelude to marriage, (3) a socially accepted alternative to marriage, (4) an alternative indistinguishable from marriage. According to Kiernan, Sweden and Denmark were among the first countries to make the transition into the fourth stage. In Sweden there had already been some acceptance of pre-marital cohabitation in the 19th century. 'Stockholm marriage' was a form of cohabitation for people who migrated to urban areas and were too poor to get married. According to Trost (1978), this existing tradition facilitated the rapid establishment of cohabitation in the 1960s and 1970s. In less than a decade (1967–1973) marriage rates were cut by half. At the same time cohabitation became more common and even in the 1980s it had become an established alternative and not only a prelude to marriage in Sweden (Popenoe, 1987). In many Western countries cohabitation is now an institutionalised alternative to marriage, which is evident in actual figures: among Swedes aged 18–44 years, more than half (53%) of all cohabitants were unmarried in 2002/2005, somewhat ahead of the other Nordic and north European countries (30–40%) and in total contrast to the south European countries (0–15%) (Soons & Kalmijn, 2009; see also Hiekel, Liefbroer & Poortman, 2014).

For a long time there has been a failure to recognise the importance of cohabitation in older people's relationships and when it has been recognised it has often been problematised. A starting point for much previous research about cohabitation has been that it is a lesser version of marriage – a 'poor people's marriage' – and that there exists a gap between cohabitation and marriage, for example with regard to the stability of the union or the quality of the relationship (Cherlin, 1992; Stanley, Whitton & Markman, 2004; Wiik, Keizer & Lappegard, 2012). However, cohabitation may have different implications in later life. According to King and Scott (2005), older cohabitants are more satisfied with their relationships, and are more likely to view cohabitation as an alternative to marriage, compared to younger people, and Brown and Kawamura (2010) did not find any gap between cohabitants and marrieds in later life. It is also possible that the assumption about a cohabitation gap reveals more about the context in which the research has been carried out – contexts where marriage has a self-evident cultural and social status as the hegemonic union form. Much of the research has been carried out in the US where marriage has a more dominant status than in northern Europe. It has been argued that the assumed cohabitation gap is not a feature of the union form itself, but rather a measure of its degree of social institutionalisation (Soons

& Kalmijn, 2009). In countries where cohabitation is still a rare phenomenon (for example many southern European countries), it is often a choice for marginalised groups, while in countries where it is an institutionalised and accepted substitute for marriage it is spread among all social groups (for example the Nordic countries, the Netherlands, France, Quebec in Canada).

The institutionalisation of non-marital cohabitation meant that intimately involved individuals could be recognised as a couple *without being married* and in time this also paved the way for the possibility of being recognised as a couple *without living together* – this form of being an established couple, but retaining different households, has come to be known as Living Apart Together or LAT (Levin, 2004; Levin & Trost, 1999). LAT has been an established way of living together and a publicly recognised concept in northern Europe since the 1980s, but has increasingly become recognised also elsewhere and pioneering research on LAT in the later part of life has in recent years been published in Australia (Malta & Farquharson, 2014; Upton-Davis, 2015), the US (Benson & Coleman, 2016a, 2016b) and Canada (Funk & Kobayashi, 2014).

According to Levin, being in an LAT relationship implies something more serious than dating or 'going steady': besides having different households, it includes defining oneself as being in a couple and being viewed as a couple by others. According to Borell (2001) LAT is characterised by a low degree of organisation, with few collective resources binding the partners together, and few legal bonds or cultural conventions to fall back on. It allows the two partners to lead distinct and autonomous lives. However, in practice there is significant variation – from living separately and seeing each other intermittently to living together almost all the time but switching between apartments. In countries where LAT is established it is recognised as a more stable union form than dating and it is not necessarily a transitional form leading to marital or non-marital cohabitation. Benson and Coleman (2016a) find that older Americans living apart together do not use the concept of LAT to describe themselves, but that they see a need to distinguish themselves from 'daters' – a concept they associated with less stability and seriousness. According to Régnier-Loilier et al (2009), LAT is often a more stable union form in old age than in earlier phases of life. LAT has grown in popularity in many Western countries in the last 40 years although comparative figures are hard to come by.

Few studies present data on the prevalence of alternative union forms in later life. In the US, cohabitation in the 60+ population grew from practically zero to 2.4% between 1960 and 1990 (Chevan, 1996). This increase has continued. According to Vespa (2013), in 2012 more than 1 in 10 in the 55+ population were cohabiting. Statistics from Finland and Sweden also show a historical increase in cohabitation in the older population (Moustgaard & Martikainen, 2009; Statistics Sweden).

Comparative data of cohabitation in the older population has been hard to come by until recently. Many countries do not collect or publish statistics on non-marital cohabitation and in many countries it is not officially recognised. Below we use data from the European Social Survey to illustrate differences in the prevalence of cohabitation in the older population across Europe. Figure 4.1 presents the proportion of marital and non-marital cohabitation in eight European countries among people aged 60–90 *who live with a partner*. It shows that there are clear differences with regard to the spread of cohabitation in different parts of the Western world. In Catholic countries such as Poland and Ireland non-marital cohabitation is almost non-existent, while in the Nordic countries (Norway, Finland and Sweden) and Estonia it is a rather common phenomenon. In between we have Germany, the Netherlands and England/Wales, with more moderate levels of cohabitation in this age group.

The data in Figure 4.1 does not include people in LAT relationships. The prevalence of LAT is even more difficult to estimate than that of cohabitation since there are few published statistics. According

Figure 4.1: Marital vs. non-marital unions among cohabiting individuals aged 60–90 in nine European countries (%)

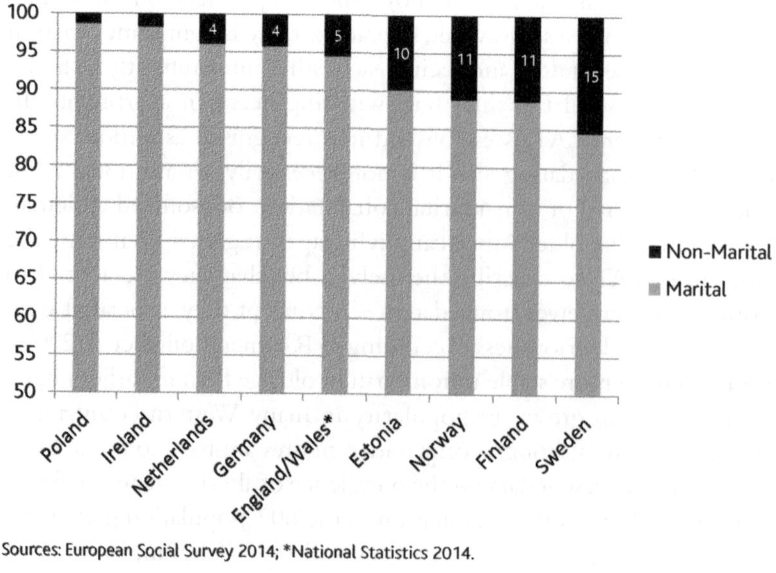

Sources: European Social Survey 2014; *National Statistics 2014.

to Régnier-Loilier et al (2009) about 4–5% of the 60–80-year-old population in France currently in a relationship were living as LATs – more women than men. A similar figure (5%) was noted by Duncan et al (2013) among older people 65+ in Britain 2011.

If we include all union forms, what is the distribution among older people? Figure 4.2 shows the prevalence of different union forms among Swedes aged 60–90 (figures from our 2012 survey). One third (32.9%) are currently single. A little more than half (53.4%) are married, while 8.6% are cohabiting and 5.1% are in an LAT union. Thus, one third of those who are not married are actually in an established intimate union. The prevalence of alternative union forms among older people is probably somewhat lower in other Western countries, where remarriage is more common after repartnering.

Figure 4.2: Union form among 60–90-year-old Swedes (%)

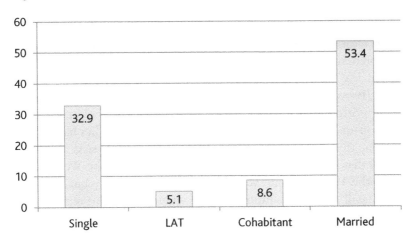

Union form in Sweden does not correlate with gender, income, education or degree of urbanity. However, it varies significantly with different aspects of time that will be considered below. The union form frequencies in Figure 4.2 raise a number of questions: do they reflect the ideal that current cohorts of older Swedes were brought up with? Or do they reflect the historical period in which they met their current partner? Or are they perhaps best understood as a reflection of the priorities characteristic of the life phase they were in when they met their partner? These are questions that are often raised implicitly in earlier research on intimacy in later life. We discuss them more explicitly below.

Are older people carriers of the ideals of marriage culture?

For a long time it was a common research assumption that marriage was the self-evident form for new intimate relationships in later life. Over 35 years ago, Lopata (1979) wrote that older widowed people had four options: to live alone, to move into some form of collective residence, to live with their children, or to remarry. There are several explanations for this focus on marriage in repartnering: the point of departure for much older research was a cultural context where marriage was the only accepted form for intimate relationships (Steitz & Welker, 1991). Some more contemporary research has also been carried out in cultural contexts where marriage remains the norm for relationships in all ages (Mehta, 2002; van den Hoonaard, 2004). The idea of a cultural lag is true in the sense that the cultural norm of marriage that prevailed when a marriage was established remains conserved in that union until it is dissolved. However, this does not necessarily reflect a cohort-typical preference for marriage.

In cultural contexts where alternative union forms are established and accepted, the assumption is often instead that older people, as a cohort effect, live by norms and traditions that dominated their formative years (Brown et al, 2006; Moore & Stratton, 2004). Older cohorts are often portrayed as physical carriers of 'cultural lag' – representatives of soon-to-be extinct traditions and values. Some studies have found that the trend towards the deinstitutionalisation of marriage (Cherlin, 2004) that has affected young and mid-life people in the West at least since the 1970s does not yet encompass older people – but speculate that it will do so in the future as a consequence of cohort replacement (Brown, Bulanda & Lee, 2005; Brown et al, 2006; Moore & Stratton, 2004; van den Hoonaard, 2004).

A few objections can be raised against the idea that older people are carriers of marriage cultural ideals. One central objection is that it builds on an anthropological assumption about people as unchanging, and a product of their upbringing (cohort belonging). Another objection is that many people in contemporary older cohorts participated in the sexual revolution and the transition to divorce culture in their youth or early adulthood. As a consequence, they are not unused to alternative ways of living together.

Are older people following the ideals of their times?

Much research instead stresses that older people tend to actively choose *not* to marry (see for example Borell, 2001; Malta & Farquharson,

2014; Talbott, 1998). Official statistics from many Western countries shows that remarriage in later life is rare and even rarer among older women than older men (see also Brown & Lin, 2012; Carr, 2004). One interpretation of this is that older people are taking part in the 'society-wide shifts that appear to affect all groups at the same time' (Cherlin, 1992, p 31), irrespective of age. Instead of sticking to 'old values' from early adulthood, older people could be assumed to be part of the normative changes that have taken place in society as part of the historical development, and to be affected by them. Such a historical development is the transformation of intimacy which has swept across large parts of the Western world over the last half century, which includes the deinstitutionalisation of marriage, or the move from a marriage to a divorce culture in which marriage becomes less determined by outside norms, and other union forms such as cohabitation and LAT are introduced as more or less equal alternatives.

In line with this historical explanation, in a Dutch study de Jong Gierveld (2004b) identified a turning point for the normalisation of alternative union forms: people 50+ repartnering before 1985 primarily chose marriage as their union form, while those repartnering in 1985 or later primarily chose LAT unions. This could be interpreted as a historical effect, connected to the diminished importance of marriage as the normative form for romantic relationships for people of all ages.

Are some union forms more adapted to later life?

A different explanation of the fact that older people tend not to (re)marry is that marriage, as well as other union forms, may have different meanings in different ages or phases of life. Marriage is often considered to be an institution connected with the security of families during the child-raising years, and is often a norm in mid-life, but not necessarily in later life when children are no longer dependent on their parents. In fact, a new marriage can be an obstacle in later life, as it ties not only two individuals together, but two families that might not appreciate the legal hassle that such an arrangement can create for future inheritance issues. In our own Swedish studies, children were often negative towards their parents remarrying, even though they were otherwise supportive of them repartnering. Also, in many countries remarrying can have negative financial effects through the loss of the widow's pension from an earlier marriage (de Jong Gierveld, 2004b; Stevens, 2004).

It has instead been argued that older people prefer alternative union forms. Some studies have pointed out that LAT relationships facilitate autonomy, which might be especially welcomed in later life when there are no common family projects (children) that demand a shared household. LAT allows for a mutually satisfying long-term emotional and sexual relationship while retaining continuity in personal identity and social interaction through an intact home. Women, in particular, have been shown to prefer LAT relationships in order to avoid re-entering into a housekeeping role that they have often experienced in an earlier marriage, or to avoid the risk of having to care for an ill older partner (Ghazanfareeon Karlsson & Borell, 2002; Malta & Farquharson, 2014). Other studies have argued that older men, in particular, might prefer cohabitation as a union form that provides many of the advantages of marriage but has few of the associated demands (Davidson, 2002).

A question of age, period or cohort?

So, out of (a) birth cohort, (b) the historical year in which the relationship was initiated and (c) the age at which the relationship started, which explanation seems to be the most important for understanding which union form older people currently live in? Below we will discuss these explanations in light of our 2012 Swedish survey data. Table 4.1 presents cross-tabulations between union form and: *birth cohort*; the *historical year* in which the relationship was initiated; and the *age* at which the individual initiated the relationship.

The cross-tabulation presented in the upper panel of Table 4.1 gives little credence to the cohort-based explanation. This panel shows the distribution of union forms for three different birth cohorts, born 1922–32, 1933–42 and 1943–52. It shows that there is no clear (significant) relationship between birth cohort and union form. Irrespective of cohort, the vast majority of those in a union are married. The second most common union form is cohabitation, closely followed by LAT. The distribution between union forms is similar for all three cohorts.

In return, the cross-tabulation in the middle panel shows strong support for the idea that union form is determined by the historical period in which the relationship was established. This panel shows the distribution of union form for six different time periods in which the relationships were established. It is clear from the table that until the beginning of the 1970s very few people chose any other form for their union besides marriage. However, marriage becomes an increasingly less common union form for relationships established in the 1970s and later. In the early 21st century, marriage has been reduced to an uncommon choice. In return the share of alternative union forms

Table 4.1: Union form in relation to the respondents' year of birth (cohort), the historical year that the relationship was initiated (period) and the respondents' age at relationship initiation (life phase) (%)

	Married	Cohabiting	LAT	Total
Year of birth (*Cohort*) ns				
1922–1932	79.7	10.8	9.5	100
1933–1942	84.0	8.9	7.1	100
1943–1952	77.3	15.4	7.3	100
Year of relationship initiation (*Period*) ***				
–1960	97.3	1.8	0.9	100
1960–69	95.5	3.5	1.0	100
1970–79	81.1	17.2	1.6	100
1980–89	72.2	19.4	8.3	100
1990–99	50.9	33.3	15.8	100
2000–	18.5	29.6	51.9	100
Age at relationship initiation (*Life Phase*) ***				
1–19	95.3	3.4	1.4	100
20–39	88.8	9.3	1.9	100
40–59	50.8	32.2	16.9	100
60–90	16.2	24.3	59.5	100

Note: ns = non significant; *** = p<.001.

(cohabitation and LAT) has grown, with cohabitation exceeding 15% in relationships established in the 1970s, and LAT reaching the same levels two decades later.

Finally, the cross-tabulation in the lower panel shows strong support for the idea that union form is determined by *life phase* – the age at which the relationship was established. This panel shows that in unions initiated before the respondents turned 40 the dominant union form was marriage. In unions formed when the respondents were in their mid-life (40–59), it was as common to choose alternative union forms as it was to get married. In unions initiated in later life (60–90) only a minority married. Instead the most common choice was LAT, followed by cohabitation.

We obviously need to be cautious in interpreting these results, since historical time overlaps with age, and most of the respondents in our data who initiated a relationship after the year 2000 were also in a later life phase, where marriage might no longer be a favoured option, regardless of historical norms. We return to this question in the multivariate tables below.

Cohort

A common expectation is that older people tend to be more conservative in their lifestyle choices than their younger counterparts. If this is true we would expect the oldest old to be married to a larger extent than the young-old – basically showing more liberal ideals for every successive cohort.

The cross-tabulation in Table 4.1 did not present any support for a cohort effect in union choice. This seems to remain true even if we break down our three cohorts on the *year the relationship was initiated* (Figure 4.3). The figure instead provides clear support for the idea of a historical (period) effect. Before 1970 nearly everybody who initiated a new relationship chose to marry, regardless of cohort belonging. In the second historical period (1970–89) marriage remains the norm,

Figure 4.3: Union form in relation to birth cohort, within three historical periods in which the relationship was initiated (year of relationship initiation) (%)

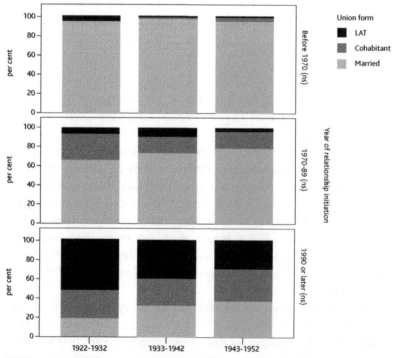

Note: P-values for cohort differences within historical periods (year at relationship initiation): ns = non significant

but cohabitation and to some extent LAT break in as alternatives to marriage, regardless of cohort belonging. In the last historical period (1990 and later) marriage is no longer the norm but a minority choice. There is no support for a cohort explanation (this is true also if we break down cohort by age at relationship initiation – data not shown). It is worth noting (although it is non-significant) that the oldest respondents (born 1922–32) seem to be the most likely to choose alternative union forms – hinting at the importance of life phase.

Historical time

It would seem that cohort belonging has very little impact on current union form. It seems reasonable to instead look closer at the relationship between historical period and life phase (age at relationship initiation).

Figure 4.4 shows that historical period remains an important explanation of chosen union form even if we break it down on the individual's age at the time of initiating the relationship. Indeed, as the figure shows, there is a clear (significant) period effect in two of the

Figure 4.4: Union form in different historical periods (year of relationship initiation), by respondents' age at relationship initiation (life phase) (%)

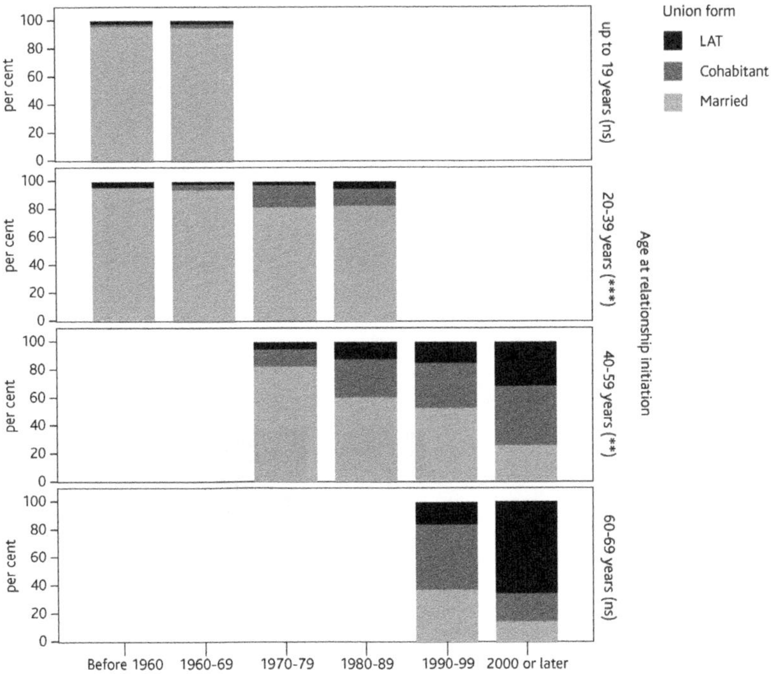

Note: P-values for year of relationship initiation within grouped age at relationship initiation (life phase); ns = non significant; ** = p<.01; *** = p<.001.

life phases (20–39 years and 40–59 years). In earlier historical periods people tended to marry to a higher extent, regardless of the life phase they were currently in. In later historical periods alternative union forms were more common, regardless of life phase (viewed panel by panel).

Life phase

Figure 4.5 presents support for the idea that the age at which the relationship was initiated has an important impact on chosen union form. This seems reasonable considering that different life phases pose different challenges to people and consequently affect their choices. The figure presents union form distribution for relationships initiated in different life phases (the age at which the relationship was initiated) broken down by three historical periods. The relationship between life

Figure 4.5: Union form in relation to life phase (age at relationship initiation), within three historical periods in which the relationship was initiated (year of relationship initiation) (%)

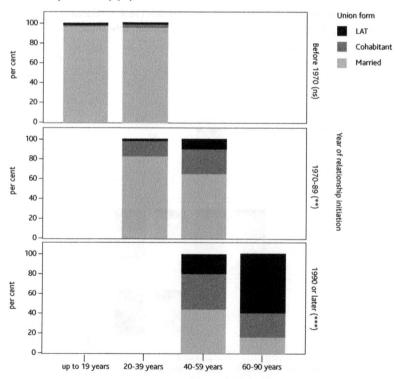

Note: P-values for age of relationship initiation within three historical periods in which the relationship was initiated (year of relationship initiation); ns = non significant; ** = p<.01; *** = p<.001.

phase and chosen union form is strong (significant) for relationships initiated after 1970 (the two lower panels). To put it more concretely, alternatives to marriage were hardly an option for relationships before 1970, regardless of the age of the respondent at the beginning of the relationship, but for the period beginning in 1970 alternative union forms are more common for those beginning their relationships in later life phases than for those who do so in earlier life phases.

Conclusion

In this chapter we have investigated the relative importance of cohort, historical period and life phase as explanations for chosen union form in people's relationships in later life, using Swedish survey data.

Historical period was more important in determining chosen union form for our Swedish respondents than cohort belonging. This finding is in line with Cherlin's (1992) assertion that he has increasingly come to 'lean more toward period-based explanations' of changing historical patterns in marriage, divorce and remarriage in the US (p vii). Thus, at least in Sweden, the social changes described by family theory, in terms of the deinstitutionalisation of marriage and the concurrent historical development of individualised and flexible relationship arrangements, seems to affect older people in the same way that has been discussed for younger people. A historical break was observable in the 1970s, after which other union forms besides marriage became potential choices for all the studied cohorts and the respondents started to experiment with alternative relationship arrangements – first, by living together without being married; later followed by the option to Live Apart Together.

The results also emphasised the importance of life phase. The older a person was at relationship initiation, the more likely that person was to currently live as LAT. In fact, the majority of those who initiated a relationship after the age of 60 chose to Live Apart Together. Previous research gives some clues to why this might be the case, based on the structural specificities of later life. In a number of articles Ghazanfareeon Karlsson and Borell (2002, 2003, 2005, 2007; see also Davidson, 2001; Davidson, 2002; Funk & Kobayashi, 2014; Malta & Farquharson, 2014) have argued that LAT is a union form particularly well suited to the specific needs and wishes of older people, allowing the preservation of separate homes and autonomous lives, for example in terms of finances, social networks and house work. Especially women, who often had prior experiences of taking care of a common home, cherished the freedom of keeping a 'home of their own'.

Another structural aspect of later life that might impact on the choice of union form is that lifetime is slowly running out (see Chapter eleven). Research on earlier life phases often describes LAT as a preparatory union form, a sort of relationship trial period, which might later turn into cohabitation or marriage if the relationship is consolidated. The finality of later life means that there might be too little time to develop a relationship to a point where it seems preferable to move in together. In our qualitative interviews many older people were hesitant to leave their current home and context because it made them feel vulnerable, and they pointed out that the consequences of major life changes carried more weight late in life. In case the relationship should suddenly end, for example by the death of the partner, they would stand without the protection of their social and kin networks. This was the case in particular for partners living at some distance from each other. These structural specificities of later life might explain why so many older people who initiate a new intimate relationship chose to live as LATs.

The results above need to be framed in a Swedish tradition of liberal relationship values. As stated in Chapter two, the Swedish individually based welfare model, combined with the historically long tradition of women's labour participation, has contributed to the normalisation of alternative union and family forms. In this sense Sweden is a special case, but similar trends can be recognised in many other Western countries, with similar transitions in family patterns, primarily in northern Europe and North America.

Our conclusion is that there is little to support the idea of older people as representatives of a cultural lag (a form of 'othering') when it comes to union form norms. Instead, our data suggests that older people are not very different from younger people in their union choices. If anything they are less traditional.

FIVE

A life of relationships

The purpose of this chapter is to attempt to bridge the macro–micro gap by showing how the historical transformation of intimacy described in earlier chapters is reflected in older individuals' relationship careers. We will challenge the idea that current generations of older people have normally lived their lives in single lifelong marriages ending in widowhood and show that their relationship careers are instead often quite complex. A second purpose of the chapter is to discuss the consequences of prior relationship experiences on interest in, and preferences for, late-life intimacy. We discuss the different implications of being widowed versus divorced for interest in repartnering and explain why divorcees are often more prepared to repartner. This is important in relation to the fact that the society of older divorcees will soon be bigger than the community of older widowed people in many Western countries (as described in Chapter three). Finally we focus on the different biographical relationship experiences of women and men and how they impact on the interest for repartnering in later life. We will conclude the chapter with a discussion of our findings in relation to the deinstitutionalisation of the life course thesis. In contrast to the previous chapters this chapter will make extensive use of biographical case descriptions and quotes to give the reader a richer understanding of what it means to have lived one's life during the historical transition to divorce culture.

Relationship careers among older Swedes

In our opening case we introduced Cohabiting Carl and Caroline, who had had rather complex relationship careers, involving marriages and remarriages, divorces and widowhood but also a number of non-marital relationships and separations. Their relationship experiences correspond directly to the normative changes following the transition from marriage to divorce culture, but they also had a concrete impact on the organisation of their current relationship – for example due to three earlier divorces Carl did not want to remarry, and due to grief after being widowed in her second marriage Caroline was totally uninterested in new romantic episodes for almost 20 years.

It is often assumed that older people have lived their adult lives in lifelong marriages lasting until widowhood – and that after widowhood they will stay single unless they remarry (Lopata, 1996). This was a common assumption in many early studies on attitudes to remarriage among widows (Steitz & Welker, 1991; Talbott, 1998) and has also been an underlying assumption in many later studies (Bennett, Arnott & Soulsby, 2013; Carr, 2004; Moorman, Booth & Fingerman, 2006). The assumption of the single prior marital relationship is also evident in later titles such as 'second couplehood' (Koren, 2011, 2015). But as the case of Carl and Caroline shows, in countries where divorce culture has been established for a long time, contemporary cohorts of older people will have experienced and been influenced by its values already during their early adult lives. These experiences, accumulated over the life course will, for a substantial group of older people, have resulted in very complex relationship careers. Indeed, Brown and Lin (2012) argue that older people often have the most complex relationship careers, as a product of having lived a long life in divorce culture.

Considering that divorce rates were already high in the 1970s in North America and northern Europe, it seems unlikely that contemporary cohorts of older people would generally have lived in single lifelong marriages. Below we illustrate the increasing complexity of the relationship careers of contemporary generations of older Swedes using both aggregate data and individual biographies.

Figure 5.1 summarises the relationship careers (numbers of partners) of a representative sample of 60–90-year-old Swedes. The first bar shows that a majority (59%) have been married only once in their lifetime (that is, they are either still married or they have previously been married once and have not remarried) while one in four (26%) have had two or more marital unions. Another 15% have never been married. If we exclude the never-marrieds, one third of those who have been married have been married more than once.

However, since alternative union forms have been accepted in Sweden for quite a long time we also need to consider cohabitation and LAT. The second bar in Figure 5.1 shows that one third of those who have cohabited (marital or non-marital cohabitation), have cohabited with more than one partner. The third bar shows the number of established relationships (married, cohabitant or LAT) an individual has had during their life. Almost half (46%) of the older individuals have had at least two established relationships, while one in four (23%) have had three or more such relationships. Consequently, the ideal of the single 'one and only' relationship (often, but not always, a lifelong marriage) is fulfilled by less than half of contemporary older Swedes. Only a small minority (7%) have never had an established relationship.

Figure 5.1: Total number of partners the respondents have (1) been married to, (2) cohabited with (marital or non-marital cohabitation), (3) had an established relationship with (married, cohabitant or LAT), and (4) had sex with (%)

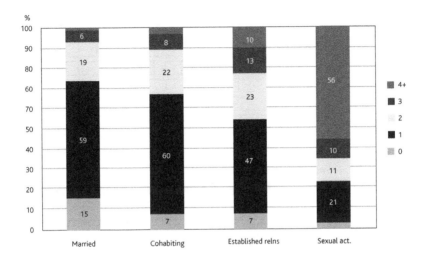

According to the ideals of marriage culture, sexual intimacy is supposed to be exclusive to marriage. However, as can be seen in bar four in Figure 5.1, in general older Swedes have had considerably more sexual partners than marital partners. The vast majority (77%) have had sex with at least two partners and a majority (56%) have had sex with four or more partners. Consequently the cultural ideal that sex should be the exclusive property of marriage is fulfilled only by a minority.

In conclusion, the aggregated data presented above about the relationship careers of older Swedish adults indicate that at least a sizeable part of the population have not lived their lives according to the institutionalised script of marriage culture. Instead many older people have very complex relationship careers, involving several partners and different union forms. Below we will continue to investigate this complexity in more detail using individual relationship biographies that show the wide range of variation between individuals. We start by presenting an overview of the relationship careers of our Swedish interviewees.

Figure 5.2 shows the distribution of unions (in different forms), as well as periods of singlehood, over the life course for our 28

Figure 5.2. Relationship careers in different union forms among 28 Swedes, aged 60–90, who have either initiated a new intimate relationship after the age of 60 or who are dating singles

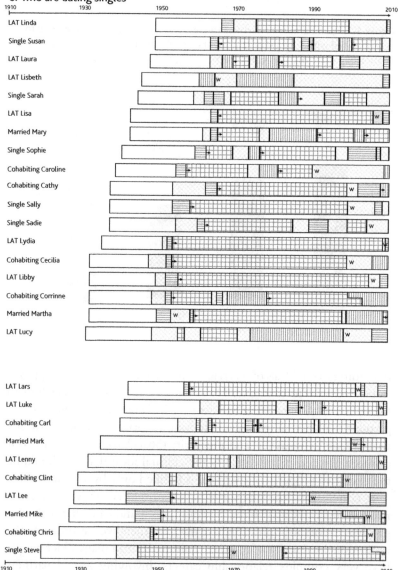

Note: Relationship dissolutions not marked with a W [widowhood] are divorces/separations.

interviewees. Many of the interviewees did not have traditional relationship careers, if by that we mean having married and lived with a partner until widowhood: 6 of the women and 6 of the men had lived in their first marriage until the death of their partner, while 11 women and 4 men were divorced from their first marriage in different phases of the life course. Before their current situation as repartnered or single, 8 of the informants had had only one prior partner, 14 had had two partners and 6 had had three (shorter dating relationships and sexual encounters not included).

The interviews illustrate the wide heterogeneity in relationship careers that the individuals have had over their life course. For example, they could take the straightforward form of the single lifelong marriage, possibly followed by a late-life 'bonus' relationship (what has been referred to as a 'second couplehood', Koren, 2011). This was the case for 87-year-old Cohabiting Chris, who lived in a single lifelong relationship until the death of his wife at the age of 81 after which he repartnered a couple of years later. But they could also take more complex forms, such as the serial relationship career, as was the case for 78-year-old Corinne:

The case of Cohabiting Corinne

Corinne had a few shorter sexual relationships from the age of 17 before meeting her future husband at the age of 20. A year after meeting they married, moved in together and soon had two children. Eleven years later her husband left her for another woman and they got divorced. During the following years she had one shorter established relationship and a couple of sexual relationships before meeting her second husband who was 12 years younger than her. They moved in together and she cohabited with him for 10 years before marrying at the age of 46. The marriage resulted in her third child. At the age of 66 she actively started looking for and found a new partner because, as she explains it, her husband thought she was too old for sex, but she 'wanted an active sex life'. Although she immediately moved in with her new partner she remained married to her former partner for another couple of years.

If we take into consideration the sequential order of the following possible relationship statuses – married, cohabitant, LAT, widowed, divorced/separated – our 28 interviews include 20 different relationship careers. Even if we look only at their relationship history prior to the current relationship, there are 15 different careers. Also, a lot of the variation took place at a relatively early age. Before the age of 40, seven of the women and four of the men had divorced at least once and two women had become widows. In total the 28 informants had

had 77 established intimate relationships in their lifetime, out of which 46 were marriages (current relationships included).

Judging from our interviewees, non-traditional relationship careers are already a reality among older Swedes. It should be noted that our interviews consist of older individuals who are either repartnered or interested in repartnering. Their relationship careers do not necessarily correspond to those of older people in lifelong marriages or singles who are *not interested* in repartnering. However, as the representative survey data in Figure 5.1 showed, they are in no way exceptional.

Irrespective of the degree to which their personal lives reflected the transition to divorce culture, the interviewees were conscious about the change that had taken place during their lifetime and often returned to it as an important reference point in their personal stories. LAT Lenny, 78 years old, describes how increasing financial security, especially for women, had been crucial for the transition:

> 'It didn't use to be this easy to separate. If you had two or three kids, then you couldn't simply say that "no, I'm fed up with this, now I leave". What would she do with three kids? And of course that contributed to the survival of many marriages although the partners weren't happy together. Today they say, on the TV, that it is better to divorce than to live unhappily. Of course it is, provided you can afford it. But it also means that people take off in different directions as soon as they are no longer happy together. You couldn't do that when I was young.'

Lenny's quote highlights the contrast between the norms he was raised with and the norms of divorce culture that later developed and how this change was conditioned on the improved financial situation of women in particular. Lenny's argument is similar to that of Beck and Beck-Gernsheim (2002), who connect the individualisation of families and intimate relationships to increasing female financial independence. Beck and Beck-Gernsheim explain this independence by increased female participation in the work force and the development of welfare states that provide material security. In Lenny's lifetime this is evident in women entering the Swedish labour force in large numbers in the 1960s and the concurrent extension of the Swedish welfare model, and especially its later reformation, where social rights are conferred on an individual rather than on a family basis. Despite his claims that it used to be difficult to divorce, Lenny's own relationship experiences could be read exactly as a description of living under the conditions of divorce culture.

The case of LAT Lenny

Lenny had his first longer relationship with his current partner Lydia at the age of 19. The relationship lasted for six months and was followed by other shorter dating/sexual relationships. At the age of 23 he had a child out of wedlock that he did not raise and has had no contact with. A few years later he met another woman and got married but the marriage was unhappy and childless and after 10 years it ended in divorce. Two years later he met the woman of his life with whom he started a 40-year-long cohabiting relationship. Lenny describes how it was only with the cohabiting relationship that his life really started. Through the relationship he gained three step-children that he retains close contact with even after the death of his partner. A year before the interview he was 'widowed'. He described widowhood as "death's waiting room". However, after a few months he was contacted by his first dating partner, LAT Lydia, who had recently become a widow, and they re-initiated their relationship.

Lenny's case is in many ways reflective of the historical transformation of intimacy – it contains multiple relationships and separations, unions in different forms and step-relationships formed as a consequence of these biographical experiences. In the interviews many informants actively reflect on how the historical transition from marriage to divorce culture is mirrored in their own relationship biographies and also how it is expressed in their personal relationship preferences. They recognised that a diverse set of ways of living together had emerged during their lifetime and they often had personal experiences of these union forms. Although most of the repartnered interviewees had previously been married, they were now happy to live in a non-marital union, according to the 'ideals of our time'. LAT Lee, an 83-year-old widower, describes this historical shift of ideals:

> 'We both belonged to the generation that necessarily had to marry. Me and my wife, we had no relationship before we got married. It was taboo at the time, in the early 50s. But now that Lucy became my partner, we felt no need to marry, instead we chose to live like others do – the way people live today.'

To conclude, the relationship careers of our informants show a wide range of complexity and historical malleability. Thus the idea that older people belong to cohorts sticking to traditional lifestyles with regard to intimate relationships can be questioned. Instead the culture of divorce has often influenced their lives and is also a central contextual condition for new intimate relationships in later life. Although these stories are gathered in the context of late modern Sweden, it is reasonable to think that contemporary cohorts of older people in other parts of Northern Europe and North America with similar historical divorce patterns will also have the same type of experiences of changing societal values over time.

Consequences of prior relationship dissolutions for late-life intimacy

Above we looked at how the transition into divorce culture has shaped the relationship biographies of current generations of older people. In this section we consider how these experiences shape late-life intimacy. As Davidson and Fennell (2002) point out: 'A first consideration in re-partnering is likely to be the nature and quality of a previous relationship' (p 6). A common metaphor used by our informants is that of having a 'backpack' of accumulated experiences. Or, as LAT Linda describes it: "Every new relationship is a new experience, and you bring it with you like a wild strawberry on a straw." Others are less poetic and talk about how prior negative relationship experiences made them wary about starting new relationships. In a study Talbott (1998) showed that widows with very bad experiences of their prior marriages were afraid to repeat these experiences by repartnering. But also those widows with very good experiences of their prior marriage tended to be sceptical about initiating new intimate relationships. However, widows with 'fairly' good experiences from prior relationships were more interested in repartnering.

A central aspect of relationship careers which weighs on intimacy choices in later life is how prior relationships have ended – through widowhood or divorce/separation. In comparison with widowed people, older divorcees are generally more interested in repartnering (see also Chapter six). In the following we focus on relationship dissolutions as specific experiences with important implications for interest in late-life repartnering.

Much gerontological research about relationship dissolutions has concerned widowhood, where the death of the partner constitutes an abrupt end to the continuity that the lifelong marriage represents. In this research loneliness is focused on as one of the biggest problems of widowhood (Carr, Ha, Utz, Williams & Umberson, 2002; Davidson, 2002; Lopata, 1996). Carr (2004) has suggested that a new intimate relationship might be a way of coping with this loneliness. In this scenario a new intimate relationship can be a way of re-establishing continuity after widowhood, for example in terms of emotional support and the continuation of a couple-oriented style of life. At the same time, however, some researchers have shown that loyalty towards the previous partner might constitute a reason for not initiating a new intimate relationship (Davidson, 2002; Moore & Stratton, 2004). In this alternative scenario, loyalty constitutes continuity with the former marriage (by continuing it alone). Lopata (1981) has coined the concept 'husband sanctification' to describe how widows idealise their lifelong marital partner and the father of their common children, and see him as irreplaceable. Bennett et al (2013) have described the corresponding phenomenon of 'wife sanctification' as an obstacle to repartnering among widowers.

An implicit assumption in much of this previous research is that the normal relationship dissolution is by widowhood from a union between two partners who have spent their whole lives together – not by divorce and not by widowhood from a second or third union. In contrast to divorce or separation, widowhood is not a *chosen* relationship dissolution. As a consequence it is more likely that widows and widowers remain attached and loyal to their former partners than it is for divorcees. Indeed, all of the informants who had been widowed described their partners in mostly positive and respectful terms. For one of the interviewees in particular – LAT Lisa – loyalty to the previous marital partner had been, and still was, a complicating factor in repartnering.

The case of LAT Lisa

68-year-old Lisa married at the age of 22 and spent 42 years with her husband until he died unexpectedly. Lisa was convinced that she would never meet another man, "I thought that there would never be another man with the same values as my husband", but two years later she found herself involved in a relationship with LAT Lars. However for Lisa, who had strong religious convictions and conservative ideals, this was highly problematic. Much of her story related her ambivalence towards her new relationship – whether she was doing right by her former husband, or not: 'Am I betraying my husband?' How should the new LAT relationship be characterised? She was adamant that the new relationship was qualitatively different from her first relationship: "My marriage – that was the self-evident, the natural. My new relationship is something out of the ordinary that I don't take for granted – they can't be compared."

Lisa is atypical of our interviewees in that she considers her new relationship to be in conflict with her former marriage. Lisa's story can be understood as a case of husband sanctification that produced strong ambivalence towards her new relationship. This was not the case for most of our repartnered informants, however her attitudes are shared by many widowed singles who express a disinterest in new relationships because no one can replace their former partner (see Chapter six) and probably by many older people currently living in lifelong marriages.

There are in principle two ways to re-establish continuity after widowhood – either by remaining loyal to the former spouse or by repartnering. LAT Lisa was torn between these two approaches. For others the repartnering strategy was less problematic. This was the case for Chris:

The case of Cohabiting Chris

Chris, 88, met his wife after a couple of years of intensive dating in his youth, including many sexual relationships: "I was a real swine, because I had new girls all the time." He had an extra-marital child at the age of 20, with whom he has had no contact. At the age of 25 he met his wife. They had one child and lived together until she died when he was 81 years old. Chris was disappointed that their sex life diminished in mid-life, but describes the marriage as very good, "She took half of my life with her in her grave." Already before her death he knew that he would have to find a new partner: "As soon as Margaret was gone, I started looking for a replacement. I think it is a tribute to her – my former wife – that I feel such a need for company. It is a little exciting, I thought. Can you start scoring at 83?" Immediately after his wife's death he started dating and after a couple of shorter dating relationships he met his current cohabiting partner Cecilia.

Chris's story is reminiscent of the partner ideal of the modern role-differentiated marriage, where men and women are seen as equal but different and where they search for their complementary match. Chris puts it poignantly: "I have the impression that a single person is just half a couple." In Chris's case this translates into an inability to live alone and the desire to immediately find a new partner after his spouse's death in order to continue his couple-oriented life.

A more common approach for combining loyalty to the former partner with continuity in couplehood was to allow a period of grief after being widowed before entering a new relationship. Some widowed partners were even brought together by the common experience of grieving for a former partner and actively collaborated on grieving. Most of our repartnered informants combined loyalty to the former partner with repartnering without any conflict, simultaneously describing the former marriage as special (where for example they had children) and the new relationship as important for later life. Often this new relationship is perceived as adding a new and different relationship rather than replacing the former one (cmpr. Stevens, 2004). It is often described as special and different – a late-life bonus or the crown of the relationship career. This was true for both men and women, even if the widowers were often more inclined to quickly start a new relationship – we will return to this issue below.

For those who have been widowed from a lifelong marriage, the former relationship represents continuity and a new relationship represents change. However, for some widowed people and most separated/divorced people, the former relationship is not the single and unique lifelong relationship. For people who have lived in a series of relationships, continuity *is* change. For these people a new relationship can constitute a natural way of dealing with a relationship dissolution, continuous with prior experiences during the life course. For divorcees, loyalty towards a former partner is unlikely to constitute an obstacle for repartnering. Our opening case of Cohabiting Carl is a typical example of such a relationship career but many other informants related similar stories of *serial repartnering*. Married Mary, aged 68 years, is one example:

The case of Married Mary

Mary met her first husband at the age of 21 and married two years later. At the age of 28 she had a child and in the same year she initiated an extra-marital affair that lasted for three years at which point they were discovered by her husband. The affair led to her first divorce, which she initiated at the age of 34. Two years after the divorce she met her second husband. For a long time they lived as cohabitants and she didn't intend to marry but gave in after a string of proposals. She describes the marriage as unfulfilling and marked by her longing for the former lover. She devoted herself to work and contemplated divorce. The second marriage lasted for another 10 years until her former lover called and told her he had become widowed. On learning the news she immediately left her husband: "I phoned my husband and said, I'm not returning home again." For Mary, her new marriage is a constant reference point in her description of her relationship career and her former marriages pale in comparison. Still she retains a polite relationship with both her former husbands: "At the grandchildren's birthdays, they [current and former husbands] all sit there together, on the same sofa."

Mary's story is contingent on late modern divorce culture and a view of relationships as means for self-fulfilment. In her story continuity *is* change. She has pursued a number of relationships during her life and has seen divorce as a natural getaway from relationships that she has not perceived as rewarding. In later life she is prepared to leave her second husband and marry her former lover. In contrast to many of those who have been widowed from lifelong marriages, Mary, as well as our other divorcees, is not constrained by loyalty towards her former partners. And even if she is deeply in love with her current husband she does not preclude repartnering if she were to become single again.

For divorcees who have lived their lives in line with the ideals of divorce culture and often divorced or separated from a number of previous unions, repartnering can be assumed to be a more natural way of dealing with relationship dissolutions. 73-year-old Single Sarah is one example of such an attitude to intimacy and how it impacts on later life:

The case of Single Sarah

Sarah dated a couple of different men in her youth and got engaged twice before marrying at the age of 23. She recalls that she wasn't convinced that her husband was the one for her, "I was standing at the altar thinking that if this doesn't work out, I can always divorce. I wasn't in love, but it was time, it was expected." She had two children in the marriage, which lasted for 14 years, but when the husband didn't want a third child she divorced and moved in with her lover. The children remained with her husband and they all collaborated on raising them in his house: "I became a maid in my former home." The new cohabiting relationship lasted on and off for a couple of years but finally fizzled out. At the age of 45 she initiated a stormy LAT relationship with a man with a drinking problem, which led to her breaking up after a few years. Shortly thereafter she met her second husband through a personal ad. Again the relationship ended after a few years due to the husband's drinking problem, "If I hadn't divorced I'd have become a widow. He drank himself to death." In later life Single Sarah leads an active dating life, involved with a handful of younger men that she has met over the Internet. She prefers younger men, she says, because of the sex and because they do not expect to be cared for. She is adamant that she is not interested in cohabiting with another man, and wants to protect her autonomy: "Men at my age are used to getting their shirts ironed and getting their food prepared."

Single Sarah's story is perhaps our most poignant illustration of a late modern relationship career – it contains a range of relationships in different union forms, renegotiated gender roles and age norms, creative takes on organising parenthood, a very open attitude towards separation and uncommitted sexual relationships. However, it lacks many of the positive connotations attributed to pure relationships by Giddens (1992). It comes closer to Bauman's (2003) description of late modern relationships as easy come, easy go, consumer goods. In fact, it is striking how many of the stories of our dating singles contain a tragic note of not being able to find and attach to that specific someone. At least for some people, the freedom afforded by the transformation of intimacy does not result in self-realisation.

Single Sarah and Married Mary relate very different relationship careers but what their stories have in common is the preparedness to break up and move on from relationships when they no longer find them fulfilling. In this sense they are both representative of the divorce cultural ideal and the individual's right to separate from an unsatisfying relationship (cmpr. Cherlin, 2009). In the sense that this preparedness represents continuity in their lives, there is nothing that suggests that this would change in later life.

The difference between how widowhood (often from lifelong relationships) and divorce (often from serial relationships) structures interest in new intimate relationships is of importance when put in the context of the fact that among older people in many parts of the Western world the society of divorcees is becoming bigger than the community of widowed people (described in Chapter three).

Gendered experiences: continuity and change in repartnering

Besides the dissolution of the previous union, another central consideration in repartnering are gendered experiences of previous relationships. Many of our informants had experienced very traditional gender roles in their first marriages, but their evaluations of these roles varied, leading to different expectations of new relationships – some wishing for role continuity while others opted for change. Some of the male and female interviewees had appreciated the clear distinction between male and female roles, leading to a wish for *continuity and reproduction* of these roles in their new relationships. This was the case for Chris and Cecilia:

The case of Cohabiting Chris and Cecilia

Chris, 87, and Cecilia, 78, both widowed, met at the local service centre restaurant. They soon initiated a relationship and after a few months Chris moved into Cecilia's house. Cecilia had been a housewife and backup to her husband who had a leading position in a large company. Chris had been the sole breadwinner in his former marriage where his wife had taken care of the home and children. "I've had a housewife all of my life and she's been a housewife all of her life." In their current relationship they are both happy to reproduce traditional gender roles. Chris was explicitly looking for an experienced housewife, "used to spoiling a male chauvinist", and Cecilia was happy to fulfil that role.

Chris described losing his wife as losing half of himself, saying that his wife took half of his life with her in her grave. For Cecilia, widowhood similarly had meant losing an important part of her identity as a loved and needed housewife. In their new relationship both Chris and Cecilia looked for continuity of their lifelong gendered identities and were thus satisfied with reproducing a traditional gendered division of labour. For Chris, who no longer worked, this meant not doing much at all, while Cecilia was doing all the housekeeping. This traditional housewife-breadwinner ideal was eloquently expressed and appreciated by Cecilia:

> 'Chris is so easy to live with. He doesn't demand much. He is a total stranger to kitchens. His wife wouldn't even let him into the kitchen. I like that he is a male chauvinist, except that I would like some company when I do the dishes. Relationships were better before, when women took care of the home and men got home from work and did their thing. It was a good division, everyone had their own turf – no arguments. We would like to tell young people that everything can't be equal, there needs to be some difference as well. Men need to be men.'

The wish to reproduce traditional gender roles, exemplified by Chris and Cecilia's story, seemed to be more common among the oldest informants, probably reflecting a generational difference, where some of the old–old interviewees had personal experience of a clear housewife/breadwinner distinction and where this distinction was central to their sense of self. For at least some of these informants, fulfilling traditional gender roles has been a central part of their identity throughout married life and could be expected to remain so in later life. For some of the men, especially in the oldest cohort, who had never taken care of a home, the discontinuation of coupled life could be very challenging and an incentive for repartnering, as expressed by 78-year-old LAT Lenny:

> 'It was difficult to be widowed. A woman she just continues to wash, cook and clean. But I had never done any of those things before. I had my responsibilities. But then, when you are widowed you have to sew in buttons. With Lydia I get much help with these things. If I suggest that we should eat a certain dish, then we buy the food together, and she cooks it.'

If some of the older informants were happy to live in accordance with traditional gender roles also in their new relationships, most of the informants, especially the young-old, wanted to *change and reconstruct* these roles in their new relationships in line with more contemporary, gender-equal norms. For many of the female informants, separation/divorce (but also widowhood) had served as a turning point that encouraged them to critically reflect on their roles in their previous unions (what Walzer, 2008, in her study of divorce, refers to as 'redoing gender') and how they would like to change these roles in a new relationship. Repartnering can be a way to reinvent gender roles and at the same time reinvent themselves, and women were often the driving agents behind such change. Some had already broken with traditional gender roles after previous divorces. This was, for example, the case for Single Sophie:

The case of Single Sophie

Sophie has been married and divorced twice, and has separated from two longer LAT relationships in later life. In her first marriage she was a housewife. After the divorce, Sophie started working and remained financially independent in her subsequent relationships. She is proud to have earned a living and raised two children on her own. In later life she remains interested in a romantic relationship but does not want to reproduce the traditional housewife role that she had in her first marriage. "Many of the men I've met have had extensive need of help with housekeeping. Some can't cook and have a great need to meet somebody. But those of us women who have worked and have a good economy, we don't need a man to help us financially. And I don't think that younger women would ever accept doing all the housekeeping that I did in my first marriage." Instead, in later life, she is mainly looking for a companion to share experiences with – not a breadwinner.

Sophie refers to the development that has taken place over her lifetime, where women have increasingly taken up employment and made a life and career outside of the household, making them increasingly financially independent from men, but also providing an alternative source of identity besides that of the housewife. For these women, taking on a housewife's duties in later life does not necessarily represent a continuity of a valuable source of their identity. Instead, for them it makes sense to opt for a renegotiation of gendered duties in later life or an LAT union that allows them to remain autonomous in relation to their partner. Some women who had lived according to a traditionally gendered script were clearly wary about taking on the role of homemaker and preferred to keep separate households for that reason. This is in line with previous findings that single older women after relationship dissolution tend to want to preserve their new-found autonomy by opting for LAT relationships (see for example Davidson, 2002; Ghazanfareeon Karlsson & Borell, 2005; Malta & Farquharson, 2014; Régnier-Loilier et al, 2009). 63-year-old Single Susan expresses the logic behind this option for a potential new relationship: "Absolutely not a cohabiting relationship! If I met a man at my age, I'll be expected to cook, clean and do the laundry. I'm pretty sure of that, and I won't do it anymore. I've done that, the whole of my life, for others."

In this section we have argued that attitudes to new intimate relationships as well as to their organisation depend on gendered experiences of previous relationships, causing people to want either to reproduce or reinvent gender roles in the new intimate relationships. Especially women want to change gender roles in repartnering. Even if these attitudes vary, they do seem to reflect a generational change, where the old–old are more likely to have lived in and based their identities on role-differentiated marriages, while the young–old had more often lived in dual earner households, where conflicts around roles and duties had been more common.

Conclusion

In this chapter we have focused on the macro-micro link and investigated how divorce culture is reflected in the relationship careers of older Swedes and how these relationship experiences shape their interest in and experience of intimacy in later life. We have shown that many older Swedes have quite complex relationship careers and we have discussed how former relationship dissolutions and gendered relationship histories affect interest in repartnering.

Kohli (1986, 2007) has described how the life course was increasingly *institutionalised* over the last two centuries, forming a more or less determined script that creates predictability for people's lives. In Chapter two we argued that in modern society marriage contributed to the organisation of the institutionalised life course by regulating the organisation of intimate and family life over the life course through the marital norm. One was, for example, expected to marry in early adulthood and stay in that lifelong marriage until widowhood in later life.

Later it has been argued that the institutionalised life course has been broken up or *deinstitutionalised* and become less predictable and more heterogeneous (Dannefer & Settersten Jr, 2010; Guillemard, 2000; O'Rand, 1996; Phillipson & Biggs, 1998). This is evident in our findings, as illustrated by Figure 5.2 above, which shows the increasing complexity of the relationship careers of current generations of older Swedes. In marriage culture, the institution of marriage helped organise the life course through establishing a script for coupling and family life where marriage was the given form and was supposed to last for a lifetime and be followed by widowhood. But for current generations of older Swedes this script has been broken up. For many older Swedes the life course has contained multiple relationships in different union forms and marriage has not been the only available choice for a union. In marriage culture, the lifelong relationship was normally initiated in early adulthood; now relationships are initiated at any point in the life course and it is hard to find a point where it is 'too late'. In marriage culture, relationship development was supposed to follow a given sequential order, where couples were supposed to first marry, then find a place to live, have sex and then have children. But again, for current generations of older Swedes, this script has not necessarily been followed. People have often had sex, moved in together and had children before marrying (if they ever married). In marriage culture, marriage was supposed to be the institutionalised form for raising a family, but current generations of older Swedes often have children –

both biological and step-children – in multiple relationships in different union forms. These complex relationship careers would seem to be reflective of an, at least partly, deinstitutionalised life course.

We have investigated two central aspects of relationship histories – prior union dissolutions and gendered relationship experiences – that impact on interest in repartnering in later life. Both these experiences can be traced back to the historical transformation of the life course, where traditional gender roles were challenged by the dissolution of the one-earner family model and by women entering the labour market. In much of the Western world this development accelerated in the latter part of the 20th century and created a new cultural imperative that encouraged women to pursue a career outside of the household and a concurrent demand, especially expressed by women, for changing gender roles also inside the family. At the same time this development challenged the marital ideal by increasing acceptance for divorce from unsatisfying unions, making this a much more common experience in the lives of contemporary generations of older people and contributing to increasingly complex relationship careers. This has important implications if we consider that the society of older divorcees will soon overtake the community of widowed people in large parts of the Western world, and already constitutes an important part of the older single community.

SIX

Attitudes towards new romantic relationships

In research on ageing and intimacy one area that has received a fair amount of interest is the attitudes of older people towards repartnering. However, this research is quite disparate and the results are hard to sum up. Many studies of older singles have shown overwhelmingly negative attitudes towards forming new relationships, while other studies have shown older people to be very interested in new relationships, although avoiding marriage. The answers depend on *who* the respondents are and *what* they are asked about. The relatively recent transition to divorce culture means that for a long time there has been a lack of concepts for talking about non-marital relationships. Also, an investigation into the epistemological preliminaries (Bourdieu, Chamboredon, Passeron & Krais, 1991) of this research reveals that the area is full of assumptions stemming from the wider research agendas that these studies are part of. For example, much research is about widowhood and consequently investigates attitudes towards new relationships as a way of managing widowed life. By framing the question in terms of the problem of widowhood the attitudes of other groups, such as divorcees and never-marrieds, towards (re)marriage and other forms of relationships (dating, cohabitation, LAT) become less visible. This can be increasingly misleading if we consider the growing society of divorcees.

The purpose of this chapter is to investigate the attitudes of older people towards intimate relationships in later life and we ask two central questions: (1) *Attitudes to what?* For example marriage, dating, a romantic partner, living together or apart? Attitudes may well differ strongly depending on what one is asking about. (2) *The attitudes of whom?* Women or men? Divorcees, widowed or never married people? Singles, LATs, cohabitants or marrieds? Older people themselves or those in their surroundings, such as children, relatives or the generalised other? Attitudes are likely to depend on who the persons holding the attitudes are and what their experiences are. Finally we consider our Swedish data to update and fill in some of the gaps in previous research. By not focusing solely on marriage we show that older people's interest in repartnering is likely higher than what has been proposed before.

Attitudes to what?

Research about attitudes towards intimate relationships in later life was for a long time haunted by the lack of an established way of talking about non-marital relationships – the lack of a clear ontological referent. A long line of more or less unclear concepts and euphemisms figure in the literature, ranging from 'gentleman friend', 'confidant', 'companion' or 'current woman' to 'going steady', 'established relationship' 'dating relationship' or 'LAT'. This problem is further accentuated by the fact that many of these concepts have different meanings in different cultural contexts. For example, cohabitation was established as a widely recognised alternative way of living together in the Nordic countries earlier than in many other parts of the world. Later LAT has become an established way of talking about living together in an established relationship without sharing a common household, but this concept is still mainly recognised in northern Europe. In the English-speaking world, dating has often been referred to in a similar sense (cmpr. K. Bulcroft & O'Connor, 1986, p 399; Malta & Farquharson, 2014), but seldom by older people themselves (Benson & Coleman, 2016a).

The lack of established concepts for talking about intimate relationships and partners meant that for a long time researchers often resorted to asking about (re)marriage, which was the only relatively universally understood concept. Perhaps it was also assumed that it would be even more difficult for older people who had grown up in marriage culture, to find words to describe non-marital relationships. In the 1970s, Lopata (1979) stated that the only repartnering option for widows was remarriage. Since then many studies from different countries have shown that in fact older people are often interested in an intimate relationship of some kind – but seldom in marriage. As early as 1984/85, in the context of the US with its internationally high remarriage rates, Talbott (1998) found that a majority of her sample of older widows were 'interested in or attracted to men' but not interested in remarriage. In another US sample from 1986, Moorman et al (2006) found little interest among widows to get remarried. A decade later in Britain, Davidson (2001) found no interest in remarriage among widows but much interest in a 'gentleman friend'. Still, focus on marriage has continued to be a central way of getting to older people's interest in romantic relationships, reflected in survey statements such as 'My life will not be complete unless I remarry' (Moorman et al, 2006) and in the titles of publications, such as 'The desire to remarry among older widows and widowers' (Carr, 2004) and '"You're not getting married for the moon and the stars" – The uncertainties of

older British widowers about the idea of new romantic relationships'
(Bennett et al, 2013).

Besides the lack of an established way of talking about non-marital
relationships, the focus on marriage can probably also be explained by
the cohort-based assumption that older people are traditional and see
marriage as the self-evident union form for an intimate relationship.
In some parts of the world this is probably true, such as in religiously
conservative parts of the Western world (see for example van den
Hoonaard, 2004) and many parts of the non-Western world (see for
example Mehta, 2002), and more so in a North American than, for
example, a German or Dutch context (Arranz Becker, Salzburger,
Lois & Nauck, 2013; Suanet, van der Pas & van Tilburg, 2013). As
we showed in Chapter four, marriage is not the norm for late-in-life
relationships in Sweden and probably not in the other Nordic countries.
Also, based on the cohort assumption, some studies assume that
marriage is the dominant option for current cohorts of older people but
speculate that marriage in later life will decrease by cohort replacement
in the future (Moore & Stratton, 2004; van den Hoonaard, 2004).

In prior research, a couple of reasons are recurrently mentioned by
older people who say they do not want to get remarried: (1) loyalty
to a deceased partner, (2) a wish to remain independent, (3) fear of
losing (yet another) partner, (4) finances (see for example Bennett et al,
2013; Bildtgård & Öberg, 2015a; Davidson, 2001; de Jong Gierveld,
2002; Malta & Farquharson, 2014; Moore & Stratton, 2004; Steitz
& Welker, 1991; Talbott, 1998). These answers reflect the lack of an
established way of talking about intimate relationships because besides
finances, the above-mentioned reasons for not wanting to remarry are
not about marriage per se: loyalty towards a former partner precludes
new intimate relationships generally. The same goes for the fear of
losing yet another partner. The wish to remain independent is mainly
directed against cohabitation, marital or not, and does not necessarily
preclude an LAT relationship.

It is really only the financial reasons that are about marriage per se.
A recurrent finding in many studies is that older people avoid getting
remarried because in many countries they will lose part of their
pension if they do. Also remarriage can be a complicating factor for
inheritance reasons because it ties not only the two partners legally
to each other but also their families. Marriage creates a legal thicket
around inheritances, which are left for the children of the two partners
to sort out after their parents' death. Consequently, older people are
often hesitant to get married.

At the beginning of the 21st century, a large number of studies had shown that marriage was not a priority for a majority of older singles in many parts of the Western world. At the same time new ways of talking about non-marital ways of living together, such as cohabitation and LAT, had become more or less established. As a consequence new studies appeared that focused on how older people organise their non-marital relationship lives. A number of studies pointed out that in fact many older people seemed to favour long-term committed relationships with another person, but not living together. According to Ghazanfareeon Karlsson and Borell (Ghazanfareeon Karlsson, 2006; Ghazanfareeon Karlsson & Borell, 2002, 2005), many older people prefer union forms that allow them to combine intimacy with independence. LAT is a form that seems uniquely suited for such priorities. By conserving separate households many of their interviewees felt it was easier to remain independent and retain continuity in both identity and social relations.

Whose attitudes?

The second question with regard to attitudes towards intimacy in later life is whose attitudes are under investigation. Is it the attitudes of singles or people in different forms of relationships? If singles, then what kinds of singles – widowed, divorced or never marrieds? Men or women?

A consequence of the dominance of marriage culture is that for a long time the problem of being involuntarily single in later life was visible primarily in terms of widowhood. The interest in attitudes towards intimacy in later life was in fact often a by-product of studies about widowhood, investigating ways of managing life after the death of a spouse. Research about older singles' attitudes to remarriage and repartnering is almost exclusively focused on widows and widowers (see for example Bennett et al, 2013; Carr, 2004; Carr & Boerner, 2013; Davidson, 2001, 2002; Mehta, 2002; Moore & Stratton, 2004; Moorman et al, 2006; Stevens, 2004; Talbott, 1998; van den Hoonaard, 2004). These studies all tend to show that the interest in remarrying among widowed people is very limited, although many express an interest in intimate relationships of different kinds. Widowers are often described as more interested in remarrying or repartnering than widows. The reasons mentioned are related to prior relationship experiences – not wanting to look after yet another man – and to social expectations, where men are more often encouraged to find a new partner.

Despite the demographic transition towards increased prevalence and incidence of divorce in later life, studies on the attitudes of divorcees towards intimacy remains almost uninvestigated. If divorcees are included it is regularly as a contrast to widowed people in a few studies based on larger statistical data sets (for example R. A. Bulcroft & Bulcroft, 1991; Mahay & Lewin, 2007). Divorcees have often been shown to have higher rates of actual repartnering than widowed people (Brown et al, 2006; Brown & Lin, 2012; de Jong Gierveld, 2004a), which points to the conclusion that older divorcees might have more open and positive attitudes to repartnering than widows and widowers.

If early research tended to focus on the attitudes of singles, a second wave of studies from the early 21st century has been interested in the attitudes of older people living as LATs towards different ways of organising their common life. In this research the gender dimension is often shown to be important. For example, in a number of studies Ghazanfareeon Karlsson and Borell (2006; 2002, 2005) have shown that women tend to be the driving force behind LAT relationships, preferring to conserve the independence of a 'home of their own'. Men, on the other hand, are often assumed to prefer unmarried cohabitation, which affords many of the same benefits as marriage without the traditional obligations (see for example Brown et al, 2005).

A third dimension concerns the attitudes of the older individual's surroundings. A clear example of the importance of context is offered by studies from more conservative and traditional cultural environments, such as Singapore (Mehta, 2002) and New Brunswick in Canada (van den Hoonaard, 2004), where children are often described as strongly opposed to their parents initiating new partnerships. Mehta explains this reticence in terms of marriage in Singapore being considered as a bond, not only between individuals but also families, which means that the marriage is not dissolved with the death of the spouse. But also in more liberal contexts, children are often reported to be negative towards their parents – and in particular their mothers – repartnering (see for example de Jong Gierveld & Merz, 2013; Dykstra, 1993). As Bulcroft and Bulcroft (1991) put it, the attitudes of children can be assumed to be an especially important reference for older parents in their relationship choices. However, the attitudes of children arguably reflect the attitudes of the wider culture, and as family norms are continuously individualised these are likely to become more and more liberal.

The Swedish case

Above we have discussed two central questions concerning attitudes to new intimate relationships in later life. What kind of intimate relationships has previous research talked about (Attitudes to what?) and which group's attitudes have been the focus of investigation (Whose attitudes?). Earlier research has tended to focus on specific single groups' (for example widows') attitudes to specific union forms (for example marriage). Representative studies of older people's attitudes to different union forms are lacking. Also, as Talbott (1998) notes, findings about older people's attitudes might not be generalisable between generations, and this might be particularly true in the area of intimacy, where normative change has been especially pervasive in the last couple of decades. Thus new and updated studies are important.

In our Swedish survey of 2012 we asked a representative group of 60–90-year-old Swedes if they 'currently preferred to be in an intimate relationship' or not. In order to capture a more general preparedness for romantic relationships, we also asked whether they would 'consider a relationship' even if they were not actively looking for one. Table 6.1 presents the results for singles by gender and marital history.

Table 6.1: Single 60–90-year-old Swedish men and women, by marital history, who (a) 'would prefer to be in' or (b) 'would consider' an intimate relationship (%)

	Never married		Widowed		Divorced		All	
	Men	Women	Men	Women	Men	Women	Men	Women
Would prefer to be in a relationship	26	15	34	9	46	25	36	15
Would consider a relationship even if not actively looking for one	58	45	51	35	72	57	61	44

In the first row of Table 6.1, the last column (All) shows, in line with earlier research, that single men are generally more interested in having a relationship (36%) than single women (15%). This pattern is the same irrespective of whether they are never-married singles, widowed singles or divorced singles. The gender difference is the greatest between widows and widowers – it is four times more common for widowed men to prefer to be in a relationship – possibly because of the different gendered experiences of previous marriages described in Chapter five. It is also more common for divorced singles than widowed singles to prefer to be in a relationship. The widows are the least interested in having a relationship (9%) while divorced men are the most interested (46%). Thus, only studying widows (and widowers) misrepresents the general interest in repartnering among singles. Still, the panel shows that a clear majority of singles are not interested in repartnering.

The second panel shows the same pattern and the same between-groups relationship as the first panel. However, it also shows that the preparedness for a new intimate relationship (if for example the right person came along) is substantially bigger than the immediate interest. This is important: many of our repartnered interviewees described how they were not actively looking for a new partner, it just happened. Thus the phrasing of the attitude question is central and determines the responses.

Older singles who were hesitant to initiate a new intimate relationship were so mainly for two reasons: primarily because they were afraid they would lose their independence (54%), and second, because they thought that no one could replace their former partner (32%). The second reason was almost only offered by widowed people – for evident reasons it was uncommon for divorced individuals to feel that their former partner was irreplaceable. There were no differences between men and women with regard to these reasons.

The attitudes of the surrounding society were generally positive. When we asked 60–90-year-old Swedes what they thought about older people in general repartnering after the age of 60 and after the age of 80, the respondents were overwhelmingly positive (97% and 91% respectively) and only very few (3% and 9%) were negative. However, as we noted above, adult children might constitute a more relevant reference point for their attitudes, and prior research often describe them as negative about their parents repartnering. Negative or judging attitudes from children were rare in our Swedish interview study. Consequently, in the survey we asked the older *single* respondents what they *believed* the attitudes of their children would be towards them repartnering, moving in together and remarrying. We also asked respondents who *had repartnered* late in life (60+) how they had *perceived* their children's attitudes.

Figure 6.1 shows that the vast majority of the older single respondents tended to perceive the attitudes of their adult children to be very positive towards them meeting a new partner. A majority also perceived their children's attitudes to be positive towards them moving in with a new partner, while a majority did not think their children would be positive towards them (re)marrying. Those who had repartnered had similar, but more positive, perceptions of their children's attitudes than the singles. Thus, in the context of late modern Sweden, the attitudes of children does not seem to constitute much of an obstacle for new relationships in later life. However – and many of our interviewees report this as well – they might constitute a reason for not remarrying.

Figure 6.1: Percentage of 60–90-year-old Swedes who agree that 'My children would be positive towards me ... (a) meeting, (b) moving in with, (c) marrying ... a new partner at my age' (%)

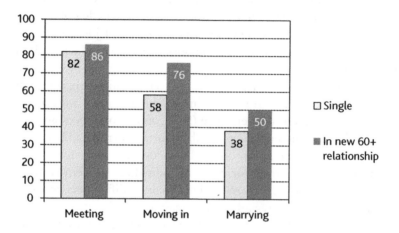

We also asked about the older respondents' attitudes towards living in different union forms.[4] The first panel in Table 6.2 shows that among those single respondents who would like to be in an intimate relationship, both men and women prefer an LAT union to a marital or non-marital cohabitation. In line with what prior research has suggested, single women are much more likely to prefer LAT (84%) than single men (55%). However, much less known is that LAT is the preferred union form also for men. Among older singles, *both men and women* prefer LAT to other union forms! Thus if we are to understand the popularity of LAT as a union form in later life, the gender explanation is not sufficient. Instead, the choice of LAT might be related as much to life phase as to gender. In later life autonomy might be important for both men and women, for example for preserving one's home intact and maintaining social networks intact.

The second panel in Table 6.2 shows that for the majority of the respondents currently living as LATs, their current union form is also their preferred union form. And this is even more pronounced among women than men. This supports the argument that LAT in later life in most cases is an alternative, and not a prelude, to marital or non-marital cohabitation. However, a sizeable minority (1 in 4) of the LATs would prefer to cohabit with their partner (more so among men, 36%, than women, 17%), which could point to a potential for future change in union form (see Chapter seven). Married and unmarried cohabitants (not shown in the table) almost always preferred their current union form.

Table 6.2: Preferred union form by gender among Swedish 60–90-year-old (a) singles who would like to have a relationship and (b) LATs (%)

	Preferred union form:			
	LAT		Cohabitation (marital or non-marital)	
	Men	Women	Men	Women
Singles	55	84	45	16
LATs	64	83	36	17

A conclusion that can be drawn from the above numbers is that a focus on remarriage risks underrepresenting older singles' interest in romantic relationships. In line with much of the research presented above, our Swedish survey data (see Figure 6.2) shows that marriage as a social institution seems to be of little importance for older people in non-marital forms of intimacy, as well as for singles. Only 9% of the LATs, 14% of the cohabitants and 16% of the singles think that it is important to be married. Not even all of the married respondents think that marriage is important (fewer than 4 in 5). These attitudes are

Figure 6.2: Swedish 60–90-year-old respondents who think it is important to be married, by union form (%)

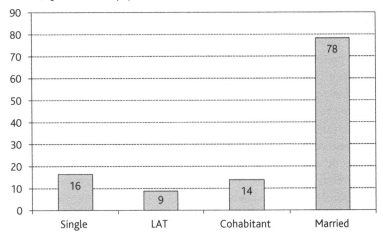

very much in contrast to their socialisation in young adulthood, where marriage was the only appropriate form for romantic relationships.

As shown in Figure 6.2, marriage remains an important institution for the part of the older population that *is already* married. But these marriages are often established earlier in life. However, a combination of historical and life-phase factors make marriage less appealing for new relationships in later life (this was clearly demonstrated in Chapter four).

Conclusion

In this chapter we have investigated older people's attitudes towards repartnering in later life. In particular we have asked what the attitudes of different groups of older people (widows, divorced, singles; men and women) are to different relationship arrangements (marriage, cohabitation and LAT). We have shown that the majority of both older women and men are not expressly looking for a new partner, but a majority of older men and a large minority of older women would consider a new relationship if the right person came along. We have also shown that a majority of older men and women would prefer an LAT relationship if they repartnered.

The above results are much in line with previous research. What they add is primarily the advantage of a more comprehensive image of different groups of older people's attitudes towards repartnering and different forms of living together in later life. The exact Swedish figures presented here might not be generalisable to other countries, but the patterns, which are very much in line with previous research, indicate that there are some mechanisms at work that are common to many Western countries. One of these mechanisms is men's and women's different relationship experiences, where many women's prior experiences of taking care of a common home might make them hesitant to cohabit (as shown in the previous chapter).

While previous research has often emphasised the insight that women tend to prefer and promote LAT unions, it is much less known that LAT is not only the preferred union form for women repartnering, *but for older people in general*. This points to a difference in the structural conditions for relationships established in different phases of life. In later life, when there is no family formation demanding financial stability and shared work efforts, a common household (marital or non-marital) may not be a priority. In fact, the preference for LAT shown above is very much in line with the results in Table 4.1, which showed that for relationships initiated late in life, LAT is the dominant union form.

In short, older singles not only prefer to live as LATs, but they also primarily initiate LAT relationships.

Finally, while the somewhat hesitant attitudes of widows towards repartnering have often been reported in prior research, the more positive attitudes of divorcees – although logically understandable, as we demonstrated in Chapter five – are much less well known. This is particularly relevant against the background of the relative growth of the society of divorcees that was shown in Chapter three. In many countries it will soon be more common to be divorced past the age of 60 than to be widowed. This lays the foundation for the prediction that repartnering in later life will increase in future cohorts of older people.

SEVEN

Initiation and development of new romantic relationships

In this chapter we aim to show how the patterns regarding attitudes and union choices uncovered in previous chapters are realised and negotiated in concrete individual lives and late-in-life relationships. The purpose of the chapter is to study the initiation and development of new late-life romantic relationships. We ask what the central issues are that need to be negotiated and resolved in order for a relationship to develop. Using four case studies, we follow the successive (but not necessary) development of late-life relationships through the negotiation of three central relationship questions: whether to initiate and continue a relationship or not; whether to move in together or not; and whether to get married or not. We show that the question of marriage is normally raised only in a later stage of a relationship's development – if ever. Thus marriage ('marriage at first sight') is seldom a relevant question for older singles.

Unveiling negotiation and change in new late-life relationships

Negotiation has often been singled out as a characteristic trait of late modern intimate relationships, where both form and content of the relationship is thought to be determined less by external norms and conventions than used to be the case in modern society, and more through agreements between relatively equal partners. This is a key feature of Giddens', Hackstaff's and Cherlin's arguments about contemporary intimacy (see Chapter two).

However, the insight that intimate relationships are characterised by negotiation and change often seems to be lost in research about older people. One reason, as we saw in Chapter six, is that until recently research has tended to focus on older singles and their *attitudes* to repartnering – rather than the *experiences* of repartnered older people. Another reason may be the assumption that older people belong to cohorts raised in marriage culture, presumably still living according to its ideals. As we showed in Chapter four, it is doubtful whether this assumption is true. Older people might in fact be freer than young adults to liberally choose the way they live together, since they rarely have nesting children. It has been argued that in later life both LAT (Ghazanfareeon Karlsson & Borell, 2002; Régnier-Loilier et al, 2009) and cohabitation (Brown et al, 2006; Brown & Wright, 2016; King & Scott, 2005) are often alternatives, rather than preludes, to marriage. However this argument might be problematic in a manner similar to the cohort hypothesis that older people prefer marriage, in that it excludes change. In this chapter we argue that it is more fruitful to ask how union form is continuously negotiated and what the central issues are that need to be resolved for a relationship to develop.

The importance of relationship development and change has been recognised more in wider social psychological perspectives. For example Levinger (1983) presents a five-stage relationship model describing the development of a relationship over time: (a) acquaintance/initial attraction, (b) build-up and increasing interdependence, (c) continuation/consolidation, including more long-term commitments, (d) deterioration or decline of interconnections, (e) ending, through death or separation. Research about new intimate relationships in later life has mostly focused on stage one and has thus missed the development of the relationships. If instead we look at the development of the relationship from the vantage point of those *already in a relationship*, we see that attitudes have at many times been ambivalent and changing during the development of the relationship, and that negotiation has been, and still is, important to the partners' life together.

The importance of negotiation and change is sometimes evident in earlier research, even if it has not been the main object of study. For example, Moore and Stratton (2004) discuss how widowers and their 'current women' negotiate an understanding regarding the degree of closeness that is comfortable and allowable in the relationship (especially regarding sexual activity), or how the benefits of the relationship are weighted against the loss of independence. Relationship change is often evident even if the partners do not immediately recognise it. For example, Stevens (2004) notes how the distinction between LAT relationships and cohabitation is often fluent, and that people describing themselves as LATs might in fact be living together most or all of the time, although keeping separate apartments. Also, as relationships develop, the desires of the partner come to have more impact on one's own attitudes and choices. This is, for example, evident in a quote from one of de Jong Gierveld's (2004b) Dutch interviews, where the informant is talking about cohabitation: 'It wasn't a motive for me, it was for him/.../ He kept on nagging about it/.../ It never was my intention to get a man' (p 95). Still, at the point of the interview she is cohabiting with the man. It is only recently that research has started to be published on the development of older people's actual relationships. For example, Watson, Bell and Stelle (2010) studied how older remarried women narrate their relationships' development and showed how their priorities changed from when they were singles to when they were married, putting less value on autonomy and more on interdependence.

Attitudes, ideals and concrete relationship arrangements change, also for older people. There are several issues that have to be negotiated after meeting a new partner, such as whether the relationship should be of a sexual nature or not; whether they should live together or not – and if they should live together, then how a common home should be built; which parts of the couple's lives should be shared; to what extent the involvement in each other's lives should extend also to each other's families (see more in Chapter nine). Even more importantly for this chapter – as the partners get more (or less) involved – priorities and attitudes are likely to change: singles who are uninterested in a new partner might change their minds when the right person shows up. Similarly, eager daters may lose spirit when they do not find a suitable partner. Daters and LATs who are convinced they will never surrender their home or their autonomy might find that the enjoyment of living together with their partner outweighs the disadvantages. Partners who want to marry might reconsider when they realise the financial disadvantages of such a union. And partners who are convinced that they will never (re)marry may find that their longing for such a commitment outweighs the obstacles. What look like definite attitudes in prospect need not be so in retrospect.

Below we use four cases currently in different relationship stages – single, LAT, cohabitant, married – to illustrate the negotiation and development of new late-life romantic relationships from initiation to cohabitation and marriage, and the central issues that have to be resolved in order for the relationship to progress. Although not all relationships go through all these stages, they represent an order of successive relationship progression in terms of establishment which is common in many contemporary Western societies, connected to higher levels of institutionalisation in terms of common resources and interpersonal dependence. First we meet Single Sally, then the LAT couple Lars and Lisa, followed by the cohabiting couple Carl and Caroline and finally Married Mark and Martha. In each case we look both at their retrospective descriptions of prior transitions within their current relationship (where relevant) and their thoughts and negotiations about potential future transitions.

Relationship ideals in singlehood: Single Sally

73-year-old Single Sally has been widowed for 11 years after an almost half-century long happy marriage with two children. She describes her unexpected transition to widowhood as the most traumatic experience of her life. For a long time after being widowed Sally was happy to remain single. Her son wanted her to find a new man who could look after her but she remained hesitant. For the first time since she met her husband at the age of 16, she was alone and enjoyed her freedom (cmpr. Davidson, 2001). Also, she did not want to risk having to experience the death of another man. She says that she enjoys her social life:

> 'My married female friends are a bit jealous of me. They think I lead a more exciting life than they do. And when I see their old men who would have been the same age as my husband if he had been alive I'm happy that I have avoided that [laughs]. Perhaps it sounds cruel but their men have Parkinson's, they are deaf and have a lot of other health problems.'

Presently Sally would ideally want to live in an established LAT relationship that would allow for both intimacy and personal autonomy:

> 'You could meet once a week and do something fun together. Perhaps go to the theatre. I like inviting people home for dinner. If he can't cook he can take me to a restaurant. Go travelling together. Above all, having somebody to 'love', to hug and have sex with. I can't really ask them to share all my interests. Old men they like golf and sailing and all that but it suits me well if they have their own lives and don't get all caught up in mine.'

After eight years as a single widow, in the last three years Sally has had three shorter dating relationship and one 2-year-long LAT relationship. None of the relationships have lasted. This is partly due to the difficulty of finding a partner with similar relationship goals. It is also due to her own personal ambivalence: on the one hand she desires an established relationship, on the other hand she wants to avoid the boredom of relationship routine and responsibilities: "I'm happy being on my own and I don't want to get married or move in with a man. I just want this 'roses and champagne stage'. Not the boring part. I've had that all my life, so enough of that."

However, underlining her ambivalence and preparedness for change, she ends the sentence: "But one should never say never." An important obstacle for Sally's romantic ambitions, typical for later life, is the frailty and functional incapacity of available older men. She wants to avoid becoming a housekeeper and she finds that this is what many men her age – who lack experience of taking care of a home – are looking for. She also wants to avoid becoming a 'nurse' and she describes how many of the men she has met have had health problems.

Her reluctance to be a caregiver was evident in the LAT relationship she had initiated three years earlier with an 80-year-old man. Together they visited many cultural activities, went sailing and travelled abroad. They had just planned a trip to Paris when he fell: "He called me in the middle of the night and had fallen out of bed and broken his femoral neck. So I hurried down to the ER and he had to have crutches and so and that wasn't exactly much fun for me. I became something of a nurse."

Soon after the incident Sally broke up with her LAT partner. She did not want to have any care responsibilities – she was happy they did not live together. In this sense Sally echoed a common concern among many of the single female interviewees – a fear of being trapped in a relationship with a chronically ill partner that would restrain the freedom of their later years. Sally also felt that with increasing age her LAT partner had become more sedentary and no longer matched her relationship goals: "I could have kept him, but he started to remind me too much of a spoiled husband. So I grew tired of him. He became boring."

Sally has tried different venues for meeting new men. She has been out on boat cruises, dancing, and she has tried Internet dating, but without any permanent success.

> 'You go out for a year or so and then you meet somebody else and it continues like that. It's not so easy to meet a man at this age. You both have your backpacks of experiences and sometimes I feel that I don't have the energy to meet yet another man and share mine.'

A year prior to the interview Sally started her most recent dating relationship, a recently widowed man. She describes having been quite attracted to him. However, again her expectations did not quite match those of her new partner, who was still grieving for his former wife and was not yet ready for a new committed relationship. "I want a somewhat more established LAT relationship and I told him so, because he wants to play the field a bit as I understand it. Perhaps he needs to give it a try [being recently widowed]. I don't know, that's how men are wired I suppose."

As their different relationship goals did not match, the relationship did not continue. Sally's story is similar to that of many of the other single informants in our study and also to the stories related in other research. Many singles are hesitant about repartnering, and two central reasons are grief of a former partner and fear of losing one's autonomy (see also Bildtgård & Öberg, 2015a; Davidson, 2001; Malta & Farquharson, 2014). Sally's story is characterised by ambivalence towards repartnering: she wants an established LAT relationship, but she fears losing her freedom and autonomy, in particular if her partner should fall ill. This was also true for many of the men she dated. For a long time she was also hesitant because she was grieving her former husband. Again this was also true for some of the men she had met. These life-phase-typical concerns play a central role in their deliberations. In order for an established relationship to be formed they need to be resolved.

From singlehood to LAT and beyond: LAT Lisa and Lars

Despite the difficulties involved in meeting a new partner, some people do manage to form an established relationship. Many, however, at least initially, choose not to live together. Living Apart Together is a way of living together that is characterised by the combination of a high degree of mutual commitment and personal autonomy in the form of a preserved 'home of one's own', a union form that has become increasingly established and institutionalised in Western Europe since the 1980s – and in the Nordic countries especially. Below we meet LAT Lars and Lisa.

LAT Lars is a 68-year-old man who was widowed eight years prior to the interview. A little more than two years ago, Lars met his current LAT partner Lisa, who is also 68 years old and who had become widowed from her lifelong marriage six months before meeting Lars. Both are former white-collar workers and both have children from their previous lifelong marriages.

Lars took the first initiative in the relationship by inviting Lisa home for dinner. He had read in the local newspaper that Lisa had been widowed. Lisa recalls their first encounter:

'He asked if I had considered having a sweetheart. "No", was my first thought – that had never crossed my mind. And that made it harmless to continue seeing each other because I had no such ambition. I was determined not to meet a new man. I thought that there would never exist any man beside my husband that I could relate to in this way – but there did.'

While Lisa had no plans to initiate a new relationship, Lars was actively dating and looking for a new partner. In order to find the best match, he ranked all women he met on qualities such as: education, cultural interest, sex appeal, homemaker ability, fashion etc, and gave them points on a scoreboard. In this way he deliberated with himself who would constitute the ideal partner. Lisa didn't meet all of his criteria, but had other qualities that made up for that.

Despite Lisa's insistence on not initiating a new romantic union, her relationship with Lars continued to develop. Five months after their initial meeting they started to describe themselves as a couple, but the relationship pathway has been paved with uncertainties, conflicts and even short break-ups. Their different relationship objectives are an issue of constant discussion, negotiation and ambivalence.

Much of Lisa's ambivalence concerns loyalty to her former husband and what she perceives as a lack of socially established norms for new intimate relationships in later life. Is it a betrayal of one's former marital partner to initiate a new relationship? How should they present themselves socially? What is a *non-marital* relationship?

'Who am I in relation to Lars? Am I betraying my husband? We haven't really found a good label for what we are. We coined a few words in the beginning: one is "friends of the heart", "symbiosis" and "lovers". We were both married for more than 40 years. That sort of couplehood is over. So what are we? How will we be perceived by others: "Are they a couple or not? They are not engaged and they are not married." Those are the only concepts we have, in our generation.'

In her ambivalence towards non-marital relationships Lisa is unrepresentative of her generation. Living in a secular society, marriage is unimportant for the vast majority of the older single Swedes (see Chapter six), also among our interviewees. Instead, Lisa's ambivalence has to be understood in the context of her strong religious upbringing and her single lifelong marital relationship.

Lars' key ambivalence emanates from his experience of a gender-skewed dating market full of older single women, and his desire to form a relationship which is different from his lifelong marriage. Lars' ideal was an 'open' relationship that could include several partners simultaneously, but Lisa didn't accept such an arrangement (neither did any of his previous dates) and Lars had had to adapt in order to continue their relationship. These different views have led to conflicts and two temporary separations, followed by reunions, and have demanded extensive negotiating efforts on their part. Lisa explains: "The amount of energy that we have spent on our relationship – I don't think either of us spent in our marriages, where everything was sort of taken for granted. Being together was simply a given, and you didn't break up because you had a conflict."

In the space of the two short sentences above, Lisa illustrates the shift from marriage to divorce culture: from a context where both the form and the contents of the relationship were externally given, to a situation where both have to be continuously negotiated. The context of divorce culture represents both potentials and threats. It allows for more diverse and individual relationship arrangements but it also lowers the threshold for relationship dissolutions. In Lars' and Lisa's case, relationship options range from breaking up to moving in together – or even marrying.

An issue of constant discussion is the option to cohabit. Lars and Lisa both believe that moving in together would constitute the financially rational choice. They can afford to have two apartments, but they live close to each other and think it is a waste to have so much space. At the same time, they are hesitant to sacrifice their personal autonomy. In this way they express hesitations that are similar to those of other singles and LAT informants, both in our data and in previous international research (see for example Davidson, 2001; Ghazanfareeon Karlsson & Borell, 2005; Malta & Farquharson, 2014; Régnier-Loilier et al, 2009). Home represents personal space but also personal history. In the latter case, the home can be a 'shrine' to the life one has led with the former spouse or partner and possibly common children. Lisa, in particular, is torn between the home she has made with her former husband and the idea of creating a new home that would instead be based on her life with Lars. If they move in together, says Lisa, it has to be in a new apartment not filled with memories of either of their former spouses or marriages. A central issue in relation to cohabitation concerns the children and questions of inheritance. As Lisa says: "Perhaps we should buy a small house and start over together. We can invest an equal sum of money so that no one has to be worried. So that the children won't have to think that somebody is wasting their inheritance."

As Talbott (1998) has pointed out, adult children are potentially important partners in the negotiation of the relationship. Some international research has found that children can often be critical of their parents repartnering. In our interviews they were more commonly portrayed as active or passive supporters. Lisa describes her children as being positive and supportive of her new union: "Mummy is worth this." Lars says his children do not interfere with his intimate relationship decisions: "My oldest daughter says 'that's your business'. The first time I presented Lisa my daughter said: 'That was the best one so far.' Lisa's children have never questioned our relationship, and neither have mine." Still, it is clear that when it comes to financial matters most older people do not perceive themselves as entirely free in relation to their children. When Lars suggested buying half of Lisa's apartment, his daughter asked him not to enter into a financial relationship, so he desisted. This represents a common theme in all of the interviews – the one area where children tend to be hesitant about their parents' relationships is when they involve financial transactions.

Lars and Lisa have somewhat different views of their responsibility for each other in the future. The promise 'for better and for worse' does not fit with Lars' ideals. He has told Lisa that if he were to become ill, she would have to leave him and get on with her life. Lars' views on the topic are typical of his strong belief that late–life relationships, because they are not aimed at reproduction and the raising of a family, ought to be aimed at personal fulfilment rather than obligations. Among our interviewees, Lars is the informant who most clearly expresses relationship ideals that approach Giddens' (1992) 'pure relationships'.

Lisa is aware of Lars' attitudes on mutual care responsibilities in the future, but she does not agree with him: "It is a hypothetical situation. Let's say we moved in together, or got married or something like that – then you don't walk away. If you have had a good relationship, then of course you'll want to stay faithful, also in times of adversity."

The future of the relationship is still uncertain. Both Lars and Lisa describe their two years together as turbulent, characterised by ambivalence and constant negotiations, and there are still a number of questions that have not been settled. Lars sums it up:

'What now? Should we move in together? Should we get married? After all, we've been going steady for two years now. It seems reasonable that we should approach a decision.

But I'm ambivalent. I don't really want to start over. I see no point in getting married. I just want to do things together, enjoy each other's company and exchange thoughts.'

Lars and Lisa's story is characterised by their ambivalence regarding the development of the relationship. They have different relationship goals and their different aims constantly threaten to break up the relationship. Their story shows the wide range of possibilities for relationship development offered by the LAT form. Among our LAT respondents there is a wide variation with regard to the degree of relationship establishment, from Lars and Lisa to very established couples who live together almost constantly, moving between homes, and who can only imagine that the relationship will dissolve through the death of one of the partners.

Lars and Lisa were hesitant to move in together. Previous research has stressed that autonomy is an important motive for not moving in together (see for example Davidson, 2001; Ghazanfareeon Karlsson & Borell, 2005; Malta & Farquharson, 2014; Régnier-Loilier et al, 2009). This was true also for our informants, including Lars and Lisa. However, for many informants this ideal lost importance as partners grew closer. This was evident in some cases where informants in established LAT relationships claimed that they would be willing to move in with their partner if he or she should fall ill, in order to be able to continue the relationship and help their partner – although they had initially agreed that it was very important to keep separate homes in order to preserve their autonomy. Some LAT informants talked about how at the beginning of the relationship they had the ideal to spend equal amounts of time in each other's homes. However, as the relationship developed this lost importance. In practice, geographical distance was often perceived as a more important and non-negotiable argument against cohabitation than autonomy. If the two partners lived far from each other, cohabitation would signify the loss of one partner's personal network of family and friends and conserving these networks was given much importance by the informants.

From singlehood to cohabitation and beyond: Cohabiting Carl and Caroline

Among our cohabiting informants, moving in together had not always been a conscious choice, but part of a process. The choice of cohabitation – like that of marriage – was generally not a choice made a priori, before meeting a partner. Instead it was a decision that was made after negotiations between two partners who had already established an LAT-relationship. In late modernity the central concern for singles is rarely whether they should cohabit/marry or not, but whether they should have a relationship or not. All our cohabitants had originally established their relationships as LAT unions. As a 79-year-old female LAT informant recalled concerning one of her prior late-life dating relationships, where they had recently met: "He fell in love with me. And he wanted us to move in together. But I said: 'That's out of the question. First we need to get to know each other.' That's what it's all about. You can't just start by cohabiting."

In many cases, LAT relationships simply developed into pseudo-cohabiting relationships as partners started living more and more together, basically moving between their apartments or favouring one apartment but staying together most of the time (cmpr. Stevens, 2004). In other cases it was a decision that slowly matured. In order to illustrate the process leading up to and beyond cohabitation we return to the opening case of Cohabiting Carl and Caroline.

Unlike the case of LAT Lisa and Lars above, neither Carl nor Caroline expressed any conflicts of loyalty towards their former marital partners. When they met Carl was 70 and Caroline 72 years old. Carl had been actively searching for a new partner since his divorce 10 years earlier, but had found it difficult to find suitable arenas for meeting a new partner: "I even tried an on-line dating service. How do you meet a new partner? Where do you go? To a night-club? But I never go to night-clubs. Or out dancing? But then you have to play that 'game' and I think it's too bothersome."

Carl, who had lived abroad for many years, had always had younger women (his former wife was 18 years younger) and had also been searching and advertising for a younger female partner after returning to Sweden. However, he had discovered that Swedish women were reluctant to date older men. After meeting his same-aged partner Caroline he had reconsidered his age ideals and found that in fact it was easier to communicate with a generational peer.

Caroline had been widowed for 20 years from a happy marriage and had, during these years, had no interest in a new intimate partner. However, when she met Carl at a local association she fell in love at first sight: "The first time I saw him I thought 'God, this is my destiny'. I was immediately attracted to him. I hadn't had a man for 20 years and I was definitely not looking for one, but he was so lovely." After having pined for Carl for a couple of weeks she told him she was in love with him. Carl was surprised, but immediately invited her to his summerhouse. It was not their intention, but they stayed there for several days. That was the start of their relationship two years prior to the interview. On New Year's Eve, one and a half years after first meeting, they got engaged.

For a few months after their first date Carl spent most of the time in Caroline's apartment. They discussed whether they should move in together, and in that case, how their home should be arranged. Just as with LAT Lars and Lisa, it was important for Carl and Caroline that neither of them should move in with or feel like a guest in the other's home, but that they should create a new common home together. However, this decision wasn't easy. Carl describes how his own house, which had also been his parental home, had been a physical manifestation of his history and his 'safe place' during his years abroad. It was difficult to separate from it, and Carl spent a lot of time in the interview explaining his attachment to his home. However, as soon as he had moved in with Caroline, the old home lost importance and the new common home became the centre of his attention. Through Caroline the new home became a strong link to the local community that he once came from.

While LAT Lars (above) was afraid of losing his independence and hesitant both about establishing an exclusive romantic relationship and about moving in together, Carl instead interpreted his and Caroline's interdependency in positive terms: for him, Caroline represented social integration, safety and 'home', something he had longed for ever since he returned to Sweden after having spent his whole adult life abroad:

> 'This closeness is so important – not being alone. With Caroline I feel at home, I feel safe. We are dependent on each other and help each other. We both grew up in the same neighbourhood, and I knew her brother and all her cousins. I knew everyone around her – but not her. That has made it very easy for me to be accepted, because everybody knew me.'

Carl's story illustrates a common point in the stories of our cohabitants, that living alone is not associated primarily with autonomy but with emptiness and isolation. As one cohabiting informant put it: "For me, a single person is only half a couple." While the LATs relate a number of disadvantages to moving in together, in particular the risk of decreased social integration, the cohabitants instead describe their union in terms of increased social integration. For example, while some LATs describe that moving in with their partner would mean that they would have to move far from their family and friends, the cohabitants typically describe how moving in with their partner has meant the comfort of having somebody around all the time to share their everyday lives.

This is also a reason why children are often positive about their parents finding a new partner (as shown in Chapter six). According to Caroline both Carl's and her children are very supportive of their new relationship. She recalls how excited her daughter was on hearing that she had 'Finally!' found a new man: "They are very happy for Carl and know that I'm taken good care of. And I think he sees his children more since I came into the picture. We like each other's children and have a great relationship."

Both Carl and Caroline describe their relationship as established and cannot imagine any other ending to the relationship than being 'widowed'. However, the union form is still under negotiation. Caroline wants to be married, but Carl resists. Carl explains his resistance with both emotional and rational arguments:

> 'Caroline is eager to get married but I resist. I've told her that I've been married three times already and it hasn't worked out. Also, what happens to my children if I should die? We have a legal agreement stating how my assets should be divided if I die [and a marriage would void that agreement]. I haven't yet reached a final decision about marriage, but the fact is that you get a lower pension if you marry.'

Caroline still hopes that Carl will marry her but finds comfort in the fact that the issue is still under negotiation:

> 'I was a little bit sad when we didn't plan to get married. I would very much have liked to, because I'm a little old fashioned. But I know that he wants me, and that we are a couple. But when somebody asks if we are married, he always replies "not yet", so I still have some hope that he will propose to me some day.'

Carl and Caroline's negotiations around marriage illustrate that even if cohabitation in later life is often presented as an alternative to marriage (see for example Brown & Kawamura, 2010), and there are important structural reasons that weigh against marriage (in particular of a financial nature), the decision always has to be negotiated, and priorities can change.

From singlehood to marriage and beyond: Married Mike and Martha

International research has shown that few older people get married and a large majority of older singles are negative about getting remarried (Bildtgård & Öberg, 2015a; Borell, 2001; Carr, 2004; Malta & Farquharson, 2014; Steitz & Welker, 1991; Talbott, 1998). Results from our interviews with older singles and LATs support these findings. However, among the cohabiting informants we found many different attitudes regarding marriage. Some informants saw their cohabiting union as self-evident and permanent (an alternative, and not a prelude, to marriage). Two betrothed informants had wanted to be married, but had chosen not to remarry in order not to lose their widow's pensions. Still, the question of whether cohabiting partners should marry or not appeared to be a question of negotiation, and circumstances could change to facilitate marriage. In most cases practical matters, such as the widow's pension or inheritance issues, made older people hesitant to marry, or they simply didn't think of marriage as important in their current phase of life. For others, negotiations on these issues eventually led to marriage. Below we describe the process from relationship initiation to marriage from the point of view of a couple who married late in life.

Married Mike is an 84-year-old remarried man with two children from his former marriage. He met and moved in with his current partner Martha while his former wife was still alive, suffering from dementia, and living in a care home. Martha is a 78-year-old remarried woman with three children from two prior relationships. Her last marriage was traumatic and led to a divorce at the age of 64 and also to the decision to remain autonomous for the rest of her life and never again initiate a new romantic relationship: "I was never going to have another man. I was going to start a new life, all on my own. I was not going to be dominated ever again."

However, a couple of months after her divorce she threw a house party for old acquaintances from her student years, including Mike. Although they were old acquaintances they had never before been romantically interested in each other and Martha was still adamant about not having a new man. Mike, who was looking for travel company, invited Martha for a trip abroad (this was, in fact, a rather common story in the interviews) although, he assures in the interview, with no intention of initiating a new relationship. On the one hand Mike was still married and on the other he believed he could no longer function sexually. However, during the trip their relationship, much to Mike's surprise, turned intimate. As for many of our cohabitants, Mike and Martha started to live together long before they formally became cohabitants (in fact they kept dual homes for many years). On their return home Mike invited Martha to temporarily move to his apartment some 300 kilometres away, concerned that she would not be able to manage her house on her own during the winter. Martha describes how the temporary cohabitation developed into a permanent one: "We became more and more bound to each other during that time and afterwards I couldn't bring myself to move out again. We never planned to become cohabitants, it just happened."

Martha's children have been positive about their relationship and marriage. However, Mike describes that his children never accepted Martha. They saw Mike's new relationship as a betrayal of their mother who was still alive but institutionalised with advanced dementia when they met. Although Mike's wife had been deceased for many years at the point of the interview, they still did not accept Martha. As a consequence, Mike's contact with both his children and grandchildren had suffered.

After having been a couple for 13 years, Mike proposed to Martha and they got married. While Cohabiting Carl (above) was hesitant to marry because it would complicate inheritance issues, this had gradually ceased to be an obstacle for Mike. The reasons were twofold – over the years his and Martha's finances had become increasingly blurred. Also, due to the conflicts with his children, he no longer felt the need to protect their inheritance: "We've had separate finances. But in the end I lost control. So I said 'why don't we just get hitched?' So we decided to do so. When we got married we drew up a new will with no prenuptial agreement."

Once the financial issue was out of the way, there were no obstacles to marriage. According to Mike marriage was not important to him, it only made the problem of ownership easier. Although Martha claims that she still wasn't interested in marriage, Mike believed that in reality she was, and proposed. Martha describes Mike's proposal, and her answer, which contradicted her decision to never be bound to another man again:

'He knew that I never wanted to be dependent on a man again. No man should ever get to decide for me again. But then there we were in a row-boat on the lake, and he said that "I've lost control over what's mine and what's yours". And then he added: "Shall we not get married after all?" And I replied "Yes, but you have to propose in the proper way." He almost fell into the water when he got down on his knees, but then I shouted "YES"'.

The case of Married Mike and Martha shows the long development of a relationship from initiation to marriage for two people who originally were not interested in repartnering at all, and the number of issues that had to be resolved in order for the relationship to develop.

Conclusion

In this chapter we have proceeded from the assumption in contemporary family theory that late modern relationships tend to be negotiated, and we have tried to illustrate the negotiations that take place in the development of relationships initiated in later life. In doing so we have wanted to show how some of the structural aspects identified earlier in the book are realised in the development of concrete relationships. While cross-sectional research has tended to give a static image of older people's relationship preferences, relationship histories better capture the dynamic process. They show how relationships tend to develop through negotiations on central issues that are raised throughout the relationship's establishment and which need to be solved in order for the relationship to develop. A central point is that these issues tend to be the same for all unions as they progress: in order for an established relationship to develop, issues regarding autonomy and potential loyalty issues towards former partners have to be resolved; in order for cohabitation to take place issues regarding autonomy, finances and the dismantling of homes need to be resolved; and in order for marriage to take place issues concerning finances and inheritance have to be resolved.

It is our contention that much prior research has put the question of older people's preferences for their relationship's arrangement in the wrong way. If in modern society the choice of initiating a relationship was limited to the question of whether one should get married or not – a package deal that included sex, cohabitation and reproduction – in late modern societies relationships tend to develop along a hierarchy of establishment, where the first question is normally whether one wants a partner or not. In this normative context almost all relationships are initiated as LAT relationships and not until the relationship is established is the question of cohabitation raised. Also, it is only after having lived together successfully for some time that the question of marriage is raised. It is thus not surprising that the preference of single older people, if they want a relationship, is LAT.

One reason why many older people who have repartnered late in life tend to live as LATs is that there are structural obstacles that have to be overcome. There are clear life-phase-related structural differences between later life and young adulthood that pose different challenges for negotiation. While for people in young adulthood living together might aid in raising common children and marriage might constitute a protective juridical framework for forming a family, in later life moving in together often means breaking up a home in which a family has already been raised, with all the accumulated memories of that family, and marriage is associated with a number of juridical problems related to those prior family constellations. In other words, while in younger adulthood, structural forces pushed relationship arrangement negotiations towards cohabitation and marriage, in later life the same structural forces tend to become obstacles for such a development. To overcome these obstacles can take time – time that older people might not have.

A common point for all our interviewees was that as soon as a transition had taken place it was no longer a question of ambivalence, and the negotiations and arguments, for and against, tended to be given little importance. Instead, ambivalence was expressed in regard to prospective decisions. Of course, many older singles and LATs will never want to cohabit and many cohabitants will never want to marry, but our intention in this chapter has been to show how priorities can change when a relationship is established and develops.

EIGHT

A new partner as a resource
for social support

The previous chapters of the book have focused on structural factors impacting on repartnering in later life and how these factors shape older people's attitudes and experiences of repartnering. The following two chapters instead focus on the consequences of repartnering for older individuals and their social network. The purpose of this chapter is to investigate the gains of repartnering in old age. We ask what a new intimate relationship can offer the individual who repartners in later life and if these rewards are different in later life than earlier in life. The chapter starts with a brief presentation of two theoretical perspectives that have been used to understand the reasons for late-life repartnering: rational choice theory and functionalism. The chapter continues by detailing different kinds of social support that a new relationship can offer the individual – companionate, emotional and practical support. The chapter will primarily be based on a review of previous research. Since our own interviews support earlier research, in this chapter they are primarily used to illustrate and provide a deeper understanding of those findings.

The gains of repartnering

Research about late-life relationship transitions has primarily focused on the *loss* of a partner through widowhood, and also, but to a much lesser extent, through divorce. Loneliness is an important consequence of widowhood for both men and women, who miss the life they had with their partner and the support he or she provided (Carr, 2004; Carr et al, 2002; Davidson, 2001, 2002; Dykstra & Gierveld, 2004; Stevens, 2004; Öberg, Andersson & Bildtgård, 2016). Some studies of divorce (Aquilino, 1994; Cooney & Dunne, 2001; Daatland, 2007; Shapiro, 2003) have furthermore suggested that parent–child relationships, especially between older fathers and their adult children, suffer negatively from a parental divorce and contribute to social isolation of the older parents (although some studies do not support these findings, for example Dykstra, 1993; K. Glaser, Stuchbury, Tomassini & Askham, 2008).

But all transitions in later life are not necessarily about loss, they can also include gains. Later life can offer the opportunity to *gain* new intimate partners. A substantial minority of older singles will find a new partner and even more are interested in repartnering. What do they stand to gain from repartnering? We know from earlier research that continuous marriage benefits older people financially, health-wise and in terms of longevity (Waite, 1995). The continuously married tend to have the best financial resources (Arber, 2004; Wilmoth & Koso, 2002), better health (Verbrugge, 1979) and lower risk of premature mortality (Drefahl, 2012; Statistics Sweden, 2016) than other civil status groups, and they are less likely to be institutionalised (Connidis, 2010; Pimouguet et al, 2016). Less is known about the effects of late-life repartnering, but some studies report that repartnered older people are more satisfied with life than divorcees and widowed people (Bildtgård & Öberg, 2015a; K. Bulcroft & O'Connor, 1986; Gray, De Vaus, Qu & Stanton, 2010; Hurd Clarke, 2005); that repartnering will often add life satisfaction – also to already good single lives (see for example Watson & Stelle, 2011); and even that women in higher-order marriages tend to be more satisfied with their lives than women in first-order marriages (Carr, Freedman & Cornman, 2016).

Two theoretical perspectives have often been applied in prior research to increase understanding of late-life repartnering. From a rational choice perspective it is hypothesised that the individual seeks the resources offered by a potential partner. The individual will consider a new relationship if he or she perceives the gains of the new relationship to be bigger than the gains of remaining single (see for example Carr, 2004; Mahay & Lewin, 2007; Vespa, 2013). A traditional idea in modern family theory (for example Becker, 1981) was that men and women fulfil different gendered roles and functions in the family: men were assumed to be socialised into a breadwinning role and to contribute financial security to the family unit, while women were assumed to be specialised in home making and social networking and to bring care and integration to the family. Rational choice theory has, for example, been used by Carr (2004) to hypothesise that men and women seek each other's complementary resources: women seek men's financial resources and men women's social resources and competences as home makers. This hypothesis is often based on the implicit assumption that older cohorts have lived their lives in accordance with a traditional breadwinner-housewife family model. It is, however, questionable how well this assumption holds up for current generations of older people in societies where gender equality is increasingly the norm, where women have (had) salaried work and where social support systems guarantee reasonable financial security also for single women.

A second theoretical perspective that has been used to understand repartnering in later life is functionalist theory. This perspective focuses on the functions that dating or a new union might fill for older single individuals and society alike. These functions might differ slightly depending on union form, such as an LAT relationship, cohabitation and marriage, and might be more or less attractive in different life phases, depending on the needs and concerns relevant to that phase. Bulcroft and Bulcroft (1991), for example, argue that a function of dating in young adulthood is to socialise new generations into taking marital roles, but that this is no longer a central function of dating in later life (and older people tend to not refer to themselves as daters for this reason, see Benson & Coleman, 2016a). Instead other functions become central, such as companionship and social integration. Another age-specific function that can be hypothesised as an extension of socio-emotional selectivity theory (Carstensen et al, 1999) is that dating and repartnering might be a way for people with poor social networks to gain emotional support.

One way of investigating what a new intimate relationship can offer the older individual who repartners is to look at what the availability of a partner can provide in terms of everyday social support. As de Jong Gierveld (2002) points out, living alone means that companionship and solidarity, as well as assistance and care, has to come from outside the household, while living together as a couple provides older men and women with the greatest possibilities for social integration. Bodenman's (2005) concept of dyadic coping captures the relevance of such a source for everyday support. Most people do not cope with everyday challenges alone (as is sometimes implied in the coping literature), but with the help of a significant other – often a partner. A partner can therefore be an especially valuable source of social support.

Below we consider the partner as a potential source of social support. Social support has been defined as 'the availability of people whom the individual trusts, on whom he can rely, and who make him feel cared for and valued as a person' (McDowell, 2006, p 152). This definition focuses on the people who are the source of support – in this chapter a new partner. Below, we will focus on three different kinds of support a new partner can offer – companionate, emotional and practical support.

Companionate support

A persistent finding in the international literature is that one of the gains of repartnering is companionship (see for example Alterovitz & Mendelsohn, 2013; K. Bulcroft & O'Connor, 1986; R.A. Bulcroft & Bulcroft, 1991; Moore & Stratton, 2004; Watson & Stelle, 2011). Below, we will focus on companionship in terms of having a partner for recreational purposes and a partner for participating in social events, and we will return to more emotional aspects in the next section.

A new intimate relationship can provide a *recreational partner* – somebody to go out with or to enjoy outdoor life and cultural events of different kinds. Davidson (2001) has shown that many widows, although not interested in marriage, express an interest in having a gentleman friend for going out to restaurants, theatre, shopping and holidays (see also Alterovitz & Mendelsohn, 2013; K. Bulcroft & O'Connor, 1986). This was true also for most of our Swedish interviewees. 63-year-old Single Susan explains what she is looking for in a new partner: "A man who I can share experiences with: Go travelling together, exercise together and do nice things together. Hike in the mountains, go on biking tours. But primarily to exercise, to maintain good health and eat good food."

A particularly common theme in our own interviews was to meet a partner over the mutual interest in travelling. Travelling appeared to be a central part of the third-age project for many of our informants, regardless of whether it meant fleeing the harsh Swedish winters or discovering new cultures. However, singles often experienced travelling as being difficult on one's own and some had initiated their relationship as part of a planned trip (see for example married Mike and Mary's story in Chapter seven). LAT Lenny, 78, describes how he and his former cohabiting partner always went to Spain for several weeks every winter, but how he found no joy in going there after her death. According to him, travelling is a couple experience.

'In Spain, whatever they say, it's couplehood that counts. On all those trips, everyone is Mr and Mss, Mr and Mss. If you do something, you do so as couples: two, four or six people. As a single person you don't ask people if you can come with them when they are going out. I tried going to Spain alone once and I was the only single out of 47 people in the bus. You just don't go there if you are alone.'

Women, who often have lifelong experience as home makers, have been found to prefer relationships that are primarily companionate in nature and preserve their autonomy through separate homes (Davidson, 2002; Ghazanfareeon Karlsson & Borell, 2005). Men are instead often assumed to prefer a shared home. According to a frequently quoted line by Davidson, women want somebody to go out with – men somebody to come home to (2002, p 51). There is excellent logic behind this assumption. However, as shown by the Swedish data presented in Chapter six, even if women prefer someone to go out with (LAT relationships) to a larger extent than older men, also a majority of older single men prefer LAT to cohabitation (someone to come home to).

As LAT Lenny noted, social life is often organised around couples. An intimate partner is often a key to being allowed to *participate in social occasions*. It has been shown that having a partner can mean a higher social status, which opens many social doors, especially for women (K. Bulcroft & O'Connor, 1986). Like LAT Lenny above, many of the interviewees recall having felt uncomfortable in social occasions or even having been banned from them after becoming single. This was the case for 78-year-old Cohabiting Cecilia. Below she compares her five years as a single widow with her life after repartnering:

> 'I was not invited to social gatherings because I was a single woman. It had to be couples. A single woman is a bit lower on the social ladder. But when I had a man beside me again, suddenly I was popular. I wasn't a threat any more. Even if you are old you are a threat to married women when you are single.'

Older women, who have often been in charge of family social ties, tend to have more social capital than older men, but ironically, as in the case of Cecilia, they might not always be able to benefit fully from it without a male partner. Older single men have been found to be less socially integrated than older single women, and to benefit from the social capital of new female partners. It has even been suggested that older men gain better contact with their own children as a consequence of getting a new partner (Hagestad 1986). This could explain older single men's greater interest in repartnering compared to women.

Emotional support

Emotional support is often understood to be about showing empathy and concern for other people through listening and reassurance and is normally offered by our closest personal relationships. Below we will present different kinds of emotional support that an intimate relationship can provide, such as help to cope with loneliness and grief, as well as being a source for self-disclosure and confidence sharing.

One of the most common problems for older singles, especially for those who have experienced a relationship dissolution, is loneliness. A new intimate relationship might be a way of *coping with loneliness* (K. Bulcroft & O'Connor, 1986; de Jong Gierveld, 2002; Moore & Stratton, 2004; Peters & Liefbroer, 1997; Stevens, 2004; Öberg et al, 2016). According to Öberg et al, partner status is a central predictor for loneliness: experiences of loneliness are less common among older people in relationships, regardless of union form, and most common among singles who *wish to have* a partner. Both in de Jong Gierveld's and Öberg et al's studies, repartnering alleviated loneliness among older people who had experienced a relationship dissolution. In our interviews many of the informants contrasted the lonely life they led as singles to the life they shared with their new partner. LAT Lenny describes his life as a widower as being in death's waiting room: "The first time alone was terrible. Almost like sitting in death's waiting room – it gets very lonely. I've always been a couple's person so I found it very difficult. And I started to expect that I would remain alone until death."

For Lenny, his new LAT relationship with Lydia had meant a total transformation of his life, giving him a new future. Together they fulfil the promises of the third age, travelling and going out together, but for Lenny being single promises nothing more than waiting for death. Having somebody to share everyday experiences with was an essential part of this transformation that gave meaning to his everyday experiences.

> 'We went to the movies a while ago. Together! That makes all the difference. I went to the movies on my own once – pretty boring. You go alone, watch the film, and then you go home, and when you open the door and say "hello" – then nothing! Lydia affects me in a positive way – from death's waiting room to a new life.'

Lenny claimed that the relationship had given new meaning to his life and allowed him to envision a new future. While widowhood, in a manner of speaking, had transferred Lenny to the fourth age, repartnering transferred him back to the third-age project. This was mentioned by a few of the men in the study – possibly because they have poorer emotional support networks than the women. 87-year-old

Cohabiting Chris described how meeting his new intimate partner Cecilia had changed his view of the future:

'Earlier life was in black and white, but with Cecilia it suddenly has colour again – like it had with my first wife 60 years ago. I have the same craving for her and love and romance, the same craving that an alcoholic has for liquor. My widowed brother in law is grey and grieving, lonely and dull, and sees his current life as death's waiting room. I have the time of my life!'

Stevens (2004) mentions a very concrete example of emotional support: that of helping one's widowed partner to *cope with the grief* of their deceased former partner. This was also mentioned by several of our widowed informants. They recalled that it had been a common theme of discussion with potential partners on Internet dating sites for seniors. Other informants who were currently in new unions were still actively helping each other to cope with the grief. LAT Lisa describes how her new relationship has been essential for her and her partner in handling what she calls the 'afterlife': "We can talk about our grief for our life companions in a way that we can't with people whose partners are still alive. And together we can take care of those terribly lonely Friday nights."

Another central aspect of emotional support is that of physical and psychological intimacy. In the literature many parallel keywords are mentioned that refer to the psychological aspect of intimacy, such as love and romance. A central aspect of psychological intimacy is that of having somebody who can share and confirm one's everyday experiences, such as the experience of a meal, or as in the quote from LAT Lenny above, the appreciation of a film, and thereby validate the reality of those experiences.

A special object that needs validation is the self. This is closely related to Luhmann's (1986) argument that a central function of an intimate partner in contemporary society is to provide a stable reference point for personal identity, in a world where identity is much more fluent than in traditional society. This point is emphasised even more in Giddens' (1992) work on late modernity, where the relationship becomes a central resource for the reflective individual's self-project. We can add that validation through a relationship can be a central part of self-realisation in the third age. A common theme in prior research is the importance of having a confidant who can provide such emotional support. Bulcroft and O'Connor (1986) found that *self-disclosure* was an important part of older people's motives for dating and Stevens (2004) found that it was an important part of repartnered older people's new relationships. Similarly, Alterovitz and Mendelsohn (2013) found that the search for a soulmate to share confidences with was a central priority among older Internet daters. Older men, in particular, have been found to rely on their partner for sharing confidences and single older men are often assumed to be searching for a confidant when repartnering. Older single women are instead often assumed to have a wider network of confidants and to thus be less interested in repartnering for the sake of finding someone to share confidences with (Carr, 2004).

A second aspect of intimacy is physical closeness. Being touched is a central aspect of being confirmed as a physical being, but for older singles sources of physical intimacy can be scarce, sometimes leading to a deficit that is colloquially referred to as 'skin hunger'. A consequence of repartnering is gaining a new source for physical intimacy, through sexual activity but also through everyday caressing. Cohabiting Cecilia describes the importance of physical intimacy:

> 'We hug and caress a lot. When we fall asleep we lie back to back, close to each other. And we give each other tenderness, warmth and some sort of life and strength. They say that single people, who sleep alone – that it shortens their life a little bit. Chris had a lovely grandma and they used to sleep back to back when he was a child. And he says that he used to have so much tenderness with her as a kid and now, towards the end of his life, he has it with me.'

In practice psychological and physical intimacy can often go together. LAT Lisa describes how she and Lars work through the grief of their respective deceased partners both through conversation and through sex: "Sometimes you need to comfort the body because there is nothing that can give comfort to the soul, when you have been through these big losses."

Sex is often an important part of physical intimacy in new late-life relationships and consequently of the emotional support that a new partner can offer. We will return to the theme of sex in later life in Chapter ten.

Practical support

Support from a partner can also be of a practical nature. Prior research mentions financial support, household work and personal assistance as potential gains of a new relationship.

As we described above, in modern family theory it is often assumed that men will bring their *financial resources* to a new relationship (Arber, 2004; Davidson, 2002). However, this assumption can be questioned in a society where men and women are often financially independent. In our interview study it was very uncommon that partners pooled their resources unless they were (re)married (which is uncommon). Instead it was clear that the informants did not see their financial resources as fully their own, but to a large extent as a part of their children's future inheritance. Informants were generally very keen to preserve their financial resources for their children and also not to be perceived as if they were exploiting their partner (and consequently their partner's children) financially. The norm was to 'go Dutch': the informants often described quite advanced strategies for keeping their finances separate, ranging from dividing up rent, adding up and splitting receipts and calculating and splitting costs for everyday expenses. Below LAT Lisa describes how they keep track of and split their car costs: "So far we both cover our own costs. If we ride in my car or his car we keep a record of the kilometres and then we even out the costs. Because I don't want anybody to think that I'm living off Lars or that he is living off me."

In our data financial resources do not appear to be a reason for repartnering. However, our results on this issue might reflect that Swedish women (and men) tend to be financially self-sufficient, and that as a consequence individuals are less likely to seek their partner's financial resources. Also, according to the Swedish theory of love (see Chapter three), genuine love is only possible between independent partners. In other contexts the hypothesis that women seek men's financial resources might, however, still be valid. For example Brown and Shinohara (2013) use it in a contemporary American study on dating.

For household work the logic may be the opposite. Men who have lived in relationships with traditional gendered role divisions might be searching for women's care and household skills. Stevens (2004), for example, found that a partner could be somebody to swap gendered household services with. In our data one group of men had more or less explicitly searched for a woman who could take *care of the household*. There were also corresponding examples of women, especially among the old-old informants, who were happy to take on a traditional homemaker role and found it to be satisfying. This was, for example, the case with Cohabiting Chris, 87, and Cecilia, 78. Below Chris describes his need for a partner offering him practical support:

> 'I planned a personal ad: "Male chauvinist wishes to meet an experienced housewife, used to spoiling a male chauvinist", because that was exactly what I was looking for. As a widower I did almost nothing. My daughter came once a week, vacuumed and emptied the laundry basket and I got clean clothes back. I didn't cook – I went to the service centre for lunch. But every morning I made up my own bed and prepared a cup of tea – all by myself.'

Cecilia did not mind providing this support, saying: "Relationships were better before, when women took care of the home and men got home from work and did their thing." However, most female informants did not want to take up the role of homemaker in a new intimate relationship (see for example Davidson, 2002; Ghazanfareeon Karlsson & Borell, 2005; Malta & Farquharson, 2014; Régnier-Loilier et al, 2009). Cohabiting Corinne described how in her new relationship the traditional gender roles had been reversed:

> 'Clint takes care of everything, really. He does the shopping, cleaning, laundry and cooking. He does the cleaning, because it is good for his health. I could clean of course or do the laundry but I don't want to take it from him, because it keeps Clint going. I try to force him to do what he can so that he won't just be sitting passively at home.'

Corinne's example shows how gender roles can be renegotiated in new intimate relationships. However, many women with experiences of traditionally gendered relationships were instead wary about moving in together with a new partner. In our interviews there seemed to be a generational difference, where the old-old (roughly 75+) were more likely to have lived in and expected relationships with a traditionally gendered division of labour, while the young-old had more heterogeneous experiences and tended to be more critical of traditionally gendered arrangements.

A final aspect of practical support which is often mentioned in the literature is *personal assistance* (see for example Moore & Stratton, 2004; Stevens, 2004) A new partner can give care individually by monitoring the behaviour of the other person (Umberson, 1992) – pushing them to go to the doctor, take walks, participate in activities, making sure that they keep clean – or more directly by practically aiding them with these issues. The following two quotes by Cohabiting Carl and Married Mark exemplify how a partner can contribute care in everyday life. Cohabiting Carl describes how he and Caroline care for each other:

> 'We depend on each other and help each other a lot. She has a bad back and I often give her massages and make sure that she doesn't carry anything heavy. I go with her to her doctor's appointments. She has a crutch but when we walk together I support her – we always go arm in arm. I make sure that she doesn't slip. And she takes care of me. She cut my hair this morning. She makes sure that I take my medicine and helps me with my eye drops. She takes care of me and it is very cosy.'

Married Mark stresses the importance of Mary's care for remaining youthful: "I believe that this relationship keeps me young. It's because of the way that Mary picks hair off my nose and makes sure that I stay fresh and that I clean up around myself."

The interviewees point out that it is important to feel needed (cmpr. Stevens, 2004). To have a person that relies on you provides a meaning to one's existence. However, many older people are hesitant to take on a caring responsibility for a new partner. This is one reason why many singles do not want a new relationship, and why those who do often opt for an LAT union. Single Susan describes how she was invited to lunch in the home of a man who was romantically interested in her, but it did not turn out well: "He showed me his fridge. It was full of medicines. He showed me how he used his medicine or pill organiser. And I'm not especially interested in nursing. I never went back."

This prospect of having to care for a new partner is particularly poignant for older women, who are likely to survive their partners. Some have experiences of offering care to former sick and dying partners and do not want to repeat the experience (cmpr. Talbott, 1998). There are also existential issues involved, such as not wanting to waste what little good time one has left in life on caring for another person (see more in Chapter eleven).

Conclusion

In this chapter we have tried to answer why singles repartner in later life by investigating what an older person may gain from a new late-in-life relationship. We have looked specifically at the different kinds of social support that a new partner may provide – companionate, emotional and practical support. These forms of support show the realities behind the common-sense assumption that 'a relationship prolongs life' and they show how new intimate relationships in later life might contribute social functions that decrease the risk for older people becoming institutionalised. We have also shown how a new partner may transform later life and contribute to envisioning a new future.

Two central distinctions often appear in prior research with regard to resources offered by a partner. First, it is assumed that men have more financial capital than women, while women have more social capital and care-giving skills. Consequently men and women are assumed to seek each other's complementary resources. Second, it is assumed that older people seek other resources in their partners than younger people. While in young adulthood and mid-life people are assumed to search for a partner to raise a family with, in later life this is no longer a concern, but instead people are assumed to look for somebody with whom to share the project of the third age. In later life, some of the assumptions about gender may change. Many women in contemporary Swedish cohorts of older adults have participated in the labour force and can rely on their own pensions and also on resources accumulated in earlier marriages. For this reason they may be less interested in men's financial resources but more in a companion to share the third-age project with. This may also be true for many of the young-old men who have lived in more gender-equal relationships earlier in life and who are used to taking care of a household.

The study of repartnering naturally implies a gains perspective on later life. This perspective poses some critical questions to developmental theory. Why would single older people choose to repartner instead of optimising their already existing social network? There are two possible answers to this question that we would like to propose. The first, complementing socio-emotional selectivity theory, would understand repartnering in terms of *compensation* for poor support networks, rather than *selection* and *optimisation* within already existing ones. The second answer focuses on the changing historical situation, where the emergence of the third age has pushed the limit of the fourth age, and the corresponding hypothesised withdrawal from social interaction, higher up the age ladder. In this perspective individuals are assumed to choose expansion and self-realisation until deep old age. In late modernity self-realisation is a central part of intimate relationships and with the third age self-realisation is a lifelong project. Together these processes mean that it is never 'too late' to repartner, as long as the health allows it. This critique also sheds light on how developmental theory implicitly proceeds from a naturalisation of the modern life course and the lifelong marriage in a social reality where this is no longer a certainty. Rather than viewing life as a continuous development towards death, where the continuous loss of social contacts plays a central part, our critique focuses on the importance of life phase and how the lifestyles of the third age can be extended until health no longer allows it. As LAT Lenny put it above, a new relationship can break this assumed continuity in loss and transform the future, "from death's waiting room to a new life".

NINE

Consequences for social network and support structures

The previous chapter considered repartnering from the perspective of what a new partner could contribute in terms of social support. The purpose of this chapter is instead to investigate how the introduction of a new partner affects the wider social network. We ask how a new partner is accepted into the older individual's family and social network and we ask how these existing relationships are renegotiated as a consequence. In the chapter we show that in most cases a new partner is integrated into the older individual's social network. Second, we show that the partner is viewed as a resource for autonomy both for the older individual and for their children. Third, we show that a new partner tends to replace children and friends as the preferred provider of different forms of social support. Finally, we discuss different theoretical ways of understanding older people's social support networks and relate these models to our survey data.

The impact of life transitions on linked lives

Our starting assumption is that interdependent lives (cmpr. Elder, 1994) are affected by major life transitions, such as when the individual repartners, separates, retires and more. Hagestad (1988) has shown how transitions in one individual's life create 'follow-transitions' in other interdependent lives: marriage creates daughter-in-law and son-in-law relationships, divorce creates ex-relationships and parenthood creates grandparental relationships. Previous research has studied the effects that major life transitions have for interdependent lives (Fennell, 2004; Hyde & Higgs, 2004; Kaufman & Uhlenberg, 1998; Lee, 2004; H. Marshall, 2004; Moen, Kim & Hofmeister, 2001; Owen & Flynn, 2004; van Solinge & Henkens, 2005). However this research has mostly focused on major turning points in the institutionalised life course, such as entry into first marriage in young adulthood, birth of children, retirement and widowhood. Studies of transitions in later life and their effects on interdependent lives has mostly focused on widowhood. Less is known about the effects of divorce, and even less about the effects of meeting a new partner late in life.

How does loss of a partner through widowhood or divorce affect interdependent lives? Studies have found that contacts with adult children increase after widowhood, when children step in as the primary sources of instrumental support to their parent (Dykstra, 1993). Adult children tend to compensate parents for the lost support of a former spouse, but this support tends to decrease over time (Ha, 2008). Studies of divorce suggest that parent–child relationships instead suffer from a parental divorce (Aquilino, 1994; Shapiro, 2003). Brown and Lin (2012) argue that when divorced older people no longer have a spouse on whom they can rely, they are likely to place greater demands on their children for support and this may create strains that weaken intergenerational ties. Family support to older parents, especially fathers, has often been found to be negatively affected by divorce as compared to married parents, and the effects can be long lasting (Cooney & Dunne, 2001; Daatland, 2007).

How does repartnering impact on the older individual's social network and access to social support? The limited research in this area has mainly focused on consequences for relationships with children. One suggestion is that a new partner, especially for men, increases contact with children. Hagestad (1986) found that 'second wives' kept the men connected with their families in ways they could not do well on their own.

More commonly, it has been suggested that a new partner might lead to conflicts and deteriorated contacts between generations. Adult children can be negative about their parents repartnering, as has been shown in studies by, for example, van den Hoonaard (2004) in a religious conservative rural part of Canada, and by Mehta (2002) in Singapore. Their studies clearly point to the impact of interdependent lives on older people's intimate partnership choices in communities that promote traditional values. However, in contexts that promote more individualistic values, the impact might be different.

Stevens (2004) noted that one of the issues that has to be negotiated and decided after meeting a new partner in later life is how to deal with conflicting loyalties between the partner on the one hand, and children, friends and family on the other. A new relationship might challenge family boundaries and for that reason not be welcomed by family members and friends. De Jong Gierveld and Peeters (2003) found that although interpersonal networks remain relatively intact after a person enters into a new late-in-life relationship, contact frequency tends to be negatively affected. In a later study de Jong Gierveld and Merz (2013) found that children were often negative towards their older (50+) parent's new intimate relationships. These experiences influenced them to form LAT relationships instead of moving in together, in order to avoid conflicts with their children. It should be noted that these negative reactions were mostly from children who shared the household with their parents, and who would have had to share their home with their parent's new partner. Effects might be different in a later phase of life when the repartnered parent and their children are no longer living in the same household.

To conclude, apart from a few Dutch studies, little research has addressed the consequences of new intimate relationships in later life for the social network. Still, this is a subject commonly addressed by older people living in new relationships.

Integration of social and filial networks

Although meeting a new partner is most transformative for the repartnered individuals themselves, it also involves people around them, such as family and friends, to different degrees. They are affected by the loss of time and focus which is redirected to the couple by both the repartnered individuals. In the Swedish interviews, the level to which the partner is introduced and integrated with friends and family varies. Some couples have for different reasons chosen to keep their respective circles of friends and families relatively separate. However, in our interviews it was more common that informants were integrated into their new partner's social network. Some have become accepted as more or less full members of the partner's family. A common example is how they help their partner's children with babysitting, or in resolving problems. This was the case for married Mike:

> 'When we told her [the partner's daughter] that we would get married, she said "Can I call you my step-father then?". "If you want to you can", I said, and she was so happy. And the two boys [step-sons] have had marital problems and one of them has had problems with his kids as well. So we've had conversations and I've helped them and it has all worked out quite well in the end.'

Children were generally positive in learning that their parents had found a new partner. In fact, in quite a few cases, children had been encouraging their mothers and fathers to find a partner who could look after them. In some cases they had even acted as dating coaches, teaching their parents how to put up profiles on dating websites.

As discussed in Chapter eight, a new partner can also be a key to a broader social network. Many informants had gained new friends and 'relatives' through their new partner and many claimed that the social circles were an important part of what the relationship brought to them. For many, inclusion in the partners' social network constituted a re-awakening of their social life, which was stunted when their former partner passed away or when they got separated.

Even if the dominant experience in the interviews was that of being welcomed into the new partners' social and filial network, integration had to be negotiated, and could be conflict-ridden. Integration was mainly affected by how the relationship with the former partner ended, especially if a betrayal of the former partner was involved. This was the case when the new partner was the reason for breaking up the former relationship, or if the new partnership was initiated when the former partner was still alive but suffering from dementia. In these cases social integration with the new partner's family and friends could be difficult (see for example the case of Married Mike and Martha in Chapter seven).

In contrast to what studies from other countries suggest (de Jong Gierveld & Merz, 2013; de Jong Gierveld & Peeters, 2003; Mehta, 2002; van den Hoonaard, 2004), Swedish adult children were generally very positive about their parents finding and/or cohabiting with new partners, but also rather negative about them getting married (see also Chapter six) – not for family boundary reasons, it seems, but for purely practical (legal) reasons.

In our interviews, formal integration into the family of the new partner was complicated by the legal bonds that connect parents to their children. This was particularly the case with inheritances. In this case remarriage could be a complicating factor because it ties not only the two partners legally to each other but also their families. Marriage creates legal complications around inheritances that are left for the children of the two partners to sort out after their parents' death. LAT Libby remembers how her daughter, who was otherwise positive about her new partner, was against her remarrying: "One of my daughters said 'Mom, you can't get married'. Because it gets so complicated when you have children on both sides... If one partner dies, you know, then there is a problem with two different families if you haven't properly arranged everything legally."

Even with prenuptials the legal situation was regularly perceived to be complex. As a consequence, even if the children were generally positive about their parents finding and living with a new partner, they were often sceptical about their parents getting remarried or involved in more profound financial transactions. Some of our informants explicitly refer to the legal/inheritance issue as a reason why they have chosen not to marry, taking into account the perspective of their children – proving Bulcroft and Bulcroft's (1991) point that adult children are central normative references for older parents' repartnering. However, few of our informants expressed any wish to get married. Instead, they often refer to marriage as something that was important in an earlier life phase, when they had young children, and in another historical context, when marriage was expected.

The partner as a key to autonomy

People tend to value close relationships with children and friends. At the same time, being autonomous is a strong societal value in most of the Western world (Beck & Beck-Gernsheim, 2002). A consequence of these combined values could be a wish for close relationships that are based on free personal choices. This is much in line with 'the Swedish theory of love' – that genuine love can only exist between independent individuals (see Chapter two). A central theme in our interviews is the value of being autonomous in relation to children and friends, in order to retain the free and voluntary character of these relationships: not being dependent on social support from friends to go to movies or restaurants, for example, or on children for companionship and practical help, is highly important, and a new intimate relationship is a tool for achieving that goal.

To some extent the preference for autonomy is clearly because relying on others is seen as a restriction on personal freedom – one cannot be too choosy about friends and family contacts when dependent on others, but when one is independent one can select only those contacts that are perceived as valuable. More importantly, dependency is frowned on because it might destroy the positive nature of the relationship, turning it into a duty rather than a voluntary relationship. The question of autonomy is particularly poignant in relation to adult children, and the informants recurrently stressed the importance of having a life of their own and of being able to determine themselves the nature of the relationship with their children. The difference is that between a voluntary and reciprocal meeting between the older person and their children on the one hand, and an adult child's obligation to visit and alleviate an older mother's or father's loneliness on the other. As LAT Laura describes: "I thought, even before I met my partner, that I want to have a social function with my kids. I didn't want to be the old person they have to take out on a picnic. I wanted them to invite granny because it's nice and fun."

A central concern articulated by the informants was to avoid being a burden to their adult children, who were in mid-life with children of their own and careers that kept them busy. Having a partner meant that they freed their children from the primary responsibility for everyday supervision. We illustrate this central point with two quotes from Married Mark and LAT Lenny. Mark compares the relationship his children have to him with the relationship he had to his widowed father:

> 'I think they [the children] are really happy I met Mary. Then they don't have to worry about me because I can take care of myself. So I think I freed them from a responsibility(...) I remember when my father became a widower. I had to take on a big responsibility: I went to him and took care of his finances; I took care of practical matters such as installing a fridge and trimming his hedge every year. My kids don't have to worry about that.'

Lenny describes how he unburdens his children:

> 'If an older person meets a new partner and they have a good life together it unburdens the children(...) I mean, they know that he or she is fine and won't, as you can read about in the papers, "lay there for three weeks before he was found". They know that if I'm sick, Lydia is here for me. And if she's sick I'm here for her. If I was alone, somebody else in the chain would have to take more responsibility. So I unburden her children and she unburdens mine.'

Two informants, among them Cohabiting Corinne, even stated that 'not being a burden' to one's children, or society in general, ought to be a moral imperative:

> 'Clint's children for example – think of all the work I've unburdened them from. Every time that he [is ill] – we went to the hospital the other day – they would have had to go with him instead. We ought to have a new collective moral code: Encourage your mother or father to find a new partner as soon as the former partner dies.'

A new partner becomes a resource for achieving the desired autonomy in relation to friends and family. It might seem like a contradiction that people are seeking independence in relation to people who they are interdependent with, but it seems to be very much in line with the ideals of Western individualism, and perhaps especially with its Nordic welfare state form.

Prior research has shown that older women, in particular, are keen to keep their personal autonomy, by having a separate home from their partner (Davidson, 2002; Ghazanfareeon Karlsson & Borell, 2002, 2005). In our study those in a relationship did not much stress the importance of being autonomous in relation to their partner; instead the value of independence was emphasised in relation to others, especially children. The partner was seen as a *key* to, rather than an *obstacle* to, an autonomous life. It would seem that as an overarching value independence was preferred, but our informants found it more agreeable to be dependent on the support of their partner than on that of their children, friends or the state.

Restructuring the chain of interdependent lives

Interdependent lives tend to form a 'chain', where somebody is always the first link, or the primary relationship. When that person is lost, somebody else in the social support network normally steps in to 'fill the gap' as the older person's primary relationship – normally the next 'link' in the chain. A new partner tends to enter as the first link of this chain. This was clearly expressed by Cohabiting Corinne who talked about her need for partnership and fear of being left alone, although she had children. If her partner passed away, she said, she would have to immediately find a new man, and added: "I wouldn't be able to live a single day without knowing who is the first in my life." (It should be noted that the expressed wish to *quickly replace* one's intimate partner is not common for either the women or the men in the interview data.) When our informants recount the story of their post-marital life, they regularly bring up the importance of friends and family for filling the gap left by their partner. In the absence of the former partner, who held a primary position as 'the first' in the hierarchy of relationships, others in the social support network, such as friends, children or other relatives, are drawn in to provide emotional and practical support.

In the chain of relationships, family, especially children and grandchildren, tend to be given priority as the most important relationship, when the former partner is gone. For most of the widowed informants, such as Married Mark, at least in the beginning it seemed natural to invest their time and energy in their relationships with children and grandchildren: "If I hadn't met Mary ... I would probably have found a place between my children and become a sort of service person for them – babysitting, painting windows and stuff."

In the case of transitions *into* new intimate relationships a reverse process seems to take place: when people meet a new partner, the focus tends to shift from the network of friends and family to that person, who now becomes the new natural focus of their time and energy. This reprioritisation is very concrete: some informants recount how they spend all of their time with their new partner. In some respects this seems to take the shape of a zero sum game, where there is only a fixed amount of time and energy to go around, so that when a new partner takes up an important position in a person's life, there is less time and energy for others (of course, some needs, such as sex, are not interchangeable). LAT Lisa describes how her relationship to her sister Doris was transformed after meeting her new partner Lars:

> 'When I became a widow, [I and my sister Doris] started thinking about moving in together to be able to support each other. Today I'm happy it didn't happen. Lars asked her "Have I stolen Lisa from you?" and she said "yes, but I'm happy for you." I sometimes feel that I give Lars much more time than Doris.'

The inclusion of a new partner in their lives demanded a measure of prioritisation. How that prioritisation should be made was a question that had to be taken into account when negotiating the form of the new relationship. One informant, for example, had opted for an LAT relationship because she had two grandchildren and it was important "that I have room for them as well in my life". In the interviews, explicit reference was often made to this zero–sum aspect of closer relationships. In order to make place for the new partner the older individual had to ration their time with friends and family, or time with the new partner had to be limited to allow space for other close relationships. In this chapter we conceptualise this as a restructuring of the *chain of interdependent lives* (see also Bildtgård & Öberg, 2017). This seems to be in line with de Jong Gierveld and Peeters' (2003) finding that a new partner in later life tends to decrease the contact frequency between generations. However, this does not necessarily mean that the quality of those relationships decreases. The changing pattern of intergenerational interaction is interpreted mostly in a positive fashion by our informants, as a ground for more autonomous and rewarding relationships, much in line with the Swedish theory of love.

A hierarchy of dependencies

To state the obvious – all relationships are not equally important in an individual's life. In the informants' stories a clear hierarchy of interdependent lives was hinted at: partners came first, followed by children and the state (professional caregivers) and finally friends and others. In an earlier article (Bildtgård & Öberg, 2017) we argued that this hierarchy could be understood both in terms of a naturalised normative order of responsibilities and in terms of everyday availability.

This argument is similar to *the hierarchical-compensatory model* presented by Cantor (1979). According to this model older people's support structures are normatively ordered in a hierarchical fashion, so that kin (especially partners and children) tend to be the preferred source for support, more or less irrespective of the kind of support. Only when no functional kin is available do people normally turn to others, such as friends, neighbours or formal organisations. Cantor proposes that a strong family norm might be the central explanation for the structural organisation of the older individual's support network, provided that the individual that constitutes the normatively preferred source of support lives close enough to provide the desired support.

Cantor's model has received much support in empirical studies, but it has also been criticised for not distinguishing between different kinds of support (Messeri, Silverstein & Litwak, 1993). Litwak (1985) has instead proposed *a structural-functionalist theory* of older peoples' support networks, which focuses on the functional specificity of different kinds of relationships. This 'task–specific' perspective argues that different groups such as partners, kin, friends, neighbours and formal organisations have different structural characteristics that match different forms of needs. These structural characteristics include proximity, length of commitment, lifestyle similarity, group size, motivation, level of technical knowledge and division of labour. According to Litwak, people tend to choose or prefer sources of support that best match their needs. For example, people tend to turn to partners for everyday needs that require proximity and long-term commitment, such as cooking, clothing and so on, but to formal organisations for medical needs that require a level of technical knowledge not always available among close acquaintances.

Litwak's model can be used for understanding the hierarchy that we presented above in functionalist terms. In our article about the relationship chain we used everyday availability (not necessarily geographical closeness) as an explanation for the preference of a partner as the primary provider of support. Availability is primarily represented by the partner and sometimes neighbours and friends, while children are mostly portrayed as being less available (occupied by other things) in everyday life, even if they are living in the same house or in the immediate area. This paradox of closeness and non-availability is well expressed by Single Sophie below:

> 'I'm getting more and more afraid that something should happen, and I want somebody [a partner] to be close at hand if it does. Even if they [daughter and her family] live in the same house, we don't see each other every day, so I could easily lie here for days without somebody knowing about it.'

An intimate partner is thus perceived as being physically and mentally available in everyday life. Using Litwak's model, everyday availability can be understood as a structural characteristic typical for certain kinds of groups, for example a partner sharing the older person's household, but also to some extent an LAT partner.

A more actor-oriented approach would suggest that support relationships are negotiated between individuals. This perspective is hinted at by Penning and Wu (2014) who propose that support networks are constructed actively by people during their lives in anticipation of old age. They find support for such a perspective in convoy theory (Kahn & Antonucci, 1980). An actor-oriented perspective would go well with late modern family theory's insistence that family and couple relationships are increasingly negotiated between relatively independent individuals, rather than determined by socially given, normative gender and family roles. This parallels the concept of 'families of choice', which has been used to describe family relations that are based on chosen closeness, which has its clearest example in non-heterosexual relationships (Weeks, 2007; see also Giddens, 1992). An actor-oriented perspective allows us to understand the older individual's initiation of new intimate relationships in later life as a way of proactively reconstructing the relationship chain to gain autonomy and manage their social support needs. In our interviews many informants had actively sought new partners to fill different support needs (remember, for example, Cohabiting Chris with his planned personal ad, looking for an experienced housewife, in Chapter eight).

The above presented models help in suggesting answers to the question: why are older people's networks hierarchically structured in the way they are? Why do older people tend to prioritise between their relationships the way they do? One answer is that it is because of an established normative order (Cantor). Another answer is that it is due to the nature of the need (Litwak). A third answer is that it is the result of a negotiation between individuals over time (cmpr. Penning & Wu, 2014).

The social support network

One way of approaching the question of how a new intimate partner restructures the older individual's social and filial network is to study how the inclusion of a partner affects the older individual's preferences for different kinds of social support. Whom do older Swedes in different family constellations prefer as their primary support providers? Table 9.1 shows to whom respondents would primarily turn for companionate, emotional and practical support.[5]

The results in Table 9.1 support a hierarchical model where the intimate partner is the primary source of support over the full range of analysed support forms. Panel A shows that for those who are *currently in a relationship* the intimate partner is the primary choice for companionate support (92%), emotional support (86%) and the two forms of practical support – household help (62%) and help with personal hygiene (60%). This is very much in line with the idea of a relationship hierarchy that we presented above, with intimate partners at the first choice for support provision, irrespective of form of support. It seems that the intimate partner has a somewhat universal character and is preferred for multiple support functions. As we indicated above, two such characteristics could be everyday availability and relatively long-term commitment.

Even though the primacy of the partner is universal across the different forms of support, panel A shows that it varies in dominance. The primacy of the partner is most pronounced in terms of companionate and emotional support, but somewhat less pronounced as a resource for practical support, especially concerning more complex needs such as help with personal hygiene. In these instances, as Litwak suggests, formal organisations become increasingly common choices.

Panel B shows that for *singles* there is clearer evidence of functional specialisation. In the absence of a partner, friends are the most likely preferred providers of companionate support (44%), with children as the second most common choice (22%). Other choices are more uncommon. Friends seem to have the particular characteristics sought in companions. Even though our survey does not contain any data to support this, it seems reasonable that friends are closer in lifestyle and historical experience than children, which might make them more suitable for company. For childless singles (panel C) the primacy of friends for companionate support is further accentuated (50%).

Panel B also shows that singles tend to prefer children (43%) for emotional support, while friends are the second most common choice (31%). For childless singles (panel C), friends are the most common choice for emotional support (41%) but the category 'other relatives' increases more in importance (34% compared to 15% among singles generally), which might point to the conclusion that singles compensate

Table 9.1. Preference for primary provider of four types of support among 60–90-year-old Swedes who are (a) in a union, (b) single or (c) single without children (%)

		Preferred provider of:			
		Travel company	Confidence sharing	Household help	Personal hygiene help
In a union					
A	Partner	92	86	62	60
	Child	2	6	14	9
	Friend	4	6	2	1
	Other relatives	1	1	2	2
	Home care service	--	--	13	20
	Other	0	0	3	5
	No one	1	1	4	3
Single					
B	Child	22	43	37	29
	Friend	44	31	9	4
	Other relatives	7	15	6	6
	Home care service	--	--	36	47
	Other	3	4	6	8
	No one	24	7	6	6
Childless single					
C	Friend	50	41	19	11
	Other relatives	13	34	21	14
	Home care service	--	--	45	65
	Other	7	8	4	5
	No one	30	17	11	5

for the absence of children with support from other relatives with whom they share a long-term commitment. This is known from prior research (see for example Dykstra, 2006; Keith, 2003).

Panel B also shows that when it comes to singles' preferences for practical support, friends are unlikely to be chosen as primary support providers (9% for household help, 4% for help with personal hygiene). For household help children (37%), but also the municipal home care service (36%), are much more likely to be chosen as primary sources of support. This is also true for help with personal hygiene.

This becomes even clearer when no children are available to provide practical support (panel C). Although a minority of childless singles would in this situation turn to other relatives or to friends, it is more likely that they will turn to the formal services (45% for household help, 65% for help with personal hygiene). For practical help, friends do not seem to have the qualities sought for providing support, such as continuity and long-term commitment. The risk of totally lacking practical support providers is also bigger for singles – especially childless singles – than for people in unions.

In short, those who lack a partner tend to prefer to cover their needs with help from different support providers, depending on support need, rather than just using one source. This is very much in line with Litwak's theory of functional specialisation.

In comparison to men, women are generally somewhat more prone to preferring others, beside their partner, as the primary source of support, irrespective of support type. This is much in line with previous research suggesting that men tend to be more dependent on their partners for support than vice versa. Also, old-old individuals (aged 75–90) are more prone than young-old (aged 60–74), to prefer children to other sources of support, presumably because friends and siblings are more likely to be deceased or in ill-health. However, none of these differences changes the dominant pattern – that older individuals in unions tend to prefer support from their partner to other sources.

An assumption, based on the figures in Table 9.1, could be that singles, if they should repartner, would have preferences similar to partnered individuals in panel A. This assumption cannot be validated by the data in the table, however the pattern is the same for recently established relationships (shorter than 15 years) as it is for all partnered individuals (panel A). In these recently established relationships (not shown in the table) the partner is the first choice for companionate support (87%), for emotional support (74%), for practical household support (57%), and for practical support with personal hygiene (51%). One interpretation of this finding is that the universal functionality of an intimate relationship is a feature of the 'partner' role and its characteristics rather than of the particularities of the individual relationship. For those actively looking for support in later life, finding a new partner would constitute a rational motive, as it provides a wider range of support functions combined in one individual compared to other relationships. In a partner one gets a friend, a confidant, a home help, a nurse and possibly a lover in one and the same person.

Conclusion

In this chapter we have asked how new intimate relationships in later life affect the social network. How are the social and filial networks of the older individual reorganised when they repartner and how does this affect the social support structures?

Our Swedish results pointed in a slightly different direction than previous studies: children appeared to be generally supportive of their parents' new intimate relationships, at least as long as there were no issues of loyalty with living partners and they did not plan to marry. Instead, new intimate partners tended to be integrated into the older person's existing social and filial networks, increasing social integration. The older individual's network tended to be structured in a hierarchical chain, and a new intimate relationship tended to restructure the chain so that time and energy was reprioritised and directed from other close relationships to the new partner. Finally, an intimate partner tended to have characteristics that made them preferable for many different kinds of support. This was true for both long-term and new relationships.

A central finding was that a new intimate partner was a resource for autonomy. The importance of autonomy in late-life intimate relationships has been emphasised before. Prior research has shown how older individuals prefer relationship arrangements that allow them to preserve their autonomy *in relation to their partner*. For example, Ghazanfareeon Karlsson and Borell (2002, 2005) have shown how older women in particular seek to combine intimacy and autonomy by preserving a home of their own.

The importance of preserving autonomy in the new relationship was emphasised by some of our informants as well (see for example LAT Lars and Lisa in Chapter seven). However, the results in our study contributed a different perspective on autonomy, where the partner was a resource, rather than an obstacle, for achieving autonomy – in particular *in relation to children*. A new partner made the individual less dependent on others for different forms of support – for travelling, going out to restaurants, confidences and practical help. Repartnering can in this context be seen as a rational choice. The multi-functional character of the partner makes them particularly useful for achieving autonomy. A partner allows the older person to determine the nature of the interaction with children and friends – allowing for an interaction based on choice rather than necessity.

The desire to remain autonomous in relation to children and friends can also be related to the wider discussion about the individualisation of the late modern family (Beck & Beck-Gernsheim, 2002; Giddens, 1992) in which relationships are determined less by external norms dictating intra-familial duties and more by chosen closeness. This is evident in new intimate unions. Many repartnered older LATs are positive about giving care to their partners based on 'love, not on a sense of duty' (Benson & Coleman, 2016a, p 446). But increasingly these norms also permeate long-term biological relationships, and at least older Swedes hesitate to take their children for granted as support providers or talk in terms of children's 'duties' – instead they see these relationships as connections that need to be cultivated. In this respect, the families of repartnered older people resemble 'families of choice', where older partners construct support networks out of the convoys of relationships they have accumulated over the life course, for example with children (including step-children from new and old relationships), siblings, friends and intimate partners.

The desire for autonomy is very much in line with the ideals of Western individualism, and perhaps especially the specific form of state-supported individualism which characterises the Nordic welfare states. The principles of state-supported individualism find a clear expression in Swedish law, where children have no formal juridical responsibility for their parents, and in Swedish elderly politics where a central goal is to enable people to grow old 'with preserved independence'. Earlier research has shown that older Swedes prefer being dependent on the state for welfare services rather than their kin (Daatland, 2007). The social context of Swedish state-supported individualism could explain why the informants in our study so strongly emphasise the value of not being a burden to their children, and stress that a new partner is a resource for autonomy and independence in relation to children and others. It could explain why children are generally positive about their parents finding new partners in later life, since it frees them from responsibility for their older parents. Individualism seems like a relevant explanation for the difference in our results and those in research from more traditionally family-oriented parts of the world, for example Mehta (2002) in Singapore, or van den Hoonaard (2004) in a conservative part of Canada, where adult children were shown to be more negative about their parents repartnering.

TEN

Sex in an ideology of love

While the former chapters have investigated different aspects of repartnering in later life, this chapter focuses on the importance of sex in those relationships. Even if sex is an integral part of most couple relationships and could have been studied under each of the previous chapters, we have chosen to dedicate a separate chapter to the issue in order to break the silence surrounding sex in later life. Until recently the sex life of older people was more or less invisible in family and gerontological research. When the world's first national study of sexual habits was carried out in Sweden in 1967 (Zetterberg, 1969), people 60 years or older were not included. Zetterberg concluded that to find the point at which sexual activity ceases one would have to include older age groups. Still, even at the beginning of the 21st century, the British national survey on sexual attitudes did not include people 45 years or older (Gott & Hinchliff, 2003a).

For a long time the dominant cultural storyline of older people in popular culture has been that of asexuality (Gott, 2005; Jones, 2002). The advent of Viagra and other pharmaceutical aids and the creation of the third age with new expectations for later life have spawned new cultural representations of a sexually active later life (see for example Bildtgård, 2000; Gott, 2005; Vares, 2009). It has been argued that sexual activity has become an integrated part of successful ageing (Katz & Marshall, 2003; B. L. Marshall & Katz, 2002). However, much of this 'post-Viagra' interest in older people's sexuality is inspired by and centred on the continuation of mid-life sexual practices, while other aspects tend to remain invisible (see for example Potts, Grace, Vares & Gavey, 2006). In her 2005 review, Gott stated that most studies on older people's sexuality ask 'Which people "do it" and how often?', but that the voices of older people themselves tend to be forgotten. The aim of this chapter is to contribute to breaking this silence.

This chapter is dedicated to the topic of late-life sexual intimacy. The specific focus of the chapter is the role and meaning of sex in intimate relationships in later life. In the chapter we first investigate how sexual norms have changed over the life course of contemporary cohorts of older people and how they have experienced this change. We then consider sexual intimacy as part of new intimate relationships established late in life and we question the persistent assumption that older people who date are primarily looking for companionate relationships. We show that older people's ideas about sex are deeply embedded in an *ideology of love*, where sex tends to be viewed as a natural part of a loving relationship, while sex outside of a loving relationship – also in a loveless marriage – is frowned on. Below we investigate these issues, basing ourselves mainly on the experiences of our older interviewees.

From an ideology of marriage to an ideology of love

The norms of sexual activity and the perceptions of what is appropriate sexual behaviour have shifted over the life course of current generations of older people – basically from rather restrictive sexual norms in their youth, when sex was only allowed within marriage, to increasingly liberal sexual norms in early adulthood or mid-life. In later life they tend to defend the idea that sex is a natural part of a loving relationship, but that it does not necessitate marriage. Below we investigate this change.

A marital ideology of sex

When current generations of older people were young the norm was to delay sexual intercourse until they were married (Levin, 2004). Within the marital ideal sex belonged to marriage and the reproduction of family bonds. This was also the absolutely dominant experience among our interviewees, who recalled the taboo surrounding sex and the admonitions of their parents. LAT Lee, 83, recalls:

> 'A sexual relationship was for after the wedding. My father held a long sermon about "not getting yourself or someone else into trouble". There were no contraceptive pills or such things so it would have had to be a coitus interruptus and that was very risky so you didn't dare to. You could hug and kiss and caress but nothing more.'

Parents were important authorities who upheld the marital ethic – warning their children about the consequences of extra-marital sex. Morals around sex were tightly connected to its reproductive determination and childbirth belonged to marriage. Since contraceptives were still rather unavailable or even illegal in Sweden before 1949 (Beckman, Waern, Gustafson & Skoog, 2008), the risk of an unwanted pregnancy was great, and the social sanctions for pregnancies out of wedlock were harsh, as 78-year-old LAT Libby remembers:

'I had many boyfriends. We could kiss but nothing more. Sure, there was a sexual attraction, but it didn't lead to anything. I could never have initiated a sexual relationship without being married. We had a neighbour whose daughter got pregnant and my mother thought it was horrible – she was a bad girl.'

Sex education in Swedish elementary schools became compulsory in 1955 (Beckman et al, 2008). Before that time, there were few sources that provided information about sex (Sandberg, 2011). Many of the informants recall how the taboo surrounding sex was paired with an almost complete silence regarding everything sexual. Some respondents recalled hiding books on the subject, while others were secretly informed by their peers. Married Mary, 68, describes the depth of her sexual ignorance in early adulthood:

'Schools had no sexual education. And then you were an adult woman, being courted by men and not knowing how to deal with that. My parents told me that if I got myself pregnant they would throw me out. And no one told me how you become pregnant. There was this little cartoon, I remember, that showed a man and a woman kissing, and then at the next page she was pregnant. So I believed kissing got you pregnant. Then I must have been 17 or 18 or something like that.'

Judging by the recurrent references to the strict sexual morals of their youth, the restrictions surrounding sex had left a strong impression on the informants but, as we will show below, they did not necessarily have the intended effect.

The sex debut

Even if the norm to not have sex before marriage was almost uniformly acknowledged by our Swedish interviewees, it had rarely been respected in practice. Most of our informants had had intercourse before marriage, and also in our survey the vast majority (93%) of the 60–90-year-old Swedes had had sexual intercourse before their first marriage (the median age of the sexual debut was 18). This was true for both men and women and for young-old and old-old alike – thus it was neither a gender nor a cohort phenomenon (in fact, as Trost, 1978, has shown, it was not uncommon to have children out of wedlock in Sweden even in the 19th century).

The incongruence between norms and practices is striking. To some extent it is probably due to a generous interpretation of 'sex within marriage', where it was not uncommon to have sex after having been engaged to marry or in a longer established relationship. Our survey showed that one third (35%) eventually married their first sexual partner, and this was almost twice as common among women as it was among men. Many of our interviewees likewise described how they had had their sexual debut in an established relationship where marriage was at least a possibility. For example, Cohabiting Cecilia had her sexual debut the same day that her first husband proposed to her. Cohabiting Corinne, 78, also had her sexual debut before being married, in a dating relationship at the age of 17, but legitimises it with the length of the monogamous relationship: "When I was young you couldn't imagine having intercourse before marriage. When it happened between me and Andrew it was the first time for us both. But then we had dated for almost a year. That was our moral."

Corinne never married Andrew. For a majority of older Swedes (two in three) the sexual debut was, as in the case of Corinne above, not associated with marriage at all. Clearly, although the restrictive norms of the surrounding society were definitely acknowledged by the interviewees, they were not very effective. The discrepancy between social norms and practices was even more pronounced in contexts where social control was less strict. Cohabiting Chris, 87, who grew up in a rural context where parental control was more relaxed, acknowledges that even if young women were supposed to not have sex before marriage ("they could be labelled mattresses"), norms for men were less restrictive:

> 'I never asked for my parent's permission (laughter). I was a pig, really, because I had lots of girls. It was sheer luck that there was only one [extra-marital] child as a result. I was a charmer. I had good looks, and then it's easy to get girls. And I took advantage of that, being the horny stud that I was. One [friend] was even worse; he had golden, curly, hair and was very manly. My God, the girls spread like rag rugs before him.'

Even if it was exceptional, there were among the interviewees examples of men and women who had been socialised in contexts with very liberal sexual attitudes even before the sexual revolution and where parents had been supportive of their children's sexual adventures. Cohabiting Carl, 70, was one example: "I had a girlfriend between the age of 15 and 18 and we discovered sex together. My parents were very liberal. When me and my girlfriend were together and my parents were out I lit a small red light in the window and they would know not to disturb us when they got back. That was in the middle of the 50s."

Carl's story shows that even though the norm of sexual restraint before marriage was widely recognised, it was not necessarily agreed on by everyone. Moreover, as in the case of Chris, our survey showed that a majority of older Swedes had not observed the restriction in practice.

Gendered stories of early sexual experiences

A common narrative among the interviewees was that the first marriage was a poor sexual relationship, partly due to the partners being inexperienced and partly due to lacking information about sex in the form of sexual education or even literature about sex. Many, especially women, recall how this silence meant that they were very unprepared for sex in young adulthood. 70-year-old Single Sophie recalls:

'You had no information about how we women work. You didn't know that women were also allowed to enjoy sex, so I never did in my first marriage. And I never felt the need [for sex], so of course my husband met somebody else. And I can sympathise with that, because I was totally uninterested.'

Single Sadie, 73, tells a similar story about early sexual ignorance, and compares her first marriage, where she was not seen or confirmed sexually, with her later marriage:

'You didn't know how it was supposed to feel. At the age of 20, I had never had sex. You just didn't sleep with anyone until you had found your future mate. My husband was 27 and in all honesty I don't think he had ever been with anyone before me either. So sex was a bit clumsy. And I got pregnant and we got married and the routine of everyday life took over. Our sex life was sporadic and in the last five years [before divorce] it was non-existent. Then there was my second husband who was warm and loving and confident in his caresses. Whatever we had [in the first marriage], died, because I was never touched in the right way.'

Some of the women described sex in their first marriages in terms of a duty and that they had been expected to 'volunteer' in bed. Stories of similar arrangements have been found in British studies, where sex was sometimes described in terms of a marital duty for women, akin to other household chores (Gott, 2005; Gott & Hinchliff, 2003a). Married Martha, 78, describes her negative sexual experiences with her first husband who was notoriously unfaithful to her and how she was supposed to volunteer sexually in a loveless marriage:

'My first husband wouldn't let me touch him. He thought hands were unpleasant. When he wanted to have sex there was no foreplay, no caressing – just intercourse. And then he returned to his separate bed. But I made no demands. Even when I understood that he had other women it didn't change anything in our sex life.'

While many of the women describe how the expectations of marriage culture had locked them in early marriages that had been sexually poor and where their sexual interest had eventually died out, men often contributed a complementary story by relating how their previous wives had lost interest in sex, even though they themselves had not. We will return to this topic below.

The development of more liberal sexual values

The introduction of sexual education in schools and the legalisation and increasing availability of contraceptives together with growing gender equality contributed to the sexual revolution that followed in the late 1960s and early 1970s in many Western countries. Traditional restrictive norms were challenged and replaced by more permissive sexual norms. Where sex had previously been strictly connected to reproduction it increasingly became centred on enjoyment and self-realisation. Our interviewees often return to this period as a reference point in their personal relationship biographies. A few had participated fully in the sexual revolution themselves, as in the case of 68-year-old Married Mary below:

'You weren't afraid of anything. You didn't talk about sexual diseases. I've never been on the contraceptive pill for example. Among us girls we talked about safe periods but I never knew what a safe period was – it was just a phrase. It wasn't dangerous. It was almost natural if you dated that you made love. There were no taboos. That was in the early 70s. We have experienced a lot, my generation, from the taboo surrounding sex as a school-age child to all this freedom [as a young adult].'

Cohabiting Carl, 70, describes how he and his first wife enjoyed the new sexual freedom even as a married couple. "We didn't vow to be faithful. That was in the 60s – for love and friendship. We could have other sexual relationships and then come home and discuss them together."

However, most of the interviewees did not directly partake in the sexual revolution, but recall having experienced it from the sidelines. Single Sally, 73, remembers:

'I got married in 1958. You were supposed to get married. I got engaged at 16 and married at 21 and had my first child at 23 and my second two years later – a boy and a girl. It was supposed to be like that – everybody did the same. Then along came free sexuality and the sexual revolution but then I was at home changing diapers. I could merely listen to the Beatles while I was doing the ironing.'

Even if most of the interviewees had not actively taken part in the sexual revolution their relationship lives had often been shaped by the new values of sexual self-fulfilment in the sense that they had often had sex with many partners (see Chapter five). When the interviewees evaluate the sexual revolution, they tend to be rather ambivalent. Some of the interviewed women described the marital ideology as a trap, where women were supposed to be sexually available, regardless of their own pleasure. Sex had sometimes been perceived as a duty – as something that was being done to them rather than something they were doing of their own free will (see also Gott, 2005; Gott & Hinchliff, 2003b). With the sexual revolution women had been freed to enjoy sex and be active sexual subjects. Single Sarah, 67, puts it succinctly: "Today women are allowed to take the initiative sexually. You weren't before. You were supposed to wait for your turn. Today it is more the opposite – I have the candy bag and can choose."

On the other hand, many, like 79-year-old LAT Lucy below, believed that the sexual liberation, although it was basically a positive development, went too far, in the sense that it uncoupled sex not only from marriage and reproduction, but also from love.

> 'When I was young – oh, that was a dark period. Earlier generations of women they have had a really tough time. Many women in my generation have never reached an orgasm, and that's a tragedy. And after that came the 1960s and 1970s. They claim it was free sexuality but I don't think it was very free, not for women at least. For women it was difficult.'

LAT Lucy and many of the other interviewees express a sentiment akin to that of 'out of the frying pan, into the fire'. For them marriage was a trap for earlier generations of women, where they had to be sexually available, even if the relationship was loveless and the sex was bad. With the sexual liberation, the marriage trap was dissolved but instead women were often expected to be generally available for the male sexual desire.

Adolescents as sexual 'others'

In the interviews the sexuality of contemporary adolescents was often used as a binary contrast to the restrictive ideals of their own youth. Adolescent sexual behaviour was repeatedly described in almost pornographic terms with words such as: raw-sex, disgusting, machinery-like, oversexualised, consumer sex and so on. In many cases the ideas expressed about adolescent sexuality were clearly exaggerated and based on stereotypes, but the concerns spoke eloquently about the interviewees' own sexual ideals: even though sex does not have to be confined to marriage, love and sex go together and should not be separated. Sex only for the sake of pleasure was regularly frowned on. For example, according to LAT Lisa, 68, the reversal of sexual norms is a betrayal of adolescent people:

> 'Society has become oversexualised and I think it is a betrayal of young people. I read about how young people have many sexual partners simultaneously. There is a constant exploitation that I think is negative and damaging. This is supposed to be the most precious part of our lives – that which we should nurture the most – and I think that instead we are making it ugly by exploiting it.'

In particular, the informants were critical of the separation of sex and emotion. Married Martha, 78, believes that the increased focus on sex in the media and in education has stripped it of its emotional context.

> 'I'm a little old fashioned. To me love is not just about sex, it is much, much more. I want young people to understand that there has to be feelings, tenderness, and not just sex. Of course there can be sex as well, but a romantic relationship has to be based on emotions.'

It was a recurrent concern that young people today have been misled and that they miss out on the true purpose of sex as part of a loving relationship. LAT Lee, 83, expresses these concerns:

> 'Today there is no party that doesn't end in bed and I'm troubled by that – not because I moralise but because I pity them. They lose out on the joy of really getting to know another person. Love is ruined when you take out the best part [the sex] in advance – or, rather, it never becomes the best part, it just becomes routine. Freedom and acceptance has expanded. Now there is abortion, the contraceptive pill and the morning-after pill. And then you never get to long for each other like we did – all restraints are lost.'

The concerns expressed could be seen as somewhat paradoxical when viewed in relation to their own sexual lives and their experiences of the sexual liberalisation, but there is a clear underlying logic here. The informants are not critical of the uncoupling of sex and marriage. Neither are they critical of the reversal of the marriage cultural norm that you should stay with the same partner forever. In fact, what is expressed is a clear ideology of love – you can have sex with whoever you want but it should be part of a monogamous relationship based on love. Even if this concern is expressed mainly in relation to young people – and possibly an exaggerated understanding of young people's sexual lives – it is clearly a reflection of their own relationship ideals. We will return to this issue below as we start looking at the role of sex in new intimate relationships established late in life.

The ideal of the consummate relationship

Below we show that sex tends to be viewed as an important part of relationships established late in life, but also that sex tends to be framed in terms of an ideology of love, while sex only for the pleasure of it is generally frowned on. The expressed ideal is a consummate relationship where love, sex and commitment complement and reinforce one another.

The myth of companionship

According to Gott (2005) there are two general myths or stereotypes of older people's sexuality: the myth of the asexual older person and the myth of the always sexy oldie. One aspect of the widespread myth about asexual older people, reinforced by research on repartnering in later life, is that if older single people are at all interested in repartnering it is primarily a 'companionate' relationship they are looking for (K. Bulcroft & O'Connor, 1986; R. A. Bulcroft & Bulcroft, 1991; Moore & Stratton, 2004; Stevens, 2004). The underlying assumption seems to be that sex is not essential for people who are repartnering in later life. However, our interviews suggest that this assumption needs to be nuanced: although the informants were indeed looking for a companion, sexual attraction was generally a precondition for repartnering.

One way of discussing the role of sex in new intimate relationships in later life is to use Sternberg's (1986) triangular theory of love. According to Sternberg a *consummate* relationship unites intimacy, commitment and passion/sex, while a *companionate* relationship is one which unites intimacy and commitment, but which is not passionate and sexual. According to the theory many consummate relationships lose their passionate characteristic over time and turn into companionate relationships. It might be tempting to interpret this change as driven by chronological age, but as we will show below it can just as well be related to the time one has spent together in a relationship. In our interviews it was clear that sexual attraction had been central to the formation of the new late-life unions. Although many had primarily sought a companion for travelling or going out with, they did not consider such an arrangement a couple relationship until it had become sexual, and sex was not always expected or planned. It was clear that a real couple relationship was thought to be – at least initially – a consummate relationship.

For the absolute majority of the informants sex was seen as a natural part of an intimate relationship. The informants described how a companionate relationship was not enough – a relationship had to be physical as well. Sexual attraction was viewed as important for initiating a romantic relationship. LAT Lucy, 79, describes how she met Lee through a personal ad on the Internet. Their long e-mail correspondence confirmed that she had found a soulmate. However, she wanted a sexual relationship and not just a companion:

> 'There has to be this attraction. We mailed each other several times a day. I tried to describe myself and I remember that I wrote – "both physical and emotional closeness if possible". That was what I was looking for. I wasn't just looking for a friend to go to the theatre with. But of course I could not know if there would be an attraction – you can't judge that from a mail conversation.'

But to her joy, on their first face-to-face date, she found Lee sexually attractive, and the relationship could develop. Although the ideal relationship was almost universally described as a close loving relationship, one aspect of this closeness was sexual intimacy. Single Steve, 91, describes a companionship relationship as only a "half-way relationship". He would like to have a consummate relationship, but instead has two relationships: on the one hand a purely sexual relationship with Maria who, as he put it, had sanctified her former husband and was not interested in having a new committed relationship; on the other hand a companionate relationship with Rosy who was not at all interested in a sexual relationship. Steve explains his ambivalence to this triangle-relationship:

> 'Maria explained that she didn't want another man. And then, to my surprise, she undressed and we ended up in bed and had sex. Very good sex I must say – better than with any of my wives. And sometimes I feel that's all we have. It is not ideal. I wish I could have a more exclusive relationship with Rosy instead. But she's afraid of having sex. I would prefer a consummate relationship with one person, not many. And it should be love that includes sex, because they go together. And you are interested in sex even at my age – most people are, even if they don't admit it. I can't picture any lasting love without sex, because sex is the closest you can get to another person. And I don't want a half-way relationship.'

Not all relationships started as sexual relationships. In some cases relationships developed out of long-term intimate friendships, in others from the desire for a companion. However it was only when

145

the relationship became sexual that the interviewees regarded it as a couple relationship. Married Mike, 84, who believed that he was impotent, did not from the outset consider any other possibility than a purely companionate relationship:

'You should not think that I was looking for sex. I wasn't, because I was convinced it was over [imagined impotency]. I wanted company, someone to go dancing with. And I thought I'd tell her about the situation so that she wouldn't be disappointed. So you should not think that sex was my goal with the relationship – it was company, explicitly.'

However, after only a couple of weeks Mike discovered that he could in fact perform sexually with Martha, and the relationship turned into a sexual relationship. It was only after this point that they started to think about themselves and present themselves as a couple.

To conclude, companionship is an important part of a new late-in-life relationship. But the dominant message from our interviews is that single and repartnered older people are not interested in a companionate relationship that doesn't include sex. In Sternberg's (1986) terms, they wanted a consummate relationship. This is also very much in line with our representative survey data that showed that among all 60–90-year-old Swedes 72% thought that an active sex life was important for a good relationship and 60% saw sexual attraction as a precondition for a new intimate relationship (similar results have been reported from Britain, by Tetley, Lee, Nazroo & Hinchliff, 2016). Young-old (60–74 years) men were most likely to find sex important while old-old (75–90 years) women were the least likely. In the qualitative study, our interviewees belong to a select group of older people who have repartnered or who want to repartner and who could be assumed to think sex is more important than older people in general. In conclusion, sex was seen as important, but as we shall see below the older Swedes were not interested in a purely sexual relationship.

An ideology of love

It is often argued that increased control over reproduction laid the foundation for the sexual revolution. However, older people have always had this control. Thus theoretically it could be assumed that the later phase of life, where at least women are no longer reproductive, would provide ideal conditions for casual sex and polyamorous arrangements. In reality this ideal was uncommon. Single Sarah, 67, belongs to those who prefer purely sexual encounters. After discovering Internet dating she was enjoying finding casual partners who could satisfy her sexual needs:

> 'I don't mind that it's only for sex as long as it gives me pleasure. Even if perhaps we don't go to bed on the first date, that is the explicit purpose. No one will cry, no one will say: "you only want me for the sex" (laughs). That guy [points to a photo on the dating site] I've known for a while. He calls me from time to time to see if I'm home, and then we both know what he wants. It is a little like taking some medicine: "I have a cold, please come over."'

Also for LAT Lars, 68, the ideal after widowhood was to have several parallel casual sexual arrangements.

> 'When you reach this age, there is no longer any risk of pregnancy and then you can become more liberated. I would prefer an open relationship. I mean, if you play some golf and have dinner together in the evening, it could easily lead to sex. But no woman accepts an open relationship. I've asked Lisa and she doesn't either.'

Lars thought that for a single widower later life was ideally suited for a polyamorous lifestyle since collaborating on having and raising children was no longer an issue. Despite the logic of his argument, Lars and Sarah are exceptional cases in our data. All the other interviewees were proponents of a monogamous ideology of love: sex was seen as the natural property of an exclusive relationship between two people who were in love. Also, in actual relationships, our survey results showed that it was extremely uncommon among the 60–90-year-old Swedes to have more than one sex partner simultaneously. Gott and Hinchliff (2003a) found similar negative attitudes to casual sexual encounters in their study of older British people.

Although both men and women expressed similar sexual ideals, they did not necessarily perceive the other gender's ideals as similar. In the interviews, men were often presented as sexual 'others' by the female informants who claimed that while for them love was a precondition for sex, men could more easily separate love and sex. For example, 70-year-old Single Sophie describes her experiences of Internet dating:

'The men, they are very quick. I say in my online self-presentation that I'm primarily looking for a companion to travel, go to concerts, have conversations and go out to restaurants with – *then* we can see where it leads. I'm still a romantic. But the men they want a relationship where sex comes in at a very early stage and to me that's not OK.'

Single Sadie, 73, describes a similar gender gap in attitudes to sex and stresses that for her sex and love are inseparable. She can't imagine having sex only for the pleasure of it:

'There are many people my age, especially men, who separate sex and love, but to me, and women generally I think, they go together. You don't go to bed with just anyone because it is nice to have sex, because it is related to the soul. I must feel a deep love for a person, and then sex follows naturally.'

Hinchliff and Gott (2008) have reported similar perceptions among British women, who described their own relation to sex as more complex than that of men. However, our interviewed men do not make an equivalently strong distinction between their own sexuality and that of women. Instead, they claim to subscribe to the same ideology of love as the women. They prefer a consummate relationship that includes both sex and intimacy, as described by Single Steve, 91:

'To me sex is very important, but it is not the only thing that matters. I don't want to only have sex with a person and then nothing else. It wouldn't suit me at all. I want a relationship that includes everything, not just a piece here and a piece there. Having sex with just anyone doesn't attract me at all, it never has.'

The ideal among the older men was a deep intimate relationship which included sex. LAT Luke emphasises that intimate friendship is pivotal: "When everything works the way it is supposed to, a partner is one's best friend. You have to have an emotional bond. I think Linda agrees with me that without that bond a sexual relationship is meaningless."

The observation that most older people tend to promote an ideology of love with regard to sex is also supported by Waite, Laumann, Das and Schumm (2009) in their study of older Americans, aged 57–85. In their study it was more common for women than for men to agree with the statement that they would not have sex with someone unless they were in love with them, but the gender gap decreased by age: the proportion of women who agreed that they would not have sex unless they were in love was similar in all ages (around 85%), but increased with age for men (from 57% for men aged 57–64 to 76% for men aged 75–85). The majority of both older women and men in the US would not accept a sexual relationship if it was not based on love. Similarly, in our Swedish survey, a majority (55%) of the 60–90-year-old respondents thought that having sex without love was not acceptable – this sentiment was more common among women than men. It is likely that this sentiment would have been even more conservative if the question had not concerned a general attitude, but rather their personal choices.

Sex in new late-life relationships

Below we will consider sexual experiences in new intimate relationships established late in life. We show that the sex life tends to be rekindled in new late-in-life relationships, but also that sexual repertoires tend to change as a consequence of changes in male physical performance.

Experiences of sexual re-initiation

In the story about their first sexual experiences in young adulthood, the norm was to delay intercourse until marriage in order to protect women and female reproduction from the sexual desire of men, which was perceived to be stronger than that of women. In contrast, in the interviewees' descriptions of late-in-life sexual 're-initiation', women tend to be portrayed as active agents and sex often tends to come early in the development of the relationship.

Cohabiting Cecilia, 78, describes her growing interest for finding a new partner after four years of widowhood. Cecilia's first encounter with her current cohabiting partner Chris was when she offered him a ride home in the rain from the service centre where they had been for lunch. During the ride she was invited home to Chris and soon thereafter she invited him to her house and the visits became more and more sexually intimate:

> 'The third or fourth time we met he kissed me, and I thought it was such a shy kiss. But something in me clicked. I invited him over again and we were alone out here and watched the sunset and started to kiss and cuddle. And I

wanted to do so lying down so I suggested that we should go to my bed, because we're too old to balance on the sofa. And we both wore jeans so I suggested that we should remove them. And Chris was so surprised. We didn't have sex that first time. But when I followed him out he kissed me and I removed my sweater so that he could touch my breasts. That wasn't like me at all. Then it had really clicked in me.'

Cecilia and many of the older women presented themselves as more sexually active than previously in life and as taking initiatives they had never taken before. Married Martha, 78, who after her latest divorce had decided never to have a man again, was astonished by her own initiatives to sexual intimacy with Mike. She recalls their first night together in her house:

'I can't understand that I wanted to share my bed with him that first time. He was downstairs in my sofa bed and I was upstairs in bed. And he hears me calling 'Aren't you coming up soon?' And he comes up to my bed and I make room for him so that he can lie beside me. I always sleep naked, but he had his underwear on so I said "why don't you remove them when you are going to sleep?" But we only held each other that first night.'

Some weeks later they had intercourse for the first time. Mike had been convinced that he was impotent and thought that this was a natural part of ageing. He thought he was incapable of having sexual intercourse and that this also made him undesirable as a partner. He describes his reawakened sex life with Martha: "With the help of an erection pump I came so far that I could perform intercourse. But it took a long time. If you haven't used your limb for many years it is not in a very good shape, you know."

The experience of a rekindled sexuality was shared by some of the male interviewees, who had been convinced they were impotent and that this was a natural part of the ageing process, and who consequently did not actively pursue sexual encounters. When they met their new partner in later life they instead discovered that their erectile dysfunction was due to a long period of celibacy in their prior relationship and that with some help they could perform sexually. Some female respondents, such as Cohabiting Cecilia, relate how they have helped their new partner regain their erectile function:

'I needed to help Chris [sexually] in the beginning, in many ways, because his wife had quit sex entirely in the last 20 years. And then he had been abandoned but was still faithful to her. So he thought he was unable to have sex. And then a mature woman can help by being calm and not make any fuss about it. But there was nothing wrong with him, he had just been starving sexually for such a long time.'

Many informants recalled having been thrilled about the prospect of initiating a new sexual relationship, but some informants also talked about their worries of how their ageing body would be accepted by a new partner and how they would be able to function sexually. LAT Laura, 63, recalls her fears of meeting a new partner and apprehensions about how her ageing body would be perceived by that partner:

'The body is not that of a 20-, 30-, 40-, or even a 50-year-old any longer. And you wonder what they [potential partners] will think – and that really tears your self-confidence down. It makes you shy, afraid and apprehensive. It is definitely harder to meet a new partner in later life, sexually. But that fear disappears when you've bared yourself. What you have is good enough, so you can just enjoy it. I've never been this appreciated and I've never had such a fun sex life before.'

Many worries were related to long periods of sexual inactivity. Cohabiting Caroline, 72, recalls how, after having been invited to Carl the first time, she was worried about how her body would react to having sex after a long period of celibacy.

'I hadn't had a man for 20 years, so I thought to myself "Will my hips work? Am I able to still have intercourse? How will he view me?" I told him "You have to remember that I'm a virgin", because I hadn't been with a man for so many years. I was really worried that I wouldn't be able to go through with it.'

However, her worries proved to be unfounded, and at the time of the interview they had an intense sex life. Although some of the men had thought that they could not perform sexually, they seldom expressed any similar worries.

Sexual rekindling

In their biographical stories, some female informants described their former sex lives as unfulfilling due to being uninformed and inexperienced and locked in marital relationships with equally uninformed and inexperienced husbands. A complementary story among the older men was that their former partner had not taken any sexual initiatives and gradually lost interest in sex, leaving the sex life barren, much against the male informants' own wishes. In these stories both men and women appear as displeased with their former sexual lives. In contrast, they view their new relationships as more sexually satisfying. Some male informants explicitly appreciated their new female partner for being more sexually active and taking more initiatives than their former partners. Cohabiting Chris, 87, compares his current relationship with the passion he experienced in the beginning of his first lifelong marriage in his 20s, a passion that faded in mid-life:

> 'My first wife was a wonderful mistress. When she entered the menopause she got tired of sex, so it gradually became a white marriage. And I guess I assumed that with age passion turns into love and love turns into symbiosis, until in the end you become more like siblings. But then I met Cecilia and she is as horny as I am and we have a wonderful sex life. She most often takes the initiative to sex. I value that, so that you don't feel like you are intruding but that you are welcomed. If one person is less interested, then it is hell.'

Cohabiting Carl, 70, also compares his current sex life with Caroline to his earlier marital experiences of being sexually rejected:

> 'It is a damn pain when one feels a strong sexual urge and is rejected by one's partner. I've experienced that in my earlier marriages. Caroline and I have a very rich sex life. It is fantastic. She is insatiable, and that surprises her as well, because she was a widow for 20 years before we met and had no man for all those years. And then we meet and she turns into this boiling cauldron.'

The complementary story among the women is that of having discovered themselves as sexual beings in their new relationships. Cohabiting Caroline, 72, describes how in her new relationship she feels more safe and free as a sexual being than ever before:

'We have a great sex life. I never thought I'd get to experience that. He is great and I know he thinks I am as well. I feel safer and freer than ever. I hardly recognise myself. And I had a good sex life with my previous two husbands, but I've never been this happy. Because it is only him and me – nothing disturbs. We can be erotic whenever we want to.'

In this quote Caroline refers to how the freedom of the third age offers potential for a more active and satisfying sexual life – a theme that we will return to in length in the next chapter.

The current sex life

What does the sex life of older people in new intimate relationships look like? LAT Lars speculates that sexual interest is naturally dulled in a long-term relationship but that it can be rekindled in new relationships as part of a natural curiosity in a new partner.

'The sexual part grows when you meet a new partner. In my former marriage it became routine. And my wife, she absolutely wasn't active. She didn't want to have sex and was a bit restrained. Lisa, has a strong interest in sex herself, and so did the other women [former dates].'

Lars' speculation is supported by many of the other interviewees, including Married Martha, 78, who describe the sex life they had as a new couple as active, both in comparison to the sex life they had in their prior relationships and to their current sex life in a union that had lasted for almost 14 years.

'After 13 years of cohabitation we are starting to calm down sexually. Mike said the other day: "do you remember when we were together several times a day" – he must have been counting the nights as well. We aren't together as often as before, but at least once a week. Sometimes more often. Now we've been together three nights in a row.'

This pattern is also supported by our survey data, which shows that older people in relatively new *relationships* are more sexually active than those living in longer relationships. And this is true irrespective of age (that is, decreased sexual activity does not seem to primarily be an age effect). The evidence here is very much in line with Sternberg's (1986) argument that relationships, if they survive, tend to become more companionate over time.

Previous research (Potts et al, 2006; Sandberg, 2015) has suggested that with age and decreased male function sexual activity is 'de-centred' from its focus on genital sex or intercourse to other parts of the body and other sexual repertoires. At the same time, as Waite et al (2009) show, even among older people foreplay and vaginal intercourse seem to constitute the two activities that respondents label as 'sex'. Even among the oldest US respondents in their study (aged 75–85) about 8 in 10 said that they usually or always have vaginal intercourse during sex. However, when sexual activity consists entirely of kissing, hugging, and sexual touching, this pattern is more common among the old–old (aged 75–85) than the young–old (aged 57–64). Our own data seems to support both these insights. Although almost all our respondents regularly had intercourse with their partners, they emphasised that cuddling and caressing had become more important parts of their sexual repertoires.

Many of our informants described changes in their sexual repertories that had occurred with age, often as a consequence of male erectile dysfunction. As much research notes, female sexuality tends to be shaped by their male partner's sexual abilities (see for example Carpenter, Nathanson & Kim, 2006; Gott, 2005; Waite et al, 2009). LAT Lucy, 79, describes that having an orgasm has become less important, and the foreplay and physical and emotional closeness has become more important in her late-in-life relationship: "There doesn't have to be orgasms every time. The most important thing is closeness, foreplay and that there is an attraction. You can have sexual joy even if the body doesn't function as before. I feel this belonging with Lee and that is an enormous comfort."

Some informants reflect on the changes in their sexual abilities and behaviour. They emphasise that the important part is that the sexual attraction and desire are maintained. Cohabiting Clint, 82, emphasises the importance of desire:

'Sexuality is important in all intimate relationships. Certain things are muted by age but the important thing is that they don't cease to exist. In youth, perhaps you were together two, three, four times a week – it isn't like that when you are 82. Perhaps it happens a few times a month. But it doesn't matter. The important thing is that it happens, that you continue to feel a desire for each other.'

Most commonly, the informants described a reprioritisation from sex centred on genital orgasms to sex focused on the whole body, on touching, hugging and caressing. The focus is on satisfying what is sometimes referred to as 'skin hunger'. Cohabiting Corinne, 78, describes that the most important part of her relationship with Clint is to feel needed and to have the physical closeness:

> 'Love! To feel needed. I don't really know what love is, but to feel needed – that he wants to be with me and lets me hug and caress him. I touch him all the time. I don't really care about having sex, even if we still have it. Having orgasms isn't important for me. What is important is that he desires me physically.'

LAT Lenny *and* Lydia was the only repartnered couple that did not have intercourse, due to Lenny's erectile dysfunction. They did not think that sex was important for their relationship. Lydia describes age-related changes in sexuality, especially concerning men. She says that sex is not important anymore at her age, and she instead emphasises tenderness and closeness:

> 'It changes, especially for men, after the age of 70 or so. And it doesn't bother me, because tenderness is more important to me. When you are between 75 and 80 there is nothing left. But sex is not important – you can still cuddle. It's a different kind of love, a mature love with lots of hugs and tenderness.'

Still, for the other informants, intercourse remained important.

Imagined sexual futures

Even if sex tended to be viewed as central to the establishment of an intimate relationship also in later life, the interviewees were less likely to think that an active sex life was a requirement for the continuation of an existing union. This is much in line with the assumption, based on Sternberg's (1986) triangular model of love, that relationships over time tend to lose their passionate character but remain intimate and committed companionate relationships. In the interviews it was clear that as long as mutual desire and attraction persists in the relationship, an imagined cessation of sexual intercourse in an existing relationship was not perceived as problematic.

Cohabiting Cecilia, 78, describes how they paused having sexual intercourse when her current partner was treated for cancer, but all the time they continued with their physical closeness and tenderness. She says that even if her partner Chris in the future were not able to have intercourse the tenderness they have in their relationship would be enough:

> 'If Chris should come to me now and say that – "now we have to stop having sex" – well, we would still continue to cuddle and caress. I always lie in his arms for a long while in the morning and again in the evening and that is good enough. So if my man had prostate cancer and couldn't [have intercourse] I'd still be satisfied with this tenderness.'

Similarly, Married Mike, 84, is happy about his reawakened erectile function, but if one day he cannot have sexual intercourse anymore he says it would not affect their relationship:

> 'Sex is not the goal, but a consequence of touching and caressing. Martha has said "This is great to have, but if it should cease then I won't be sad, because it is the closeness that I crave." A need for sex was a given earlier in life. It is not as important now but a consequence of being close together. But we could just as well hug and then just go to sleep. When our sex life started taking off [after his long period of celibacy] then we could have sex several times a day, but that has abated. To be honest, the power in the limb is not the same any more. We can have intercourse without me coming, but it doesn't bother me much and it doesn't bother her either. For her, the closeness is more important.'

In short, although sex was a precondition for the initiation of a romantic relationship it was not a precondition for continuing an existing established late-in-life relationship; at least it was not important to maintain the same sexual repertoire as at the beginning of the relationship.

Conclusion

Sex has for a long time been a neglected issue in gerontological research. Existing research on sex and ageing has mostly focused on sexual activity and sexual health, but, as Gott (2005) states, the voices of older people themselves have remained absent. The purpose of this chapter has been to contribute to filling this gap by adding the stories of our older interviewees and evidence from our survey.

In the chapter we have focused on the role and meaning of sex in a new intimate late-in-life relationship. We initially described the historical value change that has been a part of the biographical experiences of older people today and how these experiences formed a basis for their late-life sexual experiences and how they evaluate those experiences. We further showed that sexual attraction was a precondition for repartnering in later life. A purely companionate relationship was not seen by the informants as enough to qualify as an intimate relationship.

Good sex was recurrently framed in terms of an ideology of love: casual sexual adventures were frowned on; the sexual behaviour of adolescents was contrasted to what was perceived as the more healthy sexual behaviour of older people; older women described the sexuality of older men as more simple and pleasure oriented than their own sexuality, but the older men tended to subscribe to the same ideology of love as the older women.

Two stories were common regarding sexual experiences in new intimate relationships. The first was that sexual interest and activity had been rekindled in the new relationship and that it was often seen as sexually better than previous relationships. The second was that the sexual repertoire was to a large extent dictated by male sexual abilities and that with declining erectile function focus was decentred from genital sex to touching and caressing of the whole body.

The results presented in this chapter can be related to the historical transformation of intimacy, and the corresponding release of sexuality from its marital and reproductive determination. This historical development was clearly visible in the informants' relationship biographies, which reflected the liberalisation of sexual norms. It was also visible in their increased appreciation of the importance of sexual self-realisation. This was especially the case for women. Presently they did not think that marriage was a necessity for having a sexual relationship. Still sex was not entirely liberalised, but framed in an ideology of love.

ELEVEN

Time as a structuring condition for new intimate relationships in later life[6]

It is often claimed that 'love is ageless'. But is this really true? In this chapter we pose the question: is there something that sets intimate relationships in later life apart from relationships in earlier parts of the life course? Earlier in this book we have considered how intimate relationships in later life are shaped by historical and cultural conditions. In this chapter we will instead be focusing on how they are shaped by the particular existential structure of later life. We will argue that old age is a life phase characterised by a paradox of time: that of having lots of available free time, but little time left in life – and that this existential structure shapes intimacy in later life. We will argue that the scope of this theoretical insight is much wider than the Swedish case – or even than the topic of intimate relationships.

An existential theory of time

In recent years, there has been a rise of interest in the concept of time within the social sciences in general (for example Adam, 2004). However, in social gerontology this discussion still seems limited, especially considering that the whole topic of ageing is essentially about *time*. A review of the keywords in articles published in one important social gerontological journal, *Ageing and Society*, between 1994 and 2011, revealed only four articles that included time as a keyword.[7] Also, very few titles (for example Baars, 2013; Baars & Visser, 2007; McFadden & Atchley, 2001) deal specifically with the subject of time and ageing.

In the social philosophy of time, a central distinction is between perspectives that view time as an objective category (natural or social) external to the individual, and perspectives which view time as a subjective experience, internal to the individual's mind. The former perspective is evident in the theoretical proposition regarding the institutionalised life course that members of a society share cultural schedules of how a normal life should be organised over time, based on the objective category of chronological time (Hagestad & Neugarten,

1985; Neugarten, 1969). A number of social philosophers, from Heidegger to Mead and Schutz (Adam, 2004) have instead viewed time as a subjective experience. According to Mead and Schutz, both the past and future are constructs that are recurrently being renegotiated in order to maintain a sense of continuity in life. The subjective perspective of time is particularly evident in narrative gerontology and biographical research.

In the following we claim that it is fruitful to focus on time as a life resource and that the composition of this resource – having lots of available free time, but little lifetime left – constitutes a particular existential structure that separates old age from earlier phases of life. In this argument we have been influenced by Heidegger's work on time, where being is presented *as* time, or time as *the form* of being. In *Being and Time*, Heidegger (2008 [1927]) claims that the existential structure of (human) being is characterised by being-in-the-world (*Dasein*), in an everyday sense, alongside other beings and physical things (as opposed to some form of abstract existence). Being-in-the-world has two further characteristics: it is always already in the world (*thrown* into the world – most evidently at birth but more generally in every situation), and it is knowledgeable about itself as a being in the world (it can distance itself from its existence and understand it) and can thus imagine a different future and project itself into that future. These characteristics of being are *temporal* at their core: (human) being is in a present, marked by its history (time spent) and that of its environment, projecting itself towards a future (compare our concept of 'remaining time' below). Most importantly, being is finite – it has a beginning and an end. In other words, being *is* time, and time is a finite personal resource.

The idea that being *is* time is never clearer than in relation to the unavoidability of death, an insight which was an important part of Heidegger's work. Death is both certain and unpredictable, and it is against this finitude that the meaning of the life project is measured. The certainty of death is a challenge to the individual to live life deliberately. One way of putting this is that time wasted on inauthentic existence (not acknowledging the meaning of one's existence) cannot be regained. Analysing being *as* time allows us to see time as a finite personal resource that we are all born with in different, albeit estimable, amounts, and which can be put to use in different life projects. How is our time best spent? What shall we do with our lives in the years we have left?

Below we will argue that the existential structure of old age is characterised by the paradox of having an increased amount of available free time at one's disposal – what we call 'post-(re)productive free time' – but at the same time having little personal lifetime left – what we refer to as 'remaining time'. This existential structure creates conditions for new relationships in later life that differ from those in earlier periods in life, and these conditions can have formative power over relationship choices and be conducive to intimacy in romantic relationships.

Post-(re)productive free time

The lifestyle of the third age, after retirement and after one's children have left home, is characterised by an increase in available free time – post-(re)productive freedom – that offers a potential for engaging in new intimate relationships. Much of our lifetime is normally reserved for projects that are to some extent determined from the outside, such as tradition/necessity. The major project of the first 15–25 years of life is normally socialisation in different forms (what Laslett, 1989, calls the first age). This is followed by adult life, which for most people is primarily reserved for two projects: work and reproduction (what Laslett calls the second age). In a Marxian perspective, a large amount of personal lifetime is sold off as abstract work for an employer to put to use in production, based on the goals of the employer rather than those of the workers. For most people, work demands much of their adult lifetime. The second major adult life project is bringing up children. Traditionally this has been the life project of women in particular, who have spent much of their lifetime on this project. Both work and bringing up children demand a lot of time, and other life projects normally have to fit between these major projects (see also Hurd Clarke 2005).

In later life, people generally no longer have the responsibility for children living at home and the diverse chores that come with that responsibility. In old age, family relationships have become a question of choice rather than necessity – what we have conceptualised as *post-reproductive freedom*. For many, retirement is an even more important source of liberated time – what we have conceptualised as *post-productive freedom*. A very real difference in the conditions of life before and after retirement and parenting – at least in regions of the world where the third age has become part of the institutionalised life course – is that life after retirement is for the first time characterised by having vast amounts of *available time* for self-selected life projects, such as close or intimate relationships.

For those currently living in a new relationship, the free time generated by retirement and the empty nest directly translates into freedom to spend time with one's partner, doing and experiencing things together. The informants repeatedly talk about these new existential life conditions and describe them as providing a new, and compared to earlier in life, fundamentally different foundation for intimate relationships. 68-year-old LAT Lars describes the difference:

> 'When I was 20, a partner was a person that you started a family with; had children with, built a house and financial security with and raised kids with. And you had a job and a career and all that. But all of that is over now. The life we live now is a life of luxury in a way. It's so luxurious that it's insolent.'

The luxury that Lars is referring to is the luxury of having ample time for each other in the relationship – something that he had not experienced earlier in life.

Post-(re)productive life releases free time that can be invested in intimate relationships. The increased time spent together carries with it the *potential for deeper and more rewarding relationships* than in earlier periods of life. Many informants, such as 68-year-old Married Mary below, described the current relationship in later life as the 'crown' of their relationship life:

> 'Love is amazing, but I don't think that you can experience it before you reach our age. I really don't think so. Not this intensively and close. Because there is really nothing that gets in the way. You don't need to work, you don't need to get up in the morning. You have no kids, no parent-teacher conferences to attend. There are so many things that you have to do in life, and now that you have done them and can enjoy retirement, it's just wonderful!'

As Laslett (1989) points out, retirement opens up a life phase which, given health and reasonably good finances, holds the potential for self-development through new experiences and the active pursuit of personal interests. However, many people prefer realising these potentials *with* somebody. For some, the partner is a vehicle for enjoying the third age – for travelling, going out, visiting cultural events and so on – while for others being part of a couple is a form of self-realisation in itself. Indeed, as some informants retrospectively recall about their earlier lives as single retirees, if one does not have a partner and is not surrounded by friends and family, the *increase in free time could increase the risk of loneliness*. For singles (as well as those who are not happy in their current relationship), the post-productive freedom of retirement can become a trigger for trying to find somebody new to share their new-found free time with. Indeed, some informants started looking for a new partner in close connection to retirement, claiming that they had been quite content being alone earlier in life while they were pursuing their career or being responsible for children as a single parent. This was the case for 65-year-old LAT Lisbeth: "I didn't have any need [for a partner] before. Now I have. I felt lonely when I retired. Something was missing. I spent a lot of time alone in my apartment – it was quite simply boring. And then, when I met Björn [her new partner] everything became fun again."

The abundance of available free time after retirement is perhaps even more threatening for those who are widowed and suddenly have no one to share their time with. For widowed persons, a new intimate relationship can represent a significant turning point in life (what Denzin [1989] calls an 'epiphany' of life), changing the experience of the remaining lifetime from misery – 'death's waiting room', in the words of some informants – to a new promising future.

But access to increased available free time could also be a challenge to existing relationships. Some interviewees recounted how retirement had been a turning point in their former relationships, where suddenly they had a wealth of time together and had to face each other and evaluate their union. This raised the question of whether they wanted to continue the relationship or not. Others, who had been in age-heterogeneous unions, recounted how being out of phase with each other's retirement had created conditions where one person was eager to enjoy the possibilities of the third age while the other was still working, and how this had caused a strain on their relationship, eventually causing a break up.

To conclude, our informants recurrently talked about their new intimate relationships against the background of the new existential conditions of later life, after the responsibilities of working life and child rearing: that of having much available time to invest in intimate relationships, new or potential. However, our informants' stories were also told against the background of life's finitude – of having little time left. We develop this latter theme below.

Remaining time

If one side of the existential structure of later life is the availability of post-(re)productive free time, the other side is the growing awareness that time is 'running out'. Even if the particular socio-structural conditions of late modern society have extended the healthy lifespan and created a new life phase, the third age, which can be used for late-in-life self-realisation, there is still an inevitable end to life. If anything, with medical progress the limit to life has become more predictable than ever – most dying takes place late in life. It is interesting to note that according to disengagement theory, a driving force behind disengagement is an 'awareness of finitude', defined as the amount of time the ageing person believes that he or she has left before death (Sill, 1980). Also in Carstensen's theory of socio-emotional selectivity (Carstensen 1992; 1995; Carstensen, Isaacowitz & Charles 1999; see also Chapter two), awareness of finitude is the central reason for people to select (by decreasing) and optimise their social networks. In our Swedish research, the informants are clearly aware that the end of their lives is approaching, and they reflect on new relationships against this background. However, in contrast to the predictions by disengagement theory and socio-emotional selectivity theory, most of our informants draw the conclusion that they have to make the most of whatever time remains, and that a new partner is one way of doing so. This is more in line with Heidegger's idea that the finality of life acts as a horizon against which the lived life is measured, urging people to live life deliberately.

Even though most of our informants experienced their health as rather good, many of them had experienced potentially fatal incidents such as a heart attack or cancer, or were suffering from some kind of ailment that constantly reminded them of their mortality. If they were not unwell themselves, they often had people in their immediate surroundings who had become sick or died. A common and shocking reminder of the shortness of the remaining time was the death of a former partner, an experience which had often included closely following a sick and dying person for a period of time. As a consequence, a recurrent theme in the interviews was the realisation that life is finite and that the remaining time is relatively short, both for the individual and for the relationship – although this horizon might be more or less remote depending on the age and health of the informant. A number of insights follow from this.

'Fragile' relationships

For those in a relationship, a common insight is that the *relationship is fragile* and will most likely dissolve through the death either of oneself or one's partner. As a consequence, time together is precious, and many of the informants are grateful for every new day that they get to spend with their partner, as expressed by 68-year-old LAT Lisa below:

'Every day I'm aware that you can't take anything for granted. I'm thankful for the day that I have been given and I'm thankful for the relationship that I have right now. But I'm aware that I can't own it – that it's a gift that I receive every day. It affects me very much, this awareness that it can all end so quickly.'

Starting a new intimate relationship in later life means that being left alone is a realistic prospect, and one which many of the informants can relate to, having already experienced the passing of their former spouse. The insight that the relationship is unavoidably finite and thereby fragile deeply affects the informants' appreciation of their relationships, as is expressed explicitly in the quotation above. Some hope that they will be the first to pass away, or that they will pass away at the same time as their partner, so that they will not have to experience being left alone (again). There is also a strong feeling that the current relationship is likely to be the last; there is simply too little time left to start over yet again. LAT Lenny, 78, describes this insight: "It is better to be widowed at 60, because then you have a chance to start over. But at 75–76 I'm happy to have a chance with Inger these last years. But if you're left alone at 80–81, then you're in death's waiting room."

In the interviews, 'being left alone' in the future is almost always synonymous with being widowed. Voluntary separation is not an expected future transition, and is very seldom considered an option among informants living in new relationships initiated late in life. It is not seen as reasonable to separate this late in life. Moreover, because of the short remaining time the risk of 'growing apart' is not perceived as a possibility. LAT Lenny reflects on the conditions for relationship development in different phases of life:

'When you're young, when you're 20, 22, 23 years old. There's nothing that says that the relationship will develop like this all the time [shows two parallel lines with his hands]. Normally you will grow apart in some respect. But now, for us – we'll never be able to grow apart.'

All in all, the current relationship is perceived as something of a happy but unlikely and unexpected chance, which in contrast to earlier periods in life is not likely to repeat itself, and so is perceived as something very precious. As a consequence, it is commonly expressed that one has to be careful with the relationship and be *especially considerate* with one's partner in old age.

A sense of urgency

If one aspect of the increasing realisation of life's finitude is that relationships are fragile and partners have to care for each other, another is that life together must be lived deliberately. Although death is a constant companion, the informants often claim not to worry about it. If anything, the realisation that the remaining life together can be short increases the focus on enjoying and experiencing the present, or *seizing the day*.

One aspect of seizing the day is a *sense of urgency*: one should not leave anything for tomorrow, but fulfil one's relationship plans before it is too late. Some couples take the quick decision to marry or, as in the example of 87-year-old Cohabiting Chris below, to move in together shortly after having met, arguing that late in life there is nothing to gain from being cautious: "[We moved in together and got engaged very quickly] simply because we're so old that we don't have any time for reflection and all that. If we want something now we take it at once. We have our future behind us."

There are many stories in our Swedish interviews that show how strong this sense of urgency is. Exceptionally, and in contrast to what is said about fragile and considerate relationships above, some of our informants mentioned that they or somebody they know had left their partner when the partner developed dementia, because they perceived this as practically having been widowed and they wanted to get on with their lives before it was too late. LAT Lars even argued that one owes it to oneself to leave one's partner at the slightest sign of illness or disability, so as not to waste any of the precious remaining time:

> 'I've said [to my partner] that "if I were to fall ill now. you have to get on with your life. Let my children or the social services take care of me, because you shouldn't tie yourself up taking care of me for the rest of your life.". I would be able to [do the same thing]. I've spent my whole life being faithful, caring and responsible and now I have a few years left and I want to feel that I'm responsible only for myself. Life is short.'

For singles, however, the sense of urgency may also be a reason *not* to initiate new relationships, or may affect the choice of partner. Since finding a new relationship is intimately connected with fulfilling the promise of the third age, the health of one's partner is an important question for singles and also for some informants living in a relationship. A potential partner's ill-health can be experienced as an obstacle to realising the dreams the older singles have for their remaining time, or even as a pure waste of the precious resource of time. Many singles relate stories about having backed out of relationships with potential partners with health problems or other personal problems.

The importance of health is perhaps best expressed by the single female participants, who jealously guard their autonomy and want to avoid becoming the nurse of (yet) another man. This issue has also been reported in previous research on LAT relationships (see for example Davidson 2001 and 2002; Ghazanfareeon Karlsson & Borell 2002 and 2005; Carr 2004). The quotation from 73-year-old Single Sally below illustrates this attitude:

> 'As a relatively healthy woman I won't take the risk of having to take care of somebody. I mean, at 60 I was willing to take that risk, and I would have helped Eric [former husband] of course, because that love was so profound. But not now – it would limit my life.'

The sense of urgency is perhaps felt most strongly by the old singles, who often feel that the time for finding a new partner is quickly slipping away – that soon they will be too old to be able to enjoy a new relationship or too frail to attract a partner. For some people there is a feeling that it is already *too late*; for example, too late to create a new common household and leave behind the safety of one's home and history for an unknown future, or too late to get to know and trust a new and previously unknown partner if one's present partner should pass away. LAT Lenny describes this feeling and explains why he has repartnered with a woman he had already dated in young adulthood:

> 'If I place a personal ad, and I get an answer from a "happy 70-year-old in Skåne" [distant region], I won't be able to develop trust for that person until after another five or ten years. But when you have met in your youth and then reconnect 50 years later, then you already have that trust.'

With time, the horizon for active dating decreases and creates ambivalence towards new intimate relationships, because of the time it takes to establish a new relationship (including possibly breaking up from a former partner). This was the case for Single Sadie, who had recently met an older married man who was ready to end his lifelong marriage to be able to start over with Sadie:

> 'I'm 73 years old now. At that age you can't go about breaking up children, wife and family. They would think I was out of my mind. And then it takes a couple of years. Since I've been divorced I know. You can't just walk out of the door. You have responsibilities towards the person you live with. And I mean, how old would we be then? I could even be dead and buried. There is no point even beginning.'

As the interviewee notes, both relationship initiations and separations take time, and there is little time left in life. It could be argued that there is a certain 'expiration date' both for separations and for new relationships, and as people age in later life this date approaches. The idea of an expiration date is reminiscent of the hypothesis in socio-emotional selectivity theory, that people in later life are more disposed to optimising existing relationships than to initiating new intimate relationships. However, for most of our interviewees the expiration date is presented as a future scenario, and not a current one. It would seem that our interviewees, much in line with the idea of an extension of the lifestyles of the third age further up the age ladder, keep pushing the deadline of when it is too late to start over – but they recognise that this time will soon come.

To conclude, restricted remaining time can be a driving force towards initiating new intimate relationships in later life, but it can also be an obstacle. In any case, the remaining time horizon is highly significant for new intimate relationships. A consequence of this is that a striking number of the informants in our dataset have *returned to past relationships* or initiated relationships with former friends – people whom they already know well, sometimes even intimately – arguing that it minimises the time that it takes to connect, while it also reconnects them with their past (this phenomenon has also been described in North America by Lopata [1979] and Moore & Stratton [2004]).

Conclusion

By using time as a theorising frame in our analysis, we have shown that the existential structure of being-in-the-world (*Dasein*) in later life is characterised by the paradox of *having lots of available time but little time left,* and that this is central for understanding both the conditions for the formation of new intimate relationships and the meaning given to these relationships in later life. For Heidegger, the finality of life is an exhortation to live life deliberately. The third age offers a platform in later life for such deliberate self-realisation, which might include the cultivation of new intimate relationships.

The paradox of time is historically dependent. In contemporary Sweden, as in many other parts of the Western world, those born between and immediately after the two World Wars belong to generations who have experienced rapid economic expansion, as well as gains in health and welfare. Now they find themselves (*thrown*) in a world where life expectancy is longer than before. Even if death remains unpredictable, as Heidegger suggests, due to medical advances and systems of risk reduction, death has become a lot more predictable than it used to be historically, and most people can expect to live in relatively good health well into old age. Retirement age has not advanced accordingly. This has given rise to a new life phase between working life and deep old age. This is the background of the third age (Laslett 1989), which can be characterised as the *addition of available free time* to the average life course. For this lifetime, new projects such as new relationships can be imagined. The emergence of the third age has created a historically unique opportunity for large parts of the population to achieve their unrealised life goals – an opportunity that was previously reserved for a privileged minority with the necessary resources. The emergence of the third age has a central role in determining attitudes to, and expectations and experiences, of new intimate relationships in later life.

These existential conditions are present not only for the Swedish age groups represented in our sample, but probably in many parts of the contemporary Western world, and are consequently relevant to analysing new intimate relationships there as well. For example, Koren (2015) has shown that an awareness of finitude was an important part of the relationship experiences of older repartnered Israelis as well. Also, and importantly, this structure is probably applicable to the study of other areas of later life, besides new intimate relationships. Most obviously, it is likely that many of our findings can be generalised to older people living in life-long marriages, since the existential structure should be present in their lives as well. The existential structure of later life might be an explanation for the often noted U-type development in marital satisfaction over the life course, with an initial 'honeymoon' phase followed by a decrease in satisfaction in a mid-life, again followed by an improvement in later life (see Stinnett, Mittelstet Carter & Montgomery, 1972 and Bookwala & Jacobs, 2004; see also Cooney & Dunne, 2001).

In a broader sense, it seems reasonable that the existential structure of later life might impact on life choices and actions in areas of later life other than intimate relationships, such as the eternal bucket list – for example seeing the world, learning new foreign languages, volunteering for a worthwhile cause. Of course, all of these arguments about the applicability of the structure to different areas or contexts are of an analytical nature, and have yet to be empirically tested. Still, we would argue that the existential structure is a fruitful point of departure for social gerontological research generally.

TWELVE

Discussion

In this book we have investigated the issue of repartnering in later life. Throughout the book we have investigated the connection between individual attitudes to, and expectations and experiences of, new intimate relationships in later life, and situated historical change on a macro level and structural conditions on an existential level. We have used the Swedish case as our main example but have also conducted a comprehensive review of international research and compared our findings with research and data from other Western countries.

In Chapters two to four we investigated the structural preconditions of late-life intimacy in contemporary Western societies. We presented some influential theories on the changing life course and the transformation of intimacy in late modernity that suggest possible changes to the landscape of late-life intimacy. And we argued that the Swedish case constitutes one possible scenario for the future of late-life repartnering in Western countries more generally. We also discussed the limits of historical change against the certainty of death as an existential horizon. We continued by illustrating the changing landscape of late-life intimacy empirically using census data from a handful of European countries and the US. These data showed the impact of the prolonged healthy lifespan and new technologies on late-life intimacy. These data also illustrated the increasing incidence and prevalence of divorce in the older population, creating what we call a 'society of divorcees', which constitutes a central condition for an increase in repartnering in later life. We also presented evidence of an increasing acceptance for new ways of living together, such as non-marital cohabitation and LAT, and argued that union form in older people's relationships is explained by historical change in the form of the year that the relationship was initiated, and by individual change in the form of the age at which the relationship was initiated.

In Chapters five to ten we continued the exploration by showing how these transformations at the macro level are reflected in older Swedes' individual attitudes, expectations and experiences of late-life intimacy. We investigated how the transformation of intimacy was visible in individual relationship careers. We showed how 'the one and only lifelong marriage' is no longer the self-evident model for describing older people's relationship biographies – many older people have complex relationship careers that include divorces and serial relationships in different union forms. These relationship careers influence the interest in repartnering in later life. We investigated older people's attitudes to repartnering and preferences for different union forms and showed that divorcees were more interested in repartnering than widowed people, but also that gendered relationship experiences tend to make women more hesitant to repartner than men. For late-life relationships the preference is non-marital unions, in particular LAT unions, and this is the case not only for older single women, but also for older single men. We continued at the micro level by looking more closely at the negotiations surrounding the initiation and development of late-life intimate relationships. We argued that older people's relationships, in line with contemporary ideals, develop successively through negotiations and that a number of obstacles have to be resolved in order for the relationship to develop. Questions about cohabitation or marriage are not normally raised at the beginning of a relationship, but later as the relationship progresses. From this perspective questions about older singles' attitudes to remarriage, as measures of the interest in repartnering, are inadequate.

In Chapters eight to nine we asked what the consequences of a new intimate relationship are for the older individual. We showed how a new intimate partner can serve as a valuable source of companionate, emotional and practical support, which might increase well-being and decrease the risk of institutionalisation for the older individual. We also investigated the consequences of late-life repartnering for the older person's support network. We argued that a new partner can serve as a central source for a wide range of different support functions and consequently be a resource for the older person, to achieve autonomy and to unburden family and friends. For older individuals with complex relationship careers, the support network resembles a family of choice and a new intimate relationship can be a central part of that network.

In Chapter ten we investigated the role and meaning of sex in new late-in-life relationships from the point of view of older people themselves. We showed that sexual attraction was regularly a precondition for repartnering but also that sex was framed in terms of a strong ideology of love. Casual sexual adventures as well as sex in loveless marriages tended to be frowned on. A loving relationship, not marriage, was the ultimate principle for legitimising sex.

Finally, in Chapter eleven we considered the existential structure of later life and its impact on intimate relationships for older people. We argued that later life is characterised by the paradox of time: on the one hand, having lots of free time to cultivate intimate relationships in the third age, and on the other, having little time left in life. We showed how this paradox of time organises and impacts on new intimate relationships in a variety of ways – affording much time to cultivate a new relationship but also inspiring intensity both in finding and being with a new partner.

Below we will relate our findings to three central theoretical questions: how does late-life repartnering relate to the wider historical transformation of intimacy described by social theory? How can the concept of life phase enhance an understanding of late-life repartnering? How can the results from the Swedish case be generalised to a wider international context?

Historical change

A central change to the institutionalised life course, as a consequence of the prolongation of the healthy lifespan and increased economic security, is the emergence of the third age in large parts of the Western world in the second half of the 20th century (Laslett, 1989). The third age can be characterised as an extension of the lifestyles of mid-life into later life, creating a period between the responsibilities of the second age (work and child care) and the dependency of the fourth age, allowing space for self-development and the realisation of (remaining) life plans. The third age allows people to envision new intimate futures and to consider 'starting over' late in life. A new intimate partner is often an important resource in pursuing third-age projects, such as travelling, and going to cultural or social events. As we have shown above, it is common for older singles to look for a companion to share experiences with, rather than a partner for starting a family with (a common project earlier in life).

A precondition for considering new intimate futures in the third age is the historical transformation of intimacy that has taken place in the latter part of the 20th century, which has signified a deinstitutionalisation of the modern marital script that defined roles and obligations in the marital dyad, leaving room for negotiation of both the content and the form of unions. This development has also contributed to a deinstitutionalisation of the life course: freedom from the modern family script begets freedom from the script of the modern life course. When reproduction ceases to be the central organising principle for couple life, there is no longer any 'best before' date for initiating a new intimate relationship, as long as health allows it. While the modern life course script prescribed a lifelong marriage that was initiated early in adult life and dissolved by widowhood late in life –

creating predictability for family life – in the late modern life course relationships can be initiated and dissolved at different points in life (it is never too late) and families can be formed at multiple points over the life course. For a large proportion of today's older Swedes this is an actual life course experience – as demonstrated in Chapter five.

Even though there has been a wide cultural shift towards divorce culture, a common assumption in prior research has been that older people continue to live according to the ideals of marriage culture. We have called this idea the cultural lag hypothesis, where older people are thought to be living in accordance with the norms they were socialised into in early adulthood, isolated or unaffected by the value changes of the surrounding society.

However, the findings in this book do not give much support to this assumption, at least with regard to older Swedes. Instead, in chapter after chapter we have found that older people, both in their attitudes and practices, challenge the marriage cultural values they were brought up with. Older people's views and experiences of late-life repartnering, were very much in line with the theoretical suggestions put forward by Giddens (1991, 1992), Hackstaff (1999) and Cherlin (2004), that relationships in late modernity are primarily established through negotiation between relatively equal partners, and not determined by external form (for example marriage). A large proportion of the older Swedish population have complex relationship careers, involving serial relationships in different union forms as well as divorces and separations from these relationships. In later life few of the older singles are interested in getting married and instead prioritise non-marital partnerships. New intimate relationships are not necessarily built around the roles and obligations defined by the lifelong institutionalised marriage, but are negotiated, much as in a family of choice.

In his description of the transformation of intimacy, Giddens has been criticised for ignoring a few central limitations that restrain the flexibility of the pure relationship. One of these critiques is that couples are often buffered by linked lives that tie them together (Smart & Neale, 1999). This is perhaps most evident when there are young children that demand continuous cooperation between the parents also after a separation. Another critique is that cross-gender relationships are seldom as democratically arranged or gender equal as Giddens assumes them to be – especially when nesting children are involved (Jamieson, 1988, 1999). Finally, Giddens has been criticised for underestimating difference between social groups. One important difference is exactly that of age. Older couples might in fact fit better with Giddens' ideal type than couples in mid-life, in the sense that working life no longer places any external demands on the couple and reproduction is no longer an issue. This argument parallels Giddens' presentation of gay couples as an avant-garde for pure, negotiated, relationships. One evident similarity between gay and older couples is that the goal of the relationship is not normally reproduction, and the absence of children allows for a flexible arrangement of the couple's life together. This freedom is evident in the multitude of ways that older Swedes arrange their lives after repartnering and the ways in which they discuss these arrangements. Thus, rather than viewing older people as carriers of a cultural lag, an alternative could be to view them as an avant-garde freely exploring new ways of living together.

But there are of course differences also within the group of older people. Critique has been directed against the idea of a third age for primarily focusing on the lifestyles of middle or upper class segments of the population that have the necessary financial and health resources needed to participate in these lifestyles. Pursuing the lifestyles of the third age demands financial resources, and not all older people have the necessary means. To the extent that repartnering is motivated by a longing for somebody to share the project of the third age with, lacking financial resources constitutes a real obstacle to romantic ambitions. Some singles describe how they avoid partners that cannot match them financially because they cannot partake in their plans for the third age. Scarce financial resources remain an issue for many older people, even if this is perhaps less so in Sweden than in many other countries. Even more importantly, health is a very important resource for those who venture out on this market, and many singles openly declare that they avoid partners with health problems for fear of being trapped in an unrewarding relationship during their last few good years in life. For the large number of older people that have fragile health this illustrates a central limitation to repartnering in later life. Together with other reasons that make older singles uninterested in repartnering (see Chapter six), these obstacles may explain why a large proportion of the older singles remain uninterested in new intimate relationships in later life.

Phase of life

Our investigations into intimacy in later life have led us to appreciate the importance of life phase. In the stories of our informants life phase was a constant and important explanation for their relationship choices and experiences. We imagine the individual life course as a short instance within the floating current of historical time that we described in the prior section. Within this larger context life phase becomes important in at least three ways: biographically, through individual experience; socially, through contemporary norms and conditions for the life course; and existentially, through the universal conditions of human existence. All these aspects contribute to setting relationships in later life apart from relationships in earlier life phases.

Biographically, later life is characterised by a long life of relationship experiences. The most complex relationship careers, in terms of accumulated relationship experiences, are found in the older population. Relationship decisions are likely to be made in the light of this wealth of relationship experiences. Informants sometimes referred to their relationship experiences as their 'backpacks'. These backpacks could contain relationship models formed in prior unions, good and bad earlier experiences, former union dissolutions (by divorce or widowhood), and gendered relationship experiences. As we showed in Chapter five, this wealth of experiences impacts on older people's interest in repartnering and expectations of new intimate relationships. For some older people these experiences imply difficulties in adapting to new partners or even in imagining repartnering, while for others they imply preparedness to do so.

Socially, relationship norms are often most pronounced in the reproductive life phase (as implied by Smart & Neale [1999] in their critique of Giddens' pure relationships) and impact on couples with families. For example, as a juridical institution marriage determines financial responsibilities between family members and is thus primarily relevant for couples that have, or plan to have, common children. And since the reproductive phase of life is limited, this means that marriage is particularly relevant for unions initiated in earlier phases of life. In later life, marriage can instead be an obstacle that complicates questions of financial responsibilities – in particular questions concerning inheritance. Non-marital cohabitation can similarly be understood as a union form that simplifies rearing of children within the space of a shared household and which is therefore common for people in young adulthood and mid-life. In the phase of later life, where relationships are not normally reproductive, there are fewer advantages and less normative pressure to live together. Many older people instead choose to live together as LATs.

Existentially, as we saw in Chapter eleven, the paradox of time in later life has an important impact on the relationship priorities of older people. In the third age, after retirement and after the children have left the nest, lots of free time is made available to cultivate a relationship. A second existential aspect is the certainty of death, which implies a non-negotiable limit to the malleability of the life course and the expansion of the third age. Later life often implies a growing awareness of life's finitude, which weighs on relationship choices. In developmental theory, the finality of life has sometimes been used to explain withdrawal from social interaction. This is, for example, the case in Carstensen's socio-emotional selectivity theory where this social withdrawal is described as a way of coping with time running out by prioritising important existing relationships, but not by compensating for little remaining time by working more intensively on achieving non-realised relationship goals. From a Heideggerian perspective the finality of life could be seen as a challenge to live life deliberately, which could include a new life partner to share the promise of the third age with. Our research tends to show how an increased awareness of finality, at least for many older people, constitutes a challenge to live life expansively and intensively for as long as possible, which might include new late-in-life relationships. However, it also includes the awareness that it might soon be too late for new intimate relationships.

Discussing later life as a special life phase with its own biographical, social and existential conditions is important for understanding repartnering in later life and the particularities of late-life relationships. However these conditions are arguably also relevant for understanding later life in general.

The Swedish case

In this book the Swedish case has in many ways been portrayed as extreme, for example with regard to the high prevalence of divorce and alternative union forms among older people, and a widespread social acceptance of repartnering in later life. Since much of the empirical data in the book is Swedish, it is necessary to discuss the character of the Swedish case – is it unique and exceptional compared to other Western countries, or is it a forerunner to what might be a general development also in other Western countries?

An argument for seeing the Swedish, or at least the Nordic, case as qualitatively different from other parts of the Western world is the specific form of state-supported individualism which characterises the Nordic welfare states. According to Beck and Beck-Gernsheim (2002), one of the major reasons for modern individualism is the development of a welfare state that distributes rights on an individual basis, thus freeing the individual from prior collective dependencies, such as on the family or the local community. Perhaps this is more relevant for Sweden than for most other countries. There is, for example, a difference between American individualism, anchored in filial support structures, and Swedish welfare state-supported individualism, anchored in a universal insurance system (cmpr. Esping-Andersen, 1990). Swedish state-supported individualism (Berggren & Trägårdh, 2006) allows for high levels of personal autonomy by providing a relatively generous system of welfare services and insurances that guarantee that individuals can live their lives independent from others, financially and to some extent practically. This applies to women as well as men.

The principles of state-supported individualism find a clear expression in Swedish elderly care law. Since 1979 adult children in Sweden have had no formal juridical responsibility to take care of their older parents (although, informally, they often take a large responsibility). Instead, this responsibility falls on the state. Moreover, one goal of Swedish public elderly politics is to enable people to age 'with preserved independence' (Government Bill, 1997/98:113). Earlier research has shown strong support for this model, showing that older Swedes prefer being dependent on the state for welfare services rather than their kin (see for example Daatland, 2007), retaining what Rosenmayr and Köckeis (1963) have referred to as 'intimacy at a distance'.

A consequence of state-supported individualism is that it is financially feasible for older men and women in all social classes to live as singles without relying on financial assistance from their families, or from a new partner. This means that new intimate relationships can be formed freely, independent of financial motives and relationships with family and friends. According to Berggren and Trägårdh (2006) the normative assumption that good relationships are founded on independence (the Swedish theory of love) is the background for many Swedish social reforms.

The social context of Swedish individualism could explain why the informants in our study so strongly emphasise the value of not being a burden to their children, and stress that a new partner is a resource for autonomy and independence in relation to children and others. It could also explain why children are generally positive about their parents finding new partners in later life, since it actually frees them from responsibility for their older parents. Also, in a culture of individualism people are free to decide about their own lives and it would seem that adult children in Sweden do not view it as their 'right' to decide about their parents' love life.

It is possible that increasing global convergence in the future, with regard both to values and the organisation of societies, will make Sweden more similar to other Western countries. For example, integration of global economies puts pressure on states to harmonise and cut back on social expenditure. Similarly, within the European Union, pressures for the harmonisation of national legislation make it increasingly difficult for states to choose their own directions. In Sweden and many other countries of the world, pension systems have already been reformed so that the state will take less responsibility for older people in the future and consequently, older people might have to rely more on families and partners.

But it is also possible that the Swedish (and Nordic) case, although unique, is a forerunner in a more general historical development taking place in most of the Western world. As early as in the 1980s the American family sociologist Popenoe (1987) described Sweden as a laboratory for studying family change, arguing that much of the dynamic that was highlighted by the Swedish case was also inherent in other Western countries. According to this argument, differences in the social organisation of welfare states hide a wider development towards more financial independence for women and deinstitutionalisation of the family across the Western world. If we follow Popenoe it is reasonable to think that the development that we have seen in older Swedish people's relationships, for example with regard to union form, will also become increasingly evident in other countries. As we have shown in the book, research on repartnering in later life has increased over the last two decades also in other countries, such as the US, Great Britain, the Netherlands, Australia and Israel.

One indication of this global or at least Western change comes from the World Value Survey (Pettersson & Esmer, 2008; see also www. worldvaluesurvey.org). According to the study, Sweden is one of the world's most individualised countries, where people strongly emphasise independence and where collective affinities such as family, religion and nation are ascribed less importance. However, when the World Value Survey charts value change over time, it is apparent that other countries, also outside the Western world, have been moving in the same direction as Sweden in emphasising independence. In this scenario it seems reasonable to argue that Sweden is more of a forerunner than an exception – hinting at wider developmental trends that will soon be a reality in large parts of the world.

Methodological appendix

The results in this book are based on two Swedish family gerontological studies. The first research project, 'New Relationships in Later Life – Changing Forms of Intimacy in Late Modernity', was a qualitative interview study, financed by the Swedish Research Council for Health, Working Life and Welfare (Forte 2009-0720) and carried out between 2010 and 2011. The second project 'New Relationships in Later Life – A Quantitative Survey', was a nationwide postal survey, financed by the Swedish Foundation for Humanities and the Social Sciences (P11: 0909–1) and carried out in 2013.

The purpose of both projects was to study:

- *attitudes* to initiating new intimate relationships in later life (for example union form);
- *expectations* of what a new intimate relationship will offer the individual (for example emotionally, sexually, socially, financially and in terms of informal care);
- *experiences* of new intimate relationships in later life and the forms these relationships take (for example marriage, cohabitation, LAT, dating, casual meetings) and the impact of new relationships in later life on the experiences of ageing and life satisfaction.

Below we describe the methodology of the two studies in detail.

The qualitative interview study

The qualitative interview study had an explorative character, focusing specifically on experiences of repartnering in later life. For the study 28 participants, aged 60–90, were recruited who had initiated a new relationship after the age of 60, or who were actively searching for one. Interviewees were approached through advertisements, articles in the media and educational conferences arranged by retirees' organisations. For the recruitment we used what Patton (2002, p 243) refers to as a purposeful sampling strategy, or more specifically 'maximum variation sampling'; that is, purposefully considering a wide range of informants who could potentially provide rich information about the research question (see also Plummer, 2001). To guarantee maximum variation volunteers were selected using a predefined structured sampling framework that assured representation from men and women, young-old and old-old people, and different forms of intimacy – singles, LATs, cohabitants and marrieds – in order to capture the full diversity of the phenomenon of late life repartnering.

The qualitative interviews had an average length of two hours (ranging from 1h 05m to 3h 16m). The final sample on which the analysis is based was 28 interviews with 10 Swedish men and 18 Swedish women, aged 63–91 (average age 74 for the total group – 78.5 for men, 71 for women). The sample consisted of 6 dating singles or singles looking for a new relationship, and 22 people living in new relationships established after the age of 60 and who at the time were either married (n=4), cohabiting (n=7) or in an LAT relationship (n=11). For the 22 interviewees living in a new intimate relationship, the relationship had lasted from half a year to 14 years with an average of 5 years. Eighteen of the interviews were conducted with both parts of a couple, as separate individual interviews. All informants had children from earlier relationships and all but one had been married earlier in life.

Our selection strategy has consequences that deserve consideration. Relying on voluntary participation resulted in a sample overrepresented by urban middle and upper class heterosexuals. Even though we used recruiting ads in four local newspapers covering smaller towns and rural areas it was harder to find individuals with a rural and/or working class background who were willing to participate and they are consequently underrepresented (but not excluded) in the sample. Their experiences might therefore be less pronounced in the results. We asked specifically also for homosexual informants but got no volunteers. Consequently homosexual experiences of repartnering in later life are absent from our data, and also from the book.

The interviews were mainly carried out by either of the authors in the informants' homes (when both partners were interviewed, the interviews were carried out individually in separate parts of their homes), then transcribed in full and analysed successively. Besides background information, the interviews followed a semi-structured guide covering four major themes: (1) everyday life as a single or in a new relationship, (2) the history of the present relationship, (3) the history of relationships over the full life course, and (4) future perspectives on life as a single or in a relationship. Each of the major themes in the interview started with an open question and continued with more specific semi-structured probing questions – always followed by additional questions if needed for clarification.

The first interview theme started with the open question: 'Tell me about your life as married/cohabitant/LAT?' This introduction was followed by more specific questions, such as: 'What does it mean (financially/socially/emotionally/in terms of care) to be married/cohabitant/LAT in your current life phase?' One specific issue dealt with reactions from the informant's social network towards the new partnership, followed by questions about specific people: their own and their partner's children/grandchildren/friends/relatives. The informants were also asked to describe an ideal partner and an ideal relationship in their current phase of life.

The second interview theme started with an open question about the history of the current relationship: 'Can you please tell me about your current intimate relationship from the moment you met until today?' We followed up with semi-structured questions: what they thought about their current union form, whether something had made them hesitant about initiating and establishing their union, what the most important events or turning points in their current relationship history were, and how their relationship with their children had been affected by their new partnership.

The third interview theme considered the interviewees' relationship history, including all their intimate relationships, from the very first date and forwards. Probing questions were for example 'if you were to tell your relationship history like a book, which chapters would it include?', 'If you view your life decade by decade, which are the most important events in your relationship history?'. Furthermore the informants were asked questions about if, and in that case how, their ideals for a relationship had changed during their lifetime, consequences of ageing for meeting a partner, and experiences of changes of societal values regarding sex and intimate partnerships.

The fourth interview theme considered the informants' thoughts about the future development of the relationship and how it would affect their ageing and later life. It started with the open question: 'How do you think that your current relationship will develop in the future?' Following this opening question we asked about hypothetical situations such as providing care for and receiving care from their partner. Finally the theme included questions about plans for their funeral (for example if they should be buried together with their new partner, alone, or together with their previous partner).

A second interview guide was adapted to fit dating singles. In the first theme, the informants were asked to describe their lives as older singles looking for a partner, why they lived as singles, what their relationships ideals were, and the attitudes of their social network towards their late-life dating. The second interview theme concerned experiences of dating, casual partners and how and where they tried to find a partner. The third theme did not differ significantly from informants in couples. In the fourth theme the questions concerned the informants' thoughts about their future as singles or in a couple, and what it would mean for their ageing and later life.

The tape-recorded interviews were transcribed *in extenso* and analysed using principles from analytical induction (Znaniecki, 1969; Öberg, 1997) and grounded theory (B. G. Glaser & Strauss, 1967; Strauss & Corbin, 1994). Our goal was to theorise the informants' stories (see for example Bengtsson, 2006; Roos, 2005), rather than simply repeating or 'recycling' them (Apitzsch & Inowlocki, 2000) – that is to 'translate' the stories into meaningful family gerontological knowledge. Part of the analysis was performed deductively by coding the data according to our research questions. At the same time, inductive codes were created when new insights and hypotheses were generated through the reading of the data, working with the online software Dedoose to create memos and new codes. Theory development took place through constant comparison of cases, searching for negative cases ('counterexamples') and conceptual refinement. The goal of the analysis was to find the questions that the transcribed texts were giving answers to (Alasuutari, 1995), in order to turn the subjective stories into gerontologically interesting knowledge (cmpr. Apitzsch & Inowlocki, 2000; Ferrarotti, 2003; Roos, 2005). During every step of the research process both authors first read the texts and made individual interpretations, before reaching common consensual interpretations. In the book the analytical insights are reported thematically and illustrated using quotes and case descriptions.

The qualitative interview study has been vetted and approved by the Swedish Central Ethical Review Board (ref 2010/158; www.epn.se). All participation in the interviews was fully voluntary (as guaranteed by the sampling strategy in which we were contacted by people who wanted to tell us about their intimate lives), and all participants signed a letter of consent which included assurance of confidentiality.

The quantitative questionnaire

The second project was based on a nationwide postal survey, carried out in 2013 by the Swedish poll company SKOP, on behalf of the researchers. The purpose of adding a survey to the interviews was twofold: on the one hand to see how representative the insights generated by the qualitative interviews were, and on the other hand to generate comparative data about singles not interested in repartnering and older people in long-term relationships.

A postal survey was distributed to 3,000 Swedes aged 60–90 years. A random sample was drawn from the population register, boosted for non-married people (n=2,250) in relation to married people (n=750). The reason for the dual sampling strategy was that the main focus of the survey was to study new intimate relationships initiated 60+, and official statistics show that very few Swedes get married past the age of 60.

The survey questions were generated based on results from the qualitative interview study and previous research. The survey consisted of four sections. The first section was directed to all respondents, irrespective of their current relationship status. It covered themes like Current relationship status; Attitudes to new couple relationships; Relationship biography; Partner ideals; Social network; Sexual experiences. Section two was directed to all respondents currently in a relationship and included questions about the partner and the relationship (for example happiness, equality). The third section was directed specifically to respondents who had initiated a new relationship after their 60th birthday (these had already filled out section two) and included mainly questions about reactions from their social network to their new relationship. Finally, section four was directed to older singles and included questions about happiness with single life and attitudes to repartnering. (The authors are happy to mail a copy of the questionnaire on request.)

In total the questionnaire was returned by 1,225 respondents. Individuals who had died or moved abroad were excluded from the gross sample (n=116), which resulted in a response rate of 42.5% for the total sample. The sample of married respondents had a higher response rate (58.5%) than the sample of non-marrieds (36.5%). Concerning the married sample, a non-response analysis showed no deviation from the general married population of 60–90-year-old Swedes with regard to gender and age distribution. Concerning the non-married sample, the non-response analysis showed no deviation from the general population of non-marrieds with regard to gender distribution. There was a small but significant deviation (p<.05) from the population regarding the age distribution for women. However the deviation was not systematic but pointed in different directions for different age groups.

For the non-response analysis the poll institute SKOP phoned 500 individuals who had not responded to the questionnaire despite two reminders and asked them for their reasons for not participating. The dominant reason for not responding was that the questions were considered to be too intimate (included in the survey were questions of sexuality and evaluations of one's current and earlier relationships and so on). Low response rates are common in studies concerning people's sex lives (see for example the review of studies concerning sex in later life in Gott, 2005). It is impossible to exactly determine the consequences for our results of people not responding because they felt the questions were too intimate, but it is possible that our respondents have slightly more positive attitudes to new intimate relationships than the population as a whole.

The sample has been adjusted according to civil status, gender and age to compensate for the different probabilities to be included in the sample and for external non-response. All results in the book are weighted frequencies. The adjusted sample shows no deviation from census data collected the same year, 2013, with regard to cohabitation (scb.se). With regard to LAT there are no official statistics to compare with.

References

Adam, B. (2004). *Time*. Cambridge; Malden, MA: Polity.

Alasuutari, P. (1995). *Researching culture – Qualitative method and cultural studies*. London: Sage Publications.

Allen, K. R., Blieszner, R. & Roberto, K. A. (2000). Families in the middle and later years: A review and critique of research in the 1990s. *Journal of Marriage and the Family, 62*(4), 911–926. doi:10.1111/j.1741-3737.2000.00911.x.

Alterovitz, S. S. R. & Mendelsohn, G. A. (2009). Partner preferences across the life span: Online dating by older adults. *Psychology and Aging, 24*(2), 513–517. doi:10.1037/a0015897.

Alterovitz, S. S. R. & Mendelsohn, G. A. (2013). Relationship goals of middle-aged, young-old, and old-old internet daters: An analysis of online personal ads. *Journal of Aging Studies, 27*(2), 159–165. doi:10.1016/j.jaging.2012.12.006.

Apitzsch, U. & Inowlocki, L. (2000). Biographical analysis: A 'German' school. In P. Chamberlayne, J. Bornat & T. Wengraf (eds), *The turn to biographical methods in social science: comparative issues and examples* (pp 53–70). London; New York: Routledge.

Appadurai, A. (1996). *Modernity at large – cultural dimensions in globalization*. Minneapolis: University of Minnesota Press.

Aquilino, W. S. (1994). Later life parental divorce and widowhood – Impact on young adults assessment of parent–child relations. *Journal of Marriage and the Family, 56*(4), 908–922. doi:10.2307/353602

Arber, S. (2004). Gender, Marital Status and Ageing: Linking Material, Health and Social Resources. *Journal of Aging Studies* (18), doi.org/10.1016/j.jaging.2003.09.007.

Arber, S., Davidson, K. & Ginn, J. (2003). Changing Approaches to Gender and Later Life. In S. Arber, K. Davidson & J. Ginn (eds), *Gender & ageing: Changing roles and relationships* (pp 1–14). Maidenhead: Open University Press.

Arranz Becker, O., Salzburger, V., Lois, N. & Nauck, B. (2013). What narrows the stepgap? Closeness between parents and adult (step) children in Germany. *Journal of Marriage and Family, 75*(5), 1130–1148. doi:10.1111/jomf.12052.

Baars, J. (2013). Critical turns of aging, narrative and time. *International Journal of Ageing and Later Life, 7*(2), 143–165.

Baars, J. & Visser, H. (2007). *Aging and time: Multidisciplinary perspectives*. Amityville, N.Y.: Baywood Pub. doi: 10.3384/ijal.1652-8670.1272a7.

Bauman, Z. (2003). *Liquid love*. Cambridge: Polity.

Beck, U. & Beck-Gernsheim, E. (2002). *Individualization: Institutionalized individualism and its social and political consequences*. London; Thousand Oaks, CA: SAGE.

Becker, G. S. (1981). *A treatise on the family*. Cambridge, MA: Harvard University Press.

Beckman, N., Waern, M., Gustafson, D. & Skoog, I. (2008). Secular trends in self reported sexual activity and satisfaction in Swedish 70 year olds: cross sectional survey of four populations, 1971–2001. *BMJ*, 337(7662), 151–154. doi:10.1136/bmj.a279.

Bengtsson, V. (2006). Theorizing and social gerontology. *International Journal of Ageing and Later Life, 1*(1), 5–9. doi: 10.3384/ijal.1652-8670.06115.

Bennett, K. M., Arnott, L. & Soulsby, L. K. (2013). 'You're not getting married for the moon and the stars': The uncertainties of older British widowers about the idea of new romantic relationships. *Journal of Aging Studies, 27*(4), 499–506. doi:10.1016/j.jaging.2013.03.006.

Benson, J. J. & Coleman, M. (2016a). Older adult descriptions of living apart together. *Family Relations, 65*(3), 439–449. doi:10.1111/fare.12203.

Benson, J. J. & Coleman, M. (2016b). Older adults developing a preference for Living Apart Together. *Journal of Marriage and Family, 78*(3), 797–812. doi: 10.1111/jomf.12292.

Berggren, H. & Trägårdh, L. (2006). *Är svensken människa? Gemenskap och oberoende i det moderna Sverige [Is the Swede a human being? Community and independence in modern Sweden]*. Stockholm: Norstedt.

Berggren, H. & Trägårdh, L. (2012). Social trust and radical individualism – The paradox at heart of Nordic capitalism. In *Equality, individuality and social trust: The Nordic way* (pp 12–29): The Swedish Institute.

Bildtgård, T. (2000). The sexuality of elderly people on film: Visual limitations. *Journal of aging and identity, 5*(3), 169–183.

Bildtgård, T. & Öberg, P. (2015a). Förändrade intimitetsformer bland äldre i det senmoderna samhället [Changing forms of intimacy among older people in late modern society]. *Sociologisk Forskning, 52*(1), 5–31.

Bildtgård, T. & Öberg, P. (2015b). Time as a structuring condition behind new intimate relationships in later life. *Ageing & Society, 35*(7), 1505–1528. doi:10.1017/S0144686X14000452.

Bildtgård, T. & Öberg, P. (2017). New intimate relationships in later life – Consequences for the social and filial network? *Journal of Family Issues, 38*(3), 381–405. doi:10.1177/0192513X15579503.

Bodenmann, G. (2005). Dyadic coping and its significance for marital functioning. In T. A. Revenson, K. Kayser, & G. Bodenmann (eds), *Couples coping with stress: Emerging perspectives on dyadic coping. Decade of behavior* (pp 33–49). Washington DC: American Psychological Association.

Bookwala, J. & Jacobs, J. (2004). Age, marital processes, and depressed affect. *The Gerontologist, 44*(3), 328–338.

Borell, K. (2001). I stället för äktenskap: Åldrande och nya intimitetsformer [Instead of marriage: Aging and new forms of intimacy]. *Gerontologia, 15*(2), 147–156.

Bourdieu, P., Chamboredon, J. C., Passeron, J. C. & Krais, B. (1991). *The craft of sociology: epistemological preliminaries.* Berlin; New York: Walter de Gruyter.

Brown, S. L., Bulanda, J. R. & Lee, G. R. (2005). The significance of nonmarital cohabitation: Marital status and mental health benefits among middle-aged and older adults. *The Journals of Gerontology Series B: Psychological Sciences and Social Sciences, 60*(1), S21–S29. doi:10.1093/geronb/60.1.S21.

Brown, S. L. & Kawamura, S. (2010). Relationship quality among cohabitors and marrieds in older adulthood. *Social Science Research, 39*(5), 777–786. doi:10.1016/j.ssresearch.2010.04.010.

Brown, S. L. & Lin, I.-F. (2012). The gray divorce revolution: Rising divorce among middle-aged and older adults, 1990–2010. *The Journals of Gerontology Series B: Psychological Sciences and Social Sciences, 67*(6), 731–741. doi:10.1093/geronb/gbs089.

Brown, S. L. & Shinohara, S. K. (2013). Dating relationships in older adulthood: A national portrait. *Journal of Marriage and Family, 75*(5), 1194–1202. doi:10.1111/jomf.12065.

Brown, S. L. & Wright, M. R. (2016). Older adults' attitudes toward cohabitation: Two decades of change. *The Journals of Gerontology. Series B, Psychological Sciences and Social Sciences, 71*(4), 755–764. doi:10.1093/geronb/gbv053.

Bulcroft, K. & O'Connor, M. (1986). The importance of dating relationships on quality of life for older persons. *Family Relations, 35*(3), 397–401. doi: 10.2307/584367.

Bulcroft, R. A. & Bulcroft, K. A. (1991). The nature and functions of dating in later life. *Research on Aging, 13*(2), 244–260. doi:10.1177/0164027591132007.

Butler, R. N. & Lewis, M. I. (2002). *The new love and sex after 60* (rev. edn.). New York: Ballantine Books.

Calasanti, T. & Kiecolt, K. J. (2007). Diversity among late-life couples. *Generations: Journal of the American Society on Aging, 31*(3), 10–17.

Cantor, M. (1979). Neighbours and friends: An overlooked resource in the informal support system. *Research on Aging, 1*(4), 434–463.

Carpenter, L. M., Nathanson, C. A. & Kim, Y. J. (2006). Sex after 40?: Gender, ageism, and sexual partnering in midlife. *Journal of Aging Studies, 20*(2), 93–106. doi:10.1016/j.jaging.2005.06.003.

Carr, D. (2004). The desire to date and remarry among older widows and widowers. *Journal of Marriage and Family, 66*(4), 1051–1068. doi:10.1111/j.0022-2445.2004.00078.x.

Carr, D. & Boerner, K. (2013). Dating after late-life spousal loss: Does it compromise relationships with adult children? *Journal of Aging Studies, 27*(4), 487–498. doi:10.1016/j.jaging.2012.12.009.

Carr, D., Freedman, V. & Cornman, J. (2016). *Second time around: Remarriage, marital quality and life satisfaction among older adults.* Paper presented at the GSA Annual scientific meeting, New Orleans.

Carstensen, L. L. (1992). Social and emotional patterns in adulthood – support for socioemotional selectivity theory. *Psychology and Aging, 7*(3), 331–338. doi:10.1037/0882-7974.7.3.331.

Carstensen, L. L. (1995). Evidence for a life-span theory of socioemotional selectivity. *Current Directions in Psychological Science, 4*(5), 151–156. doi:10.1111/1467-8721.ep11512261.

Carstensen, L. L., Isaacowitz, D. M. & Charles, S. T. (1999). Taking time seriously – A theory of socioemotional selectivity. *American Psychologist, 54*(3), 165–181. doi:10.1037//0003-066x.54.3.165.

Cherlin, A. J. (1992). *Marriage, divorce, remarriage.* (rev. edn.). Cambridge, MA: Harvard University Press.

Cherlin, A. J. (2004). The deinstitutionalization of American marriage. *Journal of Marriage and Family, 66*(4), 848–861. doi:10.1111/j.0022-2445.2004.00058.x.

Cherlin, A.J. (2009). The origins of the ambivalent acceptance of divorce. *Journal of Marriage and Family, 71*(2), 226–229.

Chevan, A. (1996). As cheaply as one: Cohabitation in the older population. *Journal of Marriage and the Family, 58*(3), 656–667. doi:10.2307/353726.

Connidis, I. A. (2010). *Family ties and aging* (2nd ed.). Thousand Oaks, CA: Pine Forge Press (SAGE).

Cooney, T. M. & Dunne, K. (2001). Intimate relationships in later life – Current realities, future prospects. *Journal of Family Issues, 22*(7), 838–858. doi:10.1177/019251301022007003.

Cumming, E. & Henry, W. E. (1961). *Growing old, the process of disengagement.* New York: Basic Books.

Daatland, S. O. (2007). Marital history and intergenerational solidarity: The impact of divorce and unmarried cohabitation. *Journal of Social Issues, 63*(4), 809–825. doi: 10.1111/j.1540-4560.2007.00538.x.

Dannefer, D. & Settersten Jr, R. A. (2010). The study of the life course: Implications for social gerontology. In D. Dannefer & C. Phillipson (eds), *The SAGE handbook of social gerontology* (pp 3–19). London: SAGE Publications.

Davidson, K. (2001). Late life widowhood, selfishness and new partnership choices: a gendered perspective. *Ageing and Society, 21*(3), 297–317. doi.org/10.1017/S0144686X01008169.

Davidson, K. (2002). Gender differences in new partnership choices and constraints for older widows and widowers. *Ageing International, 27*(4), 43–60. doi: 10.1007/s12126-002-1014-0.

Davidson, K. & Fennell, G. (2002) New intimate relationships in later life. *Ageing International, 27*(4), 3–10.

Davidson, K. & Fennell, G. (eds). (2004). *Introduction: New intimate relationships in later life* (pp. vii–xv). New Brunswick: Transaction Publishers.

de Graaf, P. M. & Kalmijn, M. (2006). Divorce motives in a period of rising divorce – Evidence from a Dutch life-history survey. *Journal of Family Issues, 27*(4), 483–505. doi:10.1177/0192513x05283982.

de Jong Gierveld, J. (2002). The dilemmas of repartnering: Considerations of older men and women entering new intimate relationships late in life. *Ageing International, 27*(4), 61–78. doi: 10.1007/s12126-002-1015-z.

de Jong Gierveld, J. (2004a). Remarriage, unmarried cohabitation, living apart together: Partner relationships following bereavement or divorce. *Journal of Marriage and Family, 66*(1), 236–243.

de Jong Gierveld, J. (2004b). The dilemma of repartnering: Considerations of older men and women entering new intimate relationships late in life. In K. Davidson & G. Fennel (eds), *Intimacy in later life* (pp 85–104). New Brunswick: Transaction Publishers.

de Jong Gierveld, J. & Merz, E. M. (2013). Parents' Partnership Decision Making After Divorce or Widowhood: The Role of (Step)Children. *Journal of Marriage and Family, 75*(5), 1098–1113. doi:10.1111/jomf.12061.

Denzin, N. K. (1989). *Interpretive biography.* Newbury Park: Sage.

Drefahl, S. (2012). Do the married really live longer? The role of cohabitation and socioeconomic status. *Journal of Marriage and Family, 74*(3), 462–475. doi:10.1111/j.1741-3737.2012.00968.x.

Duncan, S., Phillips, M., Roseneil, S., Carter, J. & Stoilova, M. (2013). *Living Apart Together: Uncoupling intimacy and co-residence.* Available on: www.researchgate.net/publication/294444860_Living_apart_together_uncoupling_intimacy_and_co-residence (Accessed March 6, 2017).

Dykstra, P. A. (1993). The differential availability of relationships and the provision and effectiveness of support to older adults. *Journal of Social and Personal Relationships, 10*(3), 355–370. doi:10.1177/0265407593103004.

Dykstra, P. A. (2006). Off the beaten track – Childlessness and social integration in late life. *Research on Aging, 28*(6), 749–767. doi:10.1177/0164027506291745.

Dykstra, P. A. & de Jong Gierveld, J. D. (2004). Gender and marital-history differences in emotional and social loneliness among Dutch older adults. *Canadian Journal on Aging-Revue Canadienne Du Vieillissement, 23*(2), 141–155. doi:10.1353/cja.2004.0018.

Elder, G. H. (1994). Time, human agency and social change – perspectives on the life-course. *Social Psychology Quarterly, 57*(1), 4–15.

Esping-Andersen, G. (1990). *The three worlds of welfare capitalism.* Cambridge: Polity.

European Commission. (2009). *Healthy life years in the European Union – Facts and figures 2005.*

Evertsson, L. & Nyman, C. (2013). On the other side of couplehood: single women in Sweden exploring life without a partner. *Families, Relationships and Societies, 2*(1): 61–78.

Fennell, G. (2004). Transitions in mid-adult to late life. *Ageing International, 29*(4), 309–316.

Ferrarotti, F. (2003). *On the science of uncertainty: the biographical method in social research.* Lanham, MD: Lexington Books.

Funk, L. & Kobayashi, K. (2014). From motivations to accounts: An interpretative analysis of 'Living Apart Together' relationships in mid- to later-life couples. *Journal of Family Issues, 37*(8), 1101–1122.

Ganong, L. H. & Coleman, M. (2017). *Stepfamily relationships: development, dynamics, and interventions.* New York: Springer.

Ghazanfareeon Karlsson, S. (2006). *Tillsammans men var för sig: Om särboenderelationer mellan äldre kvinnor och män i Sverige. [Together but still apart: Elderly women and men Living Apart Together in Sweden].* Ph.D. Nr 47, Umeå University, Umeå.

Ghazanfareeon Karlsson, S. & Borell, K. (2002). Intimacy and autonomy, gender and ageing: Living apart together. *Ageing International, 27*(4), 11–26. doi:10.1007/s12126-002-1012-2.

Ghazanfareeon Karlsson, S. & Borell, K. (2005). A home of their own. Women's boundary work in LAT-relationships. *Journal of Aging Studies, 19*(1), 73–84. doi:10.1016/j.jaging.2004.03.008.

Giddens, A. (1991). *Modernity and self-identity: self and society in the late modern age.* Stanford, CA: Stanford University Press.

Giddens, A. (1992). *The transformation of intimacy: sexuality, love and eroticism in modern societies.* Cambridge: Polity.

Gilleard, C. J. & Higgs, P. (2000). *Cultures of ageing: self, citizen, and the body.* Harlow; New York: Prentice Hall.

Gilleard, C. J. & Higgs, P. (2010). Aging without agency: Theorizing the fourth age. *Aging & Mental Health, 14*(2), 121–128. doi:10.1080/13607860903228762.

Glaser, B. G. & Strauss, A. L. (1967). *The discovery of grounded theory; strategies for qualitative research.* Chicago, IL: Aldine Pub. Co.

Glaser, K., Stuchbury, R., Tomassini, C. & Askham, J. (2008). The long-term consequences of partnership dissolution for support in later life in the United Kingdom. *Ageing & Society, 28*(03). doi:10.1017/s0144686x07006642.

Gott, M. (2005). *Sexuality, sexual health and ageing.* Maidenhead: Open University Press.

Gott, M. & Hinchliff, S. (2003a). How important is sex in later life? The views of older people. *Social Science & Medicine, 56*(8), 1617–1628. doi:10.1016/s0277-9536(02)00180-6.

Gott, M. & Hinchliff, S. (2003b). Sex and ageing: A gendered issue. In S. Arber, K. Davidson, & J. Ginn (eds), *Gender and Ageing: Changing Roles and Relationships* (pp. 63–78). Maidenhead: Open University Press.

Government bill (1997/98:113) *Nationell plan för äldrepolitiken [National action plan for politics regarding senior citizens].* Available on www.regeringen.se/rattsdokument/proposition/1998/04/prop.-199798113/ (Acessed March 6, 2017).

Gray, M., De Vaus, D., Qu, L. & Stanton, D. (2010). Divorce and the wellbeing of older Australians. *Ageing and Society, 31*(03), 475–498. doi:10.1017/s0144686x10001017.

Guillemard, A. M. (2000). Age integration in Europe: Increasing or decreasing? *Gerontologist, 40*(3), 301–302. doi.org/10.1093/geront/40.3.301.

Ha, J. H. (2008). Changes in support from confidants, children, and friends following widowhood. *Journal of Marriage and Family, 70*(2), 306–318. doi:10.1111/j.1741-3737.2008.00483.x.

Hackstaff, K. B. (1999). *Marriage in a culture of divorce.* Philadelphia, PA: Temple University Press.

Hagestad, G. O. (1986). The aging society as a context for family-life. *Daedalus, 115*(1), 119–139.

Hagestad, G. O. (1988). Demographic change and the life-course – some emerging trends in the family realm. *Family Relations, 37*(4), 405–410. doi:10.2307/584111.

Hagestad, G. O. & Neugarten, B. L. (1985). Age and the life course. In R. Binstock & E. Shanas (eds), *Handbook of Aging and the Social Sciences* (2nd edn.) (pp. 35–61). New York: Van Nostrand Reinhold.

Hantrais, L. (1997) Exploring relationships between social policy and changing family forms within the European Union. *European Journal of Population, 13*(4), 339–379.

Heidegger, M. (2008 [1927]). *Being and time* (J. Macquarrie & E. Robinson, trans.). New York: HarperPerennial/Modern Thought.

Heikkinen, R.-L. (2000). Ageing in an autobiographical context. *Ageing & Society, 20*(4), 467–483.

Heikkinen, R.-L. (2004). The experience of ageing and advanced old age: a ten-year follow-up. *Ageing & Society, 24*(4), 567–582. doi:10.1017/s0144686x04001837.

Hiekel, N., Liefbroer, A. C. & Poortman, A. R. (2014). Understanding diversity in the meaning of cohabitation across Europe. *European Journal of Population, 30*(4), 391–410. doi:10.1007/s10680-014-9321-1.

Hinchliff, S. & Gott, M. (2008). Challenging social myths and stereotypes of women and aging: Heterosexual women talk about sex. *Journal of Women & Aging, 20*(1–2), 65–81. doi:10.1300/J074v20n01_06.

Hurd Clarke, L. (2005). Remarriage in later life: older women's negotiation of power, resources and domestic labor. *Journal of Women & Aging, 17*(4), 21–41. doi:10.1300/J074v17n04_03.

Hyde, M. & Higgs, P. (2004). The shifting sands of time: Results from the English longitudinal study of ageing on multiple transitions in later life. *Aging International, 29*(4), 317–332. doi: 10.1007/s12126-004-1002-7.

Inglehart, R. F. (2008). Changing values among western publics from 1970 to 2006. *West European Politics, 31*(1–2), 130–146. doi:10.1080/01402380701834747.

Inglehart, R. F. & Baker, W. E. (2000). Modernization, cultural change, and the persistence of traditional values. *American Sociological Review, 65*(1), 19–51. doi:10.2307/2657288.

Jamieson, L. (1988). *Intimacy: Personal relationships in modern societies.* Cambridge: Polity.

Jamieson, L. (1999). Intimacy transformed? A critical look at the 'pure relationship'. *Sociology: The Journal of the British Sociological Association, 33*(3), 477–494. doi:10.1017/s0038038599000310.

Jamieson, L. & Simpson, R. (2013). *Living alone: globalization, identity, and belonging*. Basingstoke; New York: Palgrave Macmillan.

Jones, R. L. (2002). 'That's very rude, I shouldn't be telling you that': Older women talking about sex. *Narrative Inquiry, 12*(1), 121–143. doi:10.1075/ni.12.1.18jon.

Jönsson, H. (1998). Känsla har ingen ålder. Om sex och ungdomlighet i pensionärsnoveller. [Emotions are age-less: Sex and youthfulness in retirement novels]. *Aldring & Eldre – Gerontologisk Magasin* 1, 20–25.

Kahn, R. L. & Antonucci, T. C. (1980). Convoys over the life course: Attachment, roles and social support. In P. B. Baltes & O. Brim (eds), *Life-span development and behavior* (pp 253–286). New York: Academic Press.

Katz, S. & Calasanti, T. (2015). Critical perspectives on successful aging: Does it 'appeal more than it illuminates'? *Gerontologist, 55*(1), 26–33. doi:10.1093/geront/gnu027.

Kaufman, G. & Uhlenberg, P. (1998). Effects of life course transitions on the quality of relationships between adult children and their parents. *Journal of Marriage and the Family, 60*(4), 924–938. doi:10.2307/353635.

Keith, P. (2003). Resources, family ties, and well-being of never married men and women. *Journal of Gerontological Social Work, 42*(2), 51–75. doi.org/10.1300/J083v42n02_05.

Kiernan, K. (2002). Cohabitation in Western Europe: Trends, issues, and implications. In A. Booth & A. Crouter (eds), *Just living together: implications of cohabitation on families, children, and social policy* (pp xi, 289). Mahwah, NJ: L. Erlbaum Associates.

King, V. & Scott, M. E. (2005). A comparison of cohabiting relationships among older and younger adults. *Journal of Marriage and Family, 67*(2), 271–285. doi:10.1111/j.0022-2445.2005.00115.x.

Klinenberg, E. (2012). *Going solo: the extraordinary rise and surprising appeal of living alone*. New York: Penguin Press.

Kohli, M. (1986). Social organization and subjective construction of the life-course. In F. E. Weinevi & L. Sherrod (eds), *Human Development and the Life-course: Multidisciplinary Perspectives*. New Jersey: Lawrence Estbaum Associates Inc Publ.

Kohli, M. (2007). The institutionalization of the life course: Looking back to look ahead. *Research in Human Development, 4*(3), 279–281. doi.org/10.1080/15427600701663122.

Koren, C. (2011). Continuity and discontinuity: The case of second couplehood in old age. *Gerontologist, 51*(5), 687–698. doi:10.1093/geront/gnr018.

Koren, C. (2015). The intertwining of second couplehood and old age. *Ageing & Society, 35*(9), 1864–1888. doi: doi.org/10.1017/S0144686X14000294.

Laslett, P. (1989). *A fresh map of life: The emergence of the third age.* London: Weidenfeld and Nicolson.

Lee, A. (2004). Signposts of aging: The transitions to later life of a sample of older gay men. *Aging International, 29*(4), 368–384. doi:10.1007/s12126-004-1005-4.

Levin, I. (2004). Living Apart Together: A new family form. *Current Sociology, 52*(2), 223–240. doi:10.1177/0011392104041809.

Levin, I. & Trost, J. (1999). Living apart together. *Community, work and family, 2*(3), 279–294.

Levinger, G. (1983). Development and change. In H. H. Kelley, E. Berscheid, A. Christensen, J. H. Harvey, T. L. Huston, G. Levinger, E. McClintock, L. A. Peplau, & D. R. Peterson (eds), *Close relationships.* New York: W.H. Freeman.

Lewin, B. (2000). *Sex in Sweden. On the Swedish sexual life.* Stockholm: The National Institute of Public Health.

Litwak, E. (1985). *Helping the elderly: The complementary roles of informal networks and formal systems.* New York: Guilford Press.

Lopata, H. Z. (1973). *Widowhood in an American city.* Cambridge, MA: Schenkman Pub. Co.; distributed by General Learning Press Morristown, N.J.

Lopata, H. Z. (1979). *Women as widows: Support systems.* New York: Elsevier, North Holland.

Lopata, H. Z. (1981). Widowhood and husband sanctification. *Journal of Marriage and Family, 43*(2), 439–450.

Lopata, H. Z. (1996). *Current widowhood: myths & realities.* Thousand Oaks, CA: Sage Publications.

Luhmann, N. (1986). *Love as passion: The codification of intimacy.* Cambridge: Polity.

Mahay, J. & Lewin, A. C. (2007). Age and the desire to marry. *Journal of Family Issues, 28*(5), 706–723. doi:10.1177/0192513x06297272.

Malta, S. & Farquharson, K. (2014). The initiation and progression of late-life romantic relationships. *Journal of Sociology, 50*(3), 237–251. doi:10.1177/1440783312442254.

Marshall, B. L. & Katz, S. (2002). Forever functional: Sexual fitness and the ageing male body. *Body & Society, 8*(4), 43–70. doi:10.1177/1357034X02008004003.

Marshall, H. (2004). Midlife loss of parents: The transition from adult child to orphan. *Aging International, 29*(4), 351–367. doi:10.1007/s12126-004-1004-5.

McDowell, I. (2006). *Measuring health: A guide to rating scales and questionnaires* (3rd ed.). Oxford; New York: Oxford University Press.

McFadden, S. H. & Atchley, R. C. (2001). *Aging and the meaning of time: A multidisciplinary exploration.* New York: Springer Pub.

McWilliams, S. & Barrett, A. E. (2014). Online dating in middle and later life: Gendered expectations and experiences. *Journal of Family Issues, 35*(3), 411–436. doi:10.1177/0192513x12468437.

Mehta, K. K. (2002). Perceptions of remarriage by widowed people in Singapore. *Aging International, 27*(4), 93–107. doi:10.1007/s12126-002-1017-x.

Messeri, P., Silverstein, M. & Litwak, E. (1993). Choosing optimal support groups – a review and reformulation. *Journal of Health and Social Behavior, 34*(2), 122–137. doi:10.2307/2137239.

Moen, P., Kim, J. E. & Hofmeister, H. (2001). Couples' work/retirement transitions, gender, and marital quality. *Social Psychology Quarterly, 64*(1), 55–71. doi:10.2307/3090150.

Montenegro, X. P. (2004). *The divorce experience: A study of divorce at midlife and beyond.* Washington, D.C.: AARP.

Moore, A.J. & Stratton, D.C. (2004). The 'current woman' in an older widower's life. In K. Davidson & G. Fennell (eds), *Intimacy in Later Life* (pp. 121–142). New Brunswick: Transaction Publishers.

Moorman, S. M., Booth, A. & Fingerman, K. L. (2006). Women's romantic relationships after widowhood. *Journal of Family Issues, 27*(9), 1281–1304. doi:10.1177/0192513x06289096

Mortimer, J. T. & Shanahan, M. J. (eds) (2003). *Handbook of the life course.* New York: Kluwer Academic/Plenum Publishers.

Moss, B. F. & Schwebel, A. I. (1993). Defining intimacy in romantic relationships. *Family Relations, 42*(1), 31–37. doi:10.2307/584918.

Moustgaard, H. & Martikainen, P. (2009). Nonmarital cohabitation among older Finnish men and women: socioeconomic characteristics and forms of union dissolution. *The Journals of Gerontology. Series B, Psychological Sciences and Social Sciences, 64*(4), 507–516. doi:10.1093/geronb/gbp024.

Neugarten, B. L. (1969). Continuities and discontinuities of psychological issues into adult life. *Human Development, 12*(2), 121–130. doi:10.1159/000270858.

Öberg, P. (1997). *Livet som berättelse. Om biografi och åldrande. [Life as narrative. On biography and ageing].* Uppsala: Uppsala University.

Öberg, P. (2000). Att åldras i ett estetiserande konsumtionssamhälle – En studie av kroppsbild [Ageing in an aestheticized consumer culture – A study of body image]. *Gerontologiska skrifter* 8, 7-31.

Öberg, P., Andersson, L. & Bildtgård, T. (2016). Skyddar en parrelation på äldre dar mot ensamhet? [Does couplehood in later life protect against loneliness?]. *Socialvetenskaplig tidskrift, 23*(1), 19–36.

O'Hara, K. (1998). *Comparative family policy: Eight countries' stories.* Canadian Policy Research Networks. Research report. Available at: www.cprn.org/doc.cfm?l=en&doc=442.

Orloff, A. S. (2006). From maternalism to 'employment for all': State policies to promote women's employment across the affluent democracies. In J. D. Levy (ed.), *The state after statism: New state activities in the age of liberalization* (pp 230–270). Cambridge, MA: Harvard University Press.

Owen, L. & Flynn, M. (2004). Changing work: Mid-to-late life transitions in employment. *Ageing International, 29*(4), 333–350. doi:10.1007/s12126-004-1003-6.

Parsons, T. & Bales, R. F. (1955). *Family: Socialization and interaction process.* New York: Free Press.

Patton, M. Q. (2002). *Qualitative research and evaluation methods* (3rd edn.). London: Sage.

Penning, M. J. & Wu, Z. (2014). Marital status, childlessness, and social support among older Canadians. *Canadian Journal on Aging/ Revue Canadienne du Vieillissement, 33*(4), 426–447. doi:10.1017/ s0714980814000385.

Peters, A. & Liefbroer, A. C. (1997). Beyond marital status: Partner history and well-being in old age. *Journal of Marriage and the Family, 59*(3), 687–699. doi:10.2307/353954.

Pettersson, T. & Esmer, Y. R. (2008). *Changing values, persisting cultures: Case studies in value change.* Leiden; Boston, MA: Brill.

Phillipson, C. & Biggs, S. (1998). Modernity and identity: Themes and perspectives in the study of older adults. *Journal of Aging and Identity, 3*(1), 11–23. doi:10.1023/A:1022888621674.

Pimouguet, C., Rizzuto, D., Schon, P., Shakersain, B., Angleman, S., Lagergren, M. & Xu, W. L. (2016). Impact of living alone on institutionalization and mortality: A population-based longitudinal study. *European Journal of Public Health, 26*(1), 182–187. doi:10.1093/ eurpub/ckv052.

Plummer, K. (2001). *Documents of life 2: an invitation to a critical humanism.* London; Thousand Oaks, CA: Sage Publications.

Popenoe, D. (1987). Beyond the nuclear family: A statistical portrait of the changing family in Sweden. *Journal of Marriage and Family, 49*(1), 173–183.

Potts, A., Grace, V. M., Vares, T. & Gavey, N. (2006). 'Sex for life'? Men's counter-stories on 'erectile dysfunction', male sexuality and ageing. *Sociology of Health & Illness, 28*(3), 306–329. doi:10.1111/j.1467-9566.2006.00494.x.

Rees Jones, I., Hyde, M., Victor, C. R., Wiggins, R. D., Gilleard, C. & Higgs, P. (2008). *Ageing in a consumer society: From passive to active consumption in Britain*. Bristol: Policy Press.

Régnier-Loilier, A., Beaujouan, E. & Villeneuve-Gokalp, C. (2009). Neither single, nor in a couple. A study of living apart together in France. *Demographic Research, 21*(4), 75–108. doi: 10.4054/DemRes.2009.21.4.

Riley, M. W. (1998). A life-course approach: Autobiographical notes. In J. Z. Giele & G. H. J. Elder (eds), *Methods in Life-course Research. Qualitative and Quantitative Approaches* (pp 28–51). London: Sage.

Ronström, O. (1998). Pensionärsnöjen och modernitet [Retirement pleasures and modernity]. In O. Ronström (ed.), *Pigga pensionärer och populärkultur [Lively retirees and popular culture]* (pp 229–278). Stockholm: Carlssons.

Roos, J.-P. (2005). Context, authenticity, referentiality, reflexivity: Back to basics in autobiography. In R. L. Miller (ed.), *Biographical research methods* (Vol. IV, pp 163–172). London; Thousand Oaks, CA: SAGE Publications.

Rosenmayr, L. & Köckeis, E. (1963). Propositions for a sociological theory of aging and the family. *UNESCO International Social Science Journal, 15*(3), 410–426.

Sandberg, L. (2011). *Getting intimate: A feminist analysis of old age, masculinity & sexuality*. Ph.D. dissertation. Linköping: Linköping University.

Sandberg, L. (2015). Sex, sexuality and later life. In J. Twigg & W. Martin (eds), *Routledge Handbook of Cultural Gerontology* (pp 218–225). London: Routledge.

Shapiro, A. (2003). Later-life divorce and parent-adult child contact and proximity – A longitudinal analysis. *Journal of Family Issues, 24*(2), 264–285. doi:10.1177/0192513x02250099.

Sill, J. S. (1980). Disengagement reconsidered: Awareness of finitude. *The Gerontologist, 20*(4), 457–462. doi:10.1093/geront/20.4.457.

Silverstein, M. & Giarrusso, R. (2010). Aging and family life: A decade review. *Journal of Marriage and Family, 72*(5), 1039–1058. doi:10.1111/j.1741-3737.2010.00749.x.

Smart, C. & Neale, B. (1999). *Family fragments?* Cambridge: Polity.

Soons, J. P. M. & Kalmijn, M. (2009). Is marriage more than cohabitation? Well-being differences in 30 European countries. *Journal of Marriage and Family,* 71(5), 1141–1157. doi: 10.1111/j.1741-3737.2009.00660.x.

Stanley, S. M., Whitton, S. W. & Markman, H. J. (2004). Interpersonal commitment and premarital or nonmarital cohabitation. *Journal of Family Issues,* 25(4), 496–519. doi:10.1177/0192513x03257797.

Statistics Sweden (2016) Gifta lever längre [Marrieds live longer]. *Välfärd [Welfare],* (3), 10–12.

Steitz, J. A. & Welker, K. G. (1991). Remarriage in later life: A critique and review of the literature. *Journal of Women & Aging,* 2(4), 81–90. doi:10.1300/J074v02n04_07.

Sternberg, R. J. (1986). A triangular theory of love. *Psychological Review,* 93(2), 119–135. doi:10.1037/0033-295x.93.2.119.

Stevens, N. (2004). Re-engaging: New partnerships in late-life widowhood. In K. Davidson & G. Fennell (eds), *Intimacy in Later Life* (pp. 47–64). New Brunswick: Transaction Publishers.

Stinnett, N. Mittelstet Carter, L. & Montgomery, J.E. (1972). Older persons' perceptions of their marriages. *Journal of Marriage and Family,* 34(4), 665–670.

Strauss, A. & Corbin, J. (1994). Grounded theory methodology. In N. K. Denzin & Y. S. Lincoln (eds), *Handbook of qualitative research.* Thousand Oaks, CA: Sage Publications.

Suanet, B., van der Pas, S. & van Tilburg, T. G. (2013). Who is in the stepfamily? Change in stepparents' family boundaries between 1992 and 2009. *Journal of Marriage and Family,* 75(5), 1070–1083. doi:10.1111/jomf.12053.

Sundström, G. & Johansson, L. (2004). *Framtidens anhörigomsorg [The future of informal care].* Stockholm: National Board of Health and Welfare (available at: http://swepub.kb.se/bib/swepub:oai:DiVA.org:hj-723).

Talbott, M. M. (1998). Older widows' attitudes towards men and remarriage. *Journal of Aging Studies,* 12(4), 429–449. doi:10.1016/s0890-4065(98)90028-7.

Tetley, J., Lee, D. M., Nazroo, J. & Hinchliff, S. (2016). Let's talk about sex – what do older men and women say about their sexual relations and sexual activities? A qualitative analysis of ELSA Wave 6 data. *Ageing & Society.* doi:10.1017/S0144686X16001203.

Thornton, A. & Young-DeMarco, L. (2001). Four decades of trends in attitudes toward family issues in the United States: The 1960s through the 1990s. *Journal of Marriage and Family, 63*(4), 1009–1037. doi:10.1111/j.1741-3737.2001.01009.x.

Tornstam, L. (2005). *Gerotranscendence: a developmental theory of positive aging*. New York: Springer Pub. Co.

Trost, J. (1978). A renewed social institution: Non-marital cohabitation. *Acta sociologica, 21*(4), 303–315.

Trost, J. & Levin, I. (2000). *Särbo : ett par – två hushåll [One couple – two housholds]*. Lund: Studentlitteratur.

Umberson, D. (1992). Gender, marital-status and the social-control of health behavior. *Social Science & Medicine, 34*(8), 907–917. doi:10.1016/0277-9536(92)90259-s.

Upton-Davis, K. (2015). Subverting gendered norms of cohabitation: Living Apart Together for women over 45. *Journal of Gender Studies, 24*(1), 104–116. doi:10.1080/09589236.2013.861346.

van den Hoonaard, D. K. (2004). Attitudes of older widows and widowers in New Brunswick, Canada, towards new partnerships. In K. Davidson & G. Fennel (eds), *Intimacy in later life* (pp 105–119). New Brunswick: Transaction Publishers.

van Solinge, H. & Henkens, K. (2005). Couples' adjustment to retirement: A multi-actor panel study. *The Journals of Gerontology Series B: Psychological Sciences and Social Sciences, 60*(1), S11–S20. doi:10.1093/geronb/60.1.S11.

Vares, T. (2009). Reading the 'sexy oldie': Gender, age(ing) and embodiment. *Sexualities, 12*(4), 503–524. doi:10.1177/1363460709105716.

Vaupel, J. W. (2010). Biodemography of human ageing. *Nature, 464*(7288), 536–542. doi:10.1038/nature08984.

Verbrugge, L. M. (1979). Marital-status and health. *Journal of Marriage and the Family, 41*(2), 267–285. doi:10.2307/351696.

Vespa, J. (2013). Relationship transitions among older cohabitors: The role of health, wealth, and family ties. *Journal of Marriage and Family, 75*(4), 933–949. doi:10.1111/jomf.12040.

Waite, L. J. (1995). Does marriage matter? *Demography, 32*(4), 483–507. doi:10.2307/2061670.

Waite, L. J., Laumann, E. O., Das, A. & Schumm, L. P. (2009). Sexuality: measures of partnerships, practices, attitudes, and problems in the National Social Life, Health, and Aging Study. *The Journals of Gerontology. Series B, Psychological Sciences and Social Sciences, 64* Suppl 1, i56–66. doi:10.1093/geronb/gbp038.

Walzer, S. (2008). Redoing gender through divorce. *Journal of Social and Personal Relationships, 25*(1), 5–21. doi:10.1177/0265407507086803.

Watson, W. K., Bell, N. J. & Stelle, C. (2010). Women narrate later life remarriage: Negotiating the cultural to create the personal. *Journal of Aging Studies, 24*(4), 302–312. doi:10.1016/j.jaging.2010.07.002.

Watson, W. K. & Stelle, C. (2011). Dating for older women: Experiences and meanings of dating in later life. *Journal of Women & Aging, 23*(3), 263–275. doi:10.1080/08952841.2011.587732.

Weeks, J. (2007). *The world we have won: The remaking of erotic and intimate life*. London; New York: Routledge.

Wiik, K. A., Keizer, R. & Lappegard, T. (2012). Relationship quality in marital and cohabiting unions across Europe. *Journal of Marriage and Family, 74*(3), 389–398. doi:10.1111/j.1741-3737.2012.00967.x.

Wilmoth, J. & Koso, G. (2002). Does marital history matter? Marital status and wealth outcomes among preretirement adults. *Journal of Marriage and Family, 64*(1), 254–268. doi:10.1111/j.1741-3737.2002.00254.x.

Wu, Z. & Penning, M. J. (1997). Marital instability after midlife. *Journal of Family Issues, 18*(5), 459–478. doi:10.1177/019251397018005001.

Wu, Z. & Schimmele, C. M. (2007). Uncoupling in late life. *Generations: Journal of the American Society on Aging, 31*(3), 41–46.

Zetterberg, H. (1969). *Om sexuallivet i Sverige: värderingar, normer, beteenden i sociologisk belysning [On sex life in Sweden: values, norms, behavior in a sociological perspective]*. Stockholm: Official Report of the Swedish Government 1969:2.

Znaniecki, F. (1969). *On humanistic sociology; selected papers*. Chicago, IL: University of Chicago Press.

Notes

1   All informants have been given new names corresponding to the following convention: singles' names start with an S, LATs' with an L, cohabitants' with a C and marrieds' with an M.

2   In the book we use the term single to describe a person who is not currently in an established intimate relationship, as opposed to the demographical convention of using the term single to describe a never-married person.

3   In this book Living Apart Together (LAT) is used to describe an established intimate relationship without shared residence, where the partners both see themselves – and are perceived by others – as a couple.

4   The question used was: 'Independent of current living arrangement, what is your preferred arrangement?' The response alternatives were: 'Alone without a partner'; 'Alone, but in an established relationship (LAT)'; 'Together with a partner (husband/wife/cohabitant)'; 'Together with another/others than a partner'.

5   Since we knew from the qualitative study that many repartnered older people had originally sought a travel companion, in the survey we used a question about preferred travel company to capture companionate support. Emotional support was captured using a question about who the individual would primarily turn to for sharing confidences. Practical support was captured by two questions: preferred source for help with household tasks, and with personal hygiene.

6   This chapter builds on an article previously published in *Ageing & Society* (Bildtgård & Öberg, 2015b).

7   Of these four articles, only two were relevant to the time concept, using 'temporality' as a keyword for discussing biographical change (Heikkinen, 2000, 2004). The other two articles used the keywords 'time volunteering' and 'time series'.

Index

A

Adam, B. 159–60
adolescents, sexuality of 142–3
adult children, attitudes towards parents
    repartnering 81–2, 94–5
age, and choice of partnership forms
    52–3, 53–4
age/birth cohorts, and marriage
    preferences 52–3, 58, 77, 87–8, 106
ageing bodies, and sexual intimacy
    150–1
Alterovitz, S.S. & Mendelsohn, G.A.
    37, 108, 112
Aquilino, W.S. 105, 120
Arber, S. et al 36, 106, 113
Arranz Becker, O. et al. 77
Australia, LAT partnerships 45
autonomy
  and individualism 7, 11, 19, 133–4,
    172
  and repartnering 49–50, 82, 92, 94,
    96, 119, 123–5, 132–3
  vs. interdependence 89
  and women 68–9, 72, 90, 102, 109,
    132, 167, 178

B

Baars, J 159
'backpack' of experiences 64–5
Bauman, Z. 14, 69
Beck, U. & Beck-Gernsheim, E.
    19–20, 62, 123, 133, 177
Beckman, N. et al 136–7
Bennett, K.M. et al 58, 65, 76–8
Benson, J.J. & Coleman, M. 45, 76,
    107, 133
bereavement
  coping with grief through
    repartnering 110–11
  impact on repartnering attitudes 57–8,
    64–7
  parent—child relationships 120

and partner 'sanctification' 65–7
  role of grieving 67
Berggren, H. & Trägårdh, L. 23, 178
Bildtgård, T. 4, 135
Bildtgård, T. & Öberg, P. 77, 92, 100,
    106, 126–7
Bodenman, G. 107
Borell, K. 45, 48
Bourdieu, P. et al 75
Brown, S.L. & Kawamura, S. 44, 99
Brown, S.L. & Lin, I.–F. 24, 31, 34, 35,
    49, 58, 79, 120
Brown, S.L. & Shinohara, S. 113
Brown, S.L. & Wright, M. 88
Brown, S.L. et al 35, 37, 48, 79, 88
Bulcroft, K. & O'Connor, M. 76, 79,
    106, 108–12, 144
Bulcroft, R. & Bulcroft, K. 79, 107–8,
    123, 144

C

Calasanti, T. & Kiecolt, K.J. 35
Canada
  family opposition to repartnering 79
  LAT partnerships 45
Cantor, M. 127, 129
care in everyday life 114–15
care of the household 113–14
caregiver roles 91, 95, 166, 183
  legislation 178
  with new partners 115–16
  not being dependent on adult
    children 124, 131, 133
Carr, D. 49, 58, 65, 76, 78, 100, 105–6,
    112, 167
Carr, D. et al 65, 105–6
Carstensen, L.L. 26–7, 107, 164, 177
case studies, cohabiting Clint & Cecilia
    36–7, 37–8
Catholic European countries, divorce
    rates 31–2
Cherlin, A.J. 15–16, 31–2, 44, 48–9,
    55, 69, 87, 174

cultural contexts and social
organisation 20–5, 174–5
and union form preferences 53–4,
173–5
house ownership 94–5, 98, 101, 103,
109
housekeeping roles 113–14
'husband sanctification' 65–6
Hyde, M. & Higgs, P. 119

I

identity and intimate relationships 17,
20, 21–4, 111
independence
and LAT 79
as reason for not getting remarried
77, 79
see also autonomy
the individual 16
individualisation of society
and autonomy 7, 11, 19, 133–4, 172
cultural and organisational factors
22–5
and the transformation of intimacy 19
Inglehart, R.F. 21
inheritance issues, and remarriage 2, 49,
77, 94–5, 100, 102, 113, 122–3, 176
institution of the life course, and
societal change 13–15
international comparisons
cultural values 20–2
divorce rates 33–5
life expectancy 30–1
marriage rates amongst older people
46–7
non-marital unions amongst older
people 45–7
power relations in modern states 22–5
Internet dating 37–9
intimate relationships
background history of institutional
arrangements 15–16, 173–5
contemporary changes to (overview)
15–20, 73–4
cultural contexts and social
organisation of 20–5, 174–5
importance of developmental
perspectives 25–8
lack of a 'common language' for 76–7
life phases approach to 25–8, 175–7
new union forms 16–18
the Swedish case (overview) 177–9
see also repartnering; union forms

Ireland, marital vs non-marital unions
46
Italy
life expectancy 30
percentage of widowed and divorced
33

J

Jamieson, L.L. 18, 174

K

Katz, S. & Marshall, B. 4, 135
Keith, P. 131
Kiernan, K. 16, 44
King, V. & Scott, M. 44, 88
Kohli, M. 13, 73
Koren, C. 58, 61, 169

L

language of non-marital partnerships
76–7
Laslett, P. 5, 13, 29–30, 40, 161–2, 169,
173
LAT (Living Apart Together)
relationships 45–7, 78
biographical case studies
Lee 63
Lenny 62–3, 71
Lisa & Lars 65–6, 92–6
Sophie 71–2
concept and history of 45
gendered preferences for 71–2, 79,
82–3
negotiation and change aspects 92–6
non-gendered preference for 84
older people's preference for 78, 109
prevalence of 46–7
who would prefer to cohabit 83
late-life divorces 34–5
legal inheritance issues, and remarriage
2, 49, 77, 94–5, 100, 102, 113,
122–3, 176
legislation
care giving 178
on divorce 32, 35
leisure pursuits 108–9
Levinger, G. 88
Levin, I. 16, 45, 136
Levin, I. & Trost, J. 45
life course, impact of societal change
13–15

T

Talbott, M.M. 48–9, 58, 64, 76–8, 80, 95, 100, 115
technology changes 14
terminology of repartnering 76–7
Tetley, J. et al 146
theory of 'being and time' (Heidegger) 27–8, 160
'third age' (Laslett) 13–15
  and self-realisation 20
Thornton, A. & Young-DeMarco, L. 24
time as 'structuring condition' for repartnering 159–70
  existential theories 159–61
  later life 'freedoms' 161–3
  sense of urgency over remaining years 163–8
Tornstam, L. 26
touch and physical intimacy 112, 155
  see also sexual intimacy
traditional cultures/values 21–5
  reproducing in new partnerships 70–1
transitions see life transitions
travel with partners 108
Trost, J. 16, 44–5, 137–8

U

Umberson, D. 114–15
UK
  attitudes to remarriage 76–7
  LAT arrangements 47
  marital status (over 60s) 36
  marital vs non-marital unions 46–7
  percentage of widowed and divorced 33
union form choices 43–56
  attitudes towards 77–8, 82–4
    Swedish preferences 82–4, 177–9
  by birth cohort 50–3, 58, 77, 87–8, 106, 452–3
  by historic period 53–4, 173–5
  by life phase 54–5, 55, 175–7
  gendered differences 50, 55, 82–4
  not to marry 48–9, 77
    LAT vs. cohabitation 50–5, 55–6, 77–9, 82–4
  preferences by gender 82–3
  those best suited to later life 49–50, 78
US
  cultural values and societal structures 23–5

divorce rates 19, 24, 76
  amongst older people 34–5
  interest in remarriage 76
  LAT partnerships 45
  marriages lasting more than 50 years 31
  percentage of widowed and divorced 33

V

vaginal intercourse 154
van den Hoonaard, D.K. 48, 77–9, 120, 122, 133–4
venues for dating 37–9
Vespa, J. 46, 106

W

Waite, L. et al 106, 148–9, 154
Walzer, S. 71
Watson, W.K. et al 89, 106, 108
Weeks, J. 17–18
welfare provisions
  impact on family and power relationships 19, 22–5
  Nordic model of 22
widowers, attitudes to repartnering 35, 78
widowhood
  decreasing trends for 32–4
  impact on attitudes to repartnering 57–8, 64–7, 78
'wife sanctification' 65
Wiik, K.A. et al 44
Wilmoth, J. & Koso, G. 106
withdrawal from society 25–6
women
  employment trends 17, 18–19, 56, 62, 72, 74, 116
  financial independence 19, 22–4, 34, 49, 62–3, 77
  and LAT preferences 50, 55, 79
  lifespan of 35–7
  'redoing gender' roles 71–2
  see also gender difference
World Values Survey 20–3
Wu, Z. & Penning, M.J. 31, 128–9
Wu, Z. & Schimmele, C.M. 31, 34

Z

Zetterberg, H. 5, 135